Is Socialism Possible in Britain?

Andrew Murray is an author and campaigner. He has served as chair of the Stop the War Coalition, chief of staff of Unite the union and as advisor to Jeremy Corbyn when he was leader of the Labour Party. His numerous books include *Off the Rails*, *Stop the War: The Story of Britain's Biggest Mass Movement* (with Lindsey German) and *The Fall and Rise of the British Left*.

Is Socialism Possible in Britain?

Reflections on the Corbyn Years

Andrew Murray

VERSO

London • New York

First published by Verso 2022
© Andrew Murray 2022

1 3 5 7 9 10 8 6 4 2

Verso
UK: 6 Meard Street, London W1F 0EG
US: 388 Atlantic Avenue, Brooklyn, NY 11217
versobooks.com

Verso is the imprint of New Left Books

ISBN-13: 978-1-83976-664-0
ISBN-13: 978-1-83976-666-4 (US EBK)
ISBN-13: 978-1-83976-665-7 (UK EBK)

British Library Cataloguing in Publication Data
A catalogue record for this book is available from the British Library

Library of Congress Cataloging-in-Publication Data

Names: Murray, Andrew, 1958– author.
Title: Is socialism possible in Britain? : reflections on the Corbyn years
／ Andrew Murray.
Description: London ; New York : Verso, 2022. | Includes bibliographical
references and index.
Identifiers: LCCN 2022017144 (print) | LCCN 2022017145 (ebook) | ISBN
9781839766640 (paperback) | ISBN 9781839766664 (ebk)
Subjects: LCSH: Labour Party (Great Britain) – History – 21st century. |
Socialism – Great Britain – History – 21st century. | Corbyn, Jeremy. |
Great Britain – Politics and government – 2007-
Classification: LCC JN1129.L32 M87 2022 (print)
| LCC JN1129.L32 (ebook)
| DDC 324.24107 – dc23／eng／20220623
LC record available at https://lccn.loc.gov/2022017144
LC ebook record available at https://lccn.loc.gov/2022017145

Typeset in Fournier MT by Hewer Text UK Ltd, Edinburgh
Printed and bound by CPI Group (UK) Ltd, Croydon, CR0 4YY

There is nothing more difficult to carry out, more doubtful of success, nor more dangerous to handle, than to institute a new order of things.

Machiavelli, *The Prince*

Contents

Introduction
The Shameful Footnote?

According to the organ of British finance capital, Jeremy Corbyn's leadership of the Labour Party was a 'shameful footnote in Labour history'.[1] Today, the *Financial Times* can relax. Normal service — to big business — has been resumed under the pallid leadership of Sir Keir Starmer.

Other views are available. Around half a million people joined Labour in the period of the shameful footnote, making it bigger than all other political parties in Britain combined. They were inspired by the opportunity of a different, socialist, politics. Over 40 per cent of the electorate voted Labour in 2017 in the hope that real change in a society degraded by inequality and austerity was possible.

Alas, it wasn't. Nevertheless, the Covid pandemic which followed hard on the heels of the 2019 general election proved that much of the Corbyn prospectus is indeed the common sense of our times. The *Telegraph* has gloomily conceded that 'numerous proto-Corbynite economic ideas have been adopted' by Boris

Johnson's administration, 'even though this was meant to be the government that consigned Corbynism to the history books'.[2]

When Corbynism does enter the history books it may indeed be as more than a footnote; perhaps rather a template for the future. For it was a bold attempt to re-establish socialism's relevance as the most compelling solution to the many problems that Britain and the world face. To quote the *FT*'s Martin Wolf: 'We are living in an era of multiple crises: Covid-19; a crisis of economic disappointment; a crisis of democratic legitimacy; a crisis of the global commons; a crisis of international relations; and a crisis of global governance.'[3] Jeremy Corbyn had something novel and important to say about each of these crises. That distinguishes him from both Boris Johnson and Keir Starmer. The latter has peevishly sought to exclude his predecessor from political life. Exorcising the reverberations of his leadership will be harder, and certainly beyond Starmer's capacities.

The last book by the present author was entitled *The Fall and Rise of the British Left*. It appeared in the autumn of 2019 and was apparently a spectacularly mistimed work, since the left in question was trembling on the threshold of a substantial and significant fall. It sought to explain how the rise of 'Corbynism' or something like it was predicated on observable political trends which the conventional wisdom had contrived to overlook.

This book attempts to look at what went wrong, and why Corbynism failed. There is a small body of literature looking at Corbyn and the movement he led, after his own fashion. Serious and insightful assessments have been written by *Sunday Times/ Times* journalists Gabriel Pogrund and Patrick Maguire and *Guardian* columnist Owen Jones.[4] They record in painstaking, not to say painful, detail, the unravelling of Corbyn's leadership. Both

books focus on parliamentary intrigue, personal rivalries, misman-
agement and bungling (real, exaggerated and invented) within
Corbyn's office and the general minutiae of Westminster life. Of
course, they also examine policy disputes, around Brexit above all.
They both offer sensitive assessments of the problems around anti-
Semitism, which unnecessarily escalated from challenging to
intractable in a short period of time. But there is a bigger picture
missing. Some of that is filled in by studies, like those by Sebastian
Payne and Deborah Mattinson, of the views of actual voters who
Labour lost.[5] Alex Nunns has written a compelling account of
Corbyn's leadership victory, later updated to include his first two
years in office. Len McCluskey's memoirs are useful too.[6] Studies
of Corbynism's historical roots and underpinning politics are
much thinner on the ground. Matt Bolton and Frederick Harry
Pitts wrote a somewhat curious account, since they both claim to
have supported Corbyn in 2015 yet oppose virtually the entirety of
his domestic and international outlook.[7] Mark Perryman produced
an anthology digging in to many of the issues raised by Corbynism's
ascent.[8] That pretty much covers the field.

Nevertheless, the defeat of the best chance of electing a government committed to socialist change in my lifetime deserves examin-
ing on a broader canvass. Many of the problems that beset the
Corbyn leadership, including all the decisive ones, will likely
confront any similar project in future in one form or another. Those
issues have to do with power in society – who holds it and how it is
exercised; the nature of the Labour Party and the history of reformism; the new 'cultural' divides associated with, but not identical to,
the rise of right-wing populism; the snares of parliamentarism; the
evolution of class; capitalist globalisation and its impact on the
nation-state's scope for initiative; the mass media; and more.

This book aims to examine these problems, refracted through the 2015–19 period in Labour and British politics. It therefore covers some of the same ground as the works mentioned above. The object is not just to describe the recent past and outline the difficulties we faced in giving effect to the hopes Corbyn aroused, but also to suggest how they can be more effectively addressed in the future. They will need to be.

Is Socialism Possible? attempts to synthesise memoir, history and analysis. It is informed in part by the author's own involvement in the team around Jeremy Corbyn, who I have known for many years. It further reflects my engagement with socialist politics, anti-war campaigning and the trade union movement since the mid 1970s. I was a member of the Communist Party until 2016, when I joined Labour at the behest of my union.

In terms of my own part in the Corbyn leadership, I was from 2015–17 no more than one of many informal advisors. Any influence I exerted came from my post as chief of staff at Unite, which was, under Len McCluskey's direction, a bulwark supporting Corbyn, above all during the 2016 Parliamentary Labour Party coup attempt. Thereafter, I was brought in to the leadership of the 2017 general election campaign to add managerial authority. From October 2017 my role was formalised as a part-time advisor in the Leader of the Opposition's Office (LOTO), seconded for part of the week. That arrangement continued until the end of Corbyn's leadership. I attended the Leader's Strategy Committee, the establishment of which I had recommended after the 2017 general election, and a number of other meetings. My responsibilities fluctuated over time, covering at one time or another 'preparing for government', international issues and various communications and mentoring roles. I offered a lot of strategic advice, some of it solicited and some of it followed. I worked particularly closely with Seumas Milne, whom I have known for over forty years, and Karie Murphy, a more recent acquaintance. Both sweated blood for the cause. I have no wish to exaggerate my own role – much of what was done, whether it was done well or not, happened without my intervention, and I was largely detached from the daily rough-and-tumble. I did enough, however, to earn the bile of the bourgeois media, from *The Economist* through to the *Sun*, which I wear as a badge of honour.

Spoiler alert: There is no kiss-and-tell here. I do not share the prevailing obsession with the overriding salience of personalities, without wishing to deny their relevance entirely. Jeremy Corbyn, a comrade and friend for many years, did not expect or wish to ever become Labour Party Leader and lacked some of the attributes to play the part successfully, even as he had other qualities which connected with many people and which led to his surprising elevation. Many have argued that he should have done this or that better or not at all, and sometimes they are right. But personality was not in any way decisive in the defeat of Corbynism, nor, in my view, would a John McDonnell leadership have fared very differently despite the shadow chancellor's different strengths and weaknesses.

In treating its themes, the present book overlaps with the ground covered in *The Fall and Rise*. I have tried to avoid repetition and have endeavoured to make this book coherent for those who have not read the previous one. Nevertheless, chapter 2 in particular treads along the path of the earlier work, and in various places I indicate where a fuller treatment of a given issue can be found in *Fall and Rise*. The fundamental argument in both books concerns the resilience of the left, and hopefully contributes to a capacity to learn from setbacks and mistakes. The period of Corbyn's leadership was a profound challenge, wherein socialists proved to have a surprising reach in society, albeit one that exceeded their grasp — although not perhaps by so very much. Corbynism is important because social conditions encompassing a global health pandemic, war, catastrophic climate change, rampant inequality and the collapse of the neoliberal model all mandate that something like it will need to be attempted again soon. For that reason, those of us who toiled in the project can join with the Leveller John Lilburne, who in 1649 turned to that posterity which 'we doubt not, shall reap the benefits of our labours, whatever shall become of us.'[9]

Acknowledgements

I am grateful to Tariq Ali at Verso for supporting this book, and Tom Hazeldine for his patient and skilful editing. Thanks to Seumas Milne and Jessica Murray for reading and commenting on drafts.

I am particularly grateful to Jeremy Corbyn for the opportunity to work with him, and to Len McCluskey at Unite for allowing me to do so. There are too many collaborators in the Corbyn leadership for me to recognise them all here, but I would like to acknowledge Seumas Milne, Karie Murphy, Jon Trickett MP, Leah Jennings, Laura Murray, Anjula Singh and Steve Howell. Socialism has been renewed by their efforts, and those of the tens of thousands who worked for a Labour victory in 2017 and 2019.

Finally, thanks to my wife, Anna, and my children, Jessica, Jack, Laura and Sally, for their support.

London
December 2021

1

New Adventures on the Parliamentary Road

'There is no such thing as Corbynism. There is socialism, there is social justice.' Thus said Jeremy Corbyn, looking to the future of the movement that bore his name, in the immediate aftermath of the crushing election defeat of December 2019.[1]

As with so much identified with his leadership of Labour, Corbyn was expressing a truth that begged further questions. What is this socialism? Nearly 130 years earlier, Friedrich Engels had waxed somewhat scornful about England's socialists. The country had, he wrote,

> Socialism of all shades: Socialism conscious and unconscious, Socialism prosaic and poetic, Socialism of the working class and of the middle class for, verily, that abomination of abominations, Socialism, has not only become respectable, but has actually donned evening dress and lounges lazily on drawing room *causeuses*.[2]

Socialism as a political movement has indeed appeared in a multitude of forms in Britain down the years from Engels to Corbyn, but socialism as a system of society has yet to put in an appearance. The Corbyn period proved to be the most recent example of a phenomena engraved in the history of the British left – a strong socialist movement that does not lead to socialism. In Engels's terms, Corbynism's socialism was probably more unconscious than conscious, as much middle class as working class, and with a strong dash of the poetic. None of the challenges it confronted were greater than the hitching of a poetic movement to that most prosaic of organisations, the Labour Party. Campaign in poetry, govern in prose, the adage tells us. But even in opposition, it has been rare for verse to tumble fluently from Labour's lips. No one has yet troubled to compose The Ballad of Pragmatic Adaptation to Prevailing Circumstances.

For all that was novel about the Corbyn movement, through history's telescope it was a canter down a familiar street called the parliamentary road to socialism. Many have set out on this highway, in Britain and elsewhere, but no one has yet reached the end. Lord (Neil) Kinnock – actually one of Labour's more lyrical former leaders, albeit an entirely unsuccessful one – told a 2016 meeting of the Parliamentary Labour Party, then girding its loins to try to defenestrate Corbyn:

> In 1918, in the shadow of the Russian revolution, they [the Labour Party] made a deliberate, conscious, ideological choice, that they would not pursue the syndicalist road, that they would not pursue the revolutionary road – it was a real choice in those days. They would pursue the parliamentary road to socialism . . . because we are a democratic socialist party, committed to a parliamentary road to power.[3]

On this point, Kinnock was right. For the best part of a century, the Labour Party ostensibly worked to establish socialism through the institutions of the British state. This objective was discarded by New Labour but restored de facto under Corbyn, although Blair's blancmange rewrite of the party's famous Clause Four was left untouched. Even Lord Kinnock believes that Labour is still set on the road to socialism, the compromises – and worse – of the moment being but way stations towards a better tomorrow. Others might disagree. Surveying the disappointments of the Wilson government in the sixties, Ralph Miliband concluded that there was no such avenue as parliamentary socialism. His son Ed, with filial obligation, is among the most recent to devote himself to proving his father's point.[4]

Two entwined questions, then, have bedevilled the left in Britain: is Labour a fit and proper vehicle for the pursuit of socialism, and can the new society of class equality, social justice, material abundance and ecological balance be attained through the institutions of the old? The first question might be considered a peculiarly British one, bearing on features of the Labour Party not found in most other social democratic parties, whereas the second has been debated endlessly in the working-class movement the world over – it divided the Second from the Third International and was central to the polemics between the Soviet and Chinese Communist Parties. Corbynism presupposed that the parliamentary road was worth another try. There is a case to be made for this gambit, particularly since it corresponds to that most esteemed of values in the British labour movement – and indeed British society at large – namely, 'common sense'. But it is no more than a case. Neither the antecedent history of the Labour Party, nor the course of events during Corbyn's leadership, offers ground for summary judgement. By first reviewing Labour's history we can identify the political traditions that briefly flowered within the party under Corbyn's care.

Socialism and Class

The first task of socialists, wrote Marx and Engels in *The Communist Manifesto*, was the 'formation of the proletariat as a class', prior to overturning 'bourgeois supremacy'.[5] That was far from a statement of the obvious in 1848. There was already plenty of socialism around – utopian plans, quack theories, fashionable masquerades. But of the working class, not so much. The Chartist movement had announced its arrival in Britain, albeit with a political programme that was not socialistic as such. In Belgium and France, the first stirrings. Elsewhere, barely a glimmer. Identifying the proletariat's world-historical significance, something Marx had first ventured as a sort of philosophical legerdemain in a polemic with his young Hegelian self a few years earlier, was a feat of successful prognostication with few parallels.[6]

Marx and Engels did not separate the organisation of the working class from the advancement of socialism within it. Having dismissed most varieties of English socialism in the passage quoted above, Engels consoled himself by attaching far greater importance to labour struggles in the East End of London, the largest concentration of workers anywhere in the world. The socialists he influenced were not to be found in the salons of the middle classes, but agitating in the gasworks and at the docks. What they had to accomplish was to fuse their doctrines – ideally in the form of 'conscious socialism', by which Engels certainly meant Marxism – with the trade unions and other institutions that the working class had created for itself. The model was August Bebel's German Social Democratic Party, which hegemonised the politics of a fast-developing German working class and saw its parliamentary representation grow from one election to the next, despite repression. Could British socialists of the *fin de siècle* belatedly effect a similar fusion with their own labour movement?

The Labour Party was not that fusion. It was the product of a class that had gone some considerable way towards organising itself without any significant input from socialists, communists or even Chartists (whose legacy of democratic social radicalism had been largely buried under mid-Victorian prosperity, craft-union respectability and imperial propaganda). The initiative in Labour's creation was taken by trade unions ideologically more influenced by liberalism than anything else, but mainly just proud of their pragmatism and empiricism. There was no commitment to socialism at the founding of the Labour Representation Committee in 1900, though socialists were present at the birth.

Initially, Labour offered no individual membership: you could only get involved through one or other of its affiliated organisations. For Engels's socialism of the drawing room, Labour had the Fabian Society of Sidney and Beatrice Webb. Scientific reformers seeking to permeate the Establishment with modern administrative schemes, the Webbs were most definitely against the class struggle. Conscious socialism was represented by the Marxist Social Democratic Federation founded by Henry Hyndman, an effective populariser of Marx's ideas who nevertheless disdained strikes and was regularly chauvinistic and intermittently anti-Semitic. For Socialism unconscious, yet perhaps poetic, there was the largest of the socialist societies, the Independent Labour Party (ILP).

The ILP's slogan might have been The Only Way Is Ethics. It was the obvious route for middle-class radicals or intellectuals to make their voice heard within the Labour Party, since the trade unions were almost entirely organised of and for manual workers. The most detailed assessment of ILP politics, by historian David Howell, identifies Carlyle, Ruskin, Dickens and Bunyan as sources of inspiration for a 'Romantic critique of capitalism'. Literary, quasi-religious and 'Merrie England' invocations of a lost rural arcadia trumped any sort of political economy. 'How can socialism be accomplished?' mused Robert Blatchford, editor of the influential *Clarion* newspaper. 'I confess I approach this question with great reluctance. The establishment and organisation of a Socialistic state are the two branches of work to which I have given least attention.'[7] According to another contemporary socialist writer, 'The speakers of the ILP, in their educational work among the trade unionists, hardly ever referred to revolution and class warfare, but started from the ethical, nonconformist and democratic sentiments which appeal most to British workmen'.[8] In the more severe but complementary judgement of a Soviet historian, ILP socialism 'was essentially a summary of ideas and wishes in respect of ethical reforms, acceptable to a great many people in Britain who were far from, and even hostile to, Marxism.'[9] ILPers generally leant towards internationalism and pacifism (although not Blatchford, who allegedly compelled his daughter to play 'Rule Britannia' every evening on the piano during the Boer War).[10]

It is not too much to see the progenitors of 'Corbynism' here, although to describe Corbyn himself as indifferent to class issues and hostile to Marxism would be as far off the mark as the super-heated polemics of the right portraying him as a Leninist revolutionary. The ILP's first ethical superstar was Ramsay MacDonald, best known today for abandoning the Labour government he had been elected to lead in 1931. Earlier in his career, MacDonald screwed his conscience up to the pitch of opposing British entry into the First World War – a stand that proved to exhaust his storehouse of principle, although by no means his penchant for florid and emotive rhetoric.

The purpose of the Labour Representation Committee (renamed the Labour Party in 1906) was to secure greater parliamentary representation for working people. Westminster lay front and centre of its strategic perspective. Not so in the wider socialist movement, however. The mainly Scottish-based Socialist Labour Party eschewed Parliament altogether in favour of a form of syndicalism, and the SDF was ambivalent. 'We must not make a superstition of the powers and possibilities of Parliament', Birmingham delegate Leonard Hall told the 1911 conference which united the SDF with other left-wing groups to form the British Socialist Party, later a core constituent of the Communist Party of Great Britain. Hall added, in terms relevant to the experience of Corbynism, that socialists 'had to create a far greater strength outside of Parliament before they could hope to make of Parliament more help than hindrance.'[11]

Labour might be parliamentarian to a fault, but its external connection to organised workers, via its foundation in affiliated trade unions, gave it electoral heft. The 'union link' has often seemed little more than a bureaucratic-financial transaction. Yet the unions have played a key part in shaping Labour's destiny, keeping the party going in tough times – without ever usurping the prerogatives of the parliamentary leadership. Even the Blairites hesitated to break, although not to considerably attenuate, this link. Combined with the first-past-the-post electoral system, it has effectively obstructed any socialist initiative to create a political party to the left of Labour with any chance of success. The first chairman of the CPGB, Arthur MacManus, told a gathering with Labour leaders in 1920 that he desired affiliation because without it, the Communists would be excluded from the broad field of working-class politics. This was an insight validated by history. Bit by bit, Labour forced Communists out of any form of participation in the party's activities. The CP worked heroically, but with only limited success – outside the factories, at least – to overcome the consequences of this exclusion.

Varieties of Reformism

The end of the First World War brought a new Labour Party constitution, written by the Webbs.[12] The most celebrated change was a sort-of advocacy of socialism, the Clause Four commitment to public ownership of the means of production, distribution and exchange. Whether the Webbs really intended socialism by this famous clause is debatable; that it was subsequently honoured overwhelmingly in the breach is not. Labour's plunge into the waters of ideology was a consequence of the Russian Revolution, which posed insurrection rather than parliamentary majoritarian-ism as the means of establishing a socialist regime, and soviets in the factories as the legislative power appropriate to working-class rule (although the soviets were soon to see their authority pass de facto and in toto to the Bolshevik Party). In Britain, a fretful head of MI5 advised the Lloyd George government that revolutionary feeling was being held in check only by the popularity of the Royal Family and of sport.[13] As the winds of revolution rattled windows in Bloomsbury, the astute Fabians realised that they needed to up their game to keep Bolshevism at bay.

This, more or less, is where Lord Kinnock comes in – or at least his historical analysis does. Faced with the mere possibility of insurrection, Labour opted for reformism instead. Reformism has come in 'soft' and 'hard' guises. The first holds that capitalism can be satisfactorily mitigated through legislation, and does not seek systemic change.[14] The second wants a socialist form of society, but believes that incremental parliamentary action is the means to securing it. Soft reformism is the tendency associated with MacDonald, Bevin, Morrison, Crosland, George Brown, Jenkins, Healey, Blair and Gordon Brown; hard reformism with Lansbury, Bevan, Foot and Benn. The two trends have coexisted, often very disharmoniously, throughout the party's history. Attlee and Wilson made at least a show of trying to straddle the divide, although Attlee apparently made only a mild demurral when his wife opined, 'you were never really a socialist were you, Clem?'[15]

Soft reformism – managing capitalism for the best – has always been hegemonic when Labour holds the keys to Downing Street. The party's first minority government came and went in 1924. Dependent on Liberal support in parliament, enslaved to Treasury orthodoxy, committed to the security of the Empire, MacDonald's ministers added next to nothing to the treasury of socialist endeavour. A second minority administration in 1929–31 fell apart when MacDonald defected to a Tory-dominated National Government after his cabinet colleagues refused to buckle to demands for austerity from the City of London. By then, trade-union militancy had been neutered by defeat in the 1926 General Strike and the high unemployment ushered in with the Great Depression.

MacDonald's legacy to the labour movement has been the invocation of his name as a dire warning against cooperation with other political forces – the phrase 'Ramsay MacCorbyn' did not pass unuttered in strategy discussions when there were suggestions of working with the Theresa May government to secure passage of a Brexit deal.

After a chaotic interlude, MacDonald was succeeded as Labour Leader by George Lansbury, MP for Bow and Bromley, in 1932. It is worth spending a moment on Lansbury because he is the most left-wing Labour Leader before Corbyn and is seen as a precursor to him. Immersed in local government in London, Lansbury's obsessions were tackling poverty, equality for all, and especially peace and disarmament. While his pacifism was more absolute and religiously informed than Corbyn's – it led him to ill-judged, indeed embarrassing, meetings with Hitler and Mussolini in his quest to avoid another war, after he had yielded the party leadership to Attlee – it is easy to see his politics rekindled in the shape of 'Corbynism'. In 2013, Dagenham Labour MP Jon Cruddas gave the inaugural George Lansbury Memorial Lecture in the East End. He said:

> Through Lansbury we can rediscover exiled traditions within Labour by returning to questions of ethics and virtue; to lost utopias; by rebuilding hope, energy and vitality through returning to issues of principle and character. It is about re-imagining what a Labour Party could be. This re-imagined socialism is romantic, not scientific; humane and warm; passionate yet humble; it is about rediscovering a political sentiment. It pushes back against party orthodoxy, careerism and transactional politics.[16]

Cruddas's remarks seem a remarkably prescient summation of what became the essence of Corbyn's appeal to the party membership, and a wider public as well, just two years later.

High Hopes

The first opportunity to implement a parliamentary transition to socialism through a *majority* Labour administration fell to Clement Attlee in 1945. It remains the most storied episode in the party's history, the example invoked to show what a Labour government is capable of. Labour entered office better prepared. First, a lot of thinking had addressed how to make social democracy work in practice since the ignominious end of the last MacDonald administration. Not all of this had been done by social democrats – in fact, two of the biggest intellectual influences on the 1945 government were Liberals. William Beveridge developed the foundations for the major extension of the welfare state, including the recommendation that a national health service be established on 'communist lines', while John Maynard Keynes's macroeconomic theories showed the way to trim the market's wings in the interests of maintaining full employment. Second, Attlee, Bevin, Morrison and other key ministers had all served in Churchill's wartime coalition government, in Attlee's case as deputy prime minister. Wartime controls and regulations – including a system of rationing that led to improvements in many working-class diets, and greater trade-union involvement in the resolution of industrial problems – laid the foundations for social democracy with a measure of cross-party consensus, although the Tories looked more eagerly for an eventual return to capitalist normality. Much as sections of the elite regarded the advent of a landslide Labour government as an inversion of the natural order of things, for the most part they felt assured that such changes as were unavoidable would be kept within boundaries they could live with.

They were not wrong. To some extent, the 1945 government needs retrieving from the roseate glow of nostalgia which has, in Labour circles and beyond, befogged it ever since.

Undoubtedly some of the measures it adopted, above all the creation of the NHS, have proved to be of lasting benefit to the working class and to the country as a whole. Likewise, the entrenchment of social services – the 'welfare state'. These advances have endured, despite repeated Tory and neoliberal attempts to undermine them. Other measures, like the public building of homes, were impactful in their time but have not been sustained.

In other respects, however, Attlee's Labour was a normal capitalist government. Even its programme of nationalisations was not the act of radicalism sometimes assumed. The industries taken into state ownership – coal and railways above all – had been decaying for more than a generation, starved of private investment. The newly established state bodies responsible for their administration were run by personnel drawn from the familiar capitalist establishment, without trade union or employee involvement in management. The story told me forty years ago by Mick McGahey, Communist leader of Scotland's mineworkers, is apposite. The young McGahey returned home from his shift on vesting day, 1 January 1947, jubilant at seeing the new sign outside his colliery announcing that it was now 'managed by the National Coal Board on behalf of the people'. This, he exulted to his father, was socialism. The older Mr McGahey, a Communist of more rigorous application, responded to his son scornfully: 'This isn't socialism,

son. Socialism is working-class power and we don't have that yet.'
He was right: nationalisation was aimed at the development of a
more efficient capitalism, the market economy still firmly in the
saddle. Working-class power it wasn't.

In fact, power stayed very much where it was. Labour introduced no constitutional reforms of note, leaving the House of
Lords, the monarchy, the civil service and the electoral system
intact, and turned a deaf ear to calls for a Scottish parliament. From
Attlee down, ministers made it clear that while they might listen to
the party membership and conference, they did not in any sense see
themselves as answerable to them – indeed, the very idea was an
abomination. The trade union affiliates were mainly in the hands of
the right: men who by nature were authoritarian, loyalist and
imbued with a collaborationist outlook inimical to industrial action.
Above all, there was continuity with Tory foreign policy under
Ernie Bevin, the former leader of the Transport and General
Workers Union, who became foreign secretary. The granting of
independence to India, under circumstances which led to a bloody
partition and huge loss of life, was an outlier. Indian independence
was a policy which would have been imposed even on Tory diehards
like Churchill – the movement to end the Raj had passed the point
of no return, and the means available to continue to coerce India
were simply insufficient to the task. It was also a matter which
Attlee handled personally, since Bevin, a prisoner to racist assumptions regarding the fitness of India for self-government, resisted to
the last. Otherwise, the Attlee government was a staunch defender
of the Empire, something even Bevin's most recent hagiographer,
New Labour's Andrew Adonis, is forced to concede as a misjudgement.[17] Bevin absorbed the imperial dogmas of the Foreign Office
wholesale and saw every global issue, including the demands of the

colonial peoples for self-determination, exclusively through the prism of an anticommunism forged by his authoritarian leadership of the Transport and General Workers' Union and the need to align British policy with Washington.[18] As the government limped towards its conclusion, it was cutting social spending in order to pay for the Korean War.

Thus, the high hopes throughout the labour movement that Attlee's Labour could build a socialist society were not fulfilled. Despite the disappointments, however, even the smaller Communist left assessed that in a hardening Cold War environment, there was no longer any way around the parliamentary road.[19] Back in Downing Street, Churchill grumblingly preserved most of Labour's nationalisations, as well as its commitment to full employment, which the Conservatives found compatible with capitalist growth during the long post-war boom. Labour was meanwhile convulsed by the schism between the followers of Nye Bevan – representing the reformism that genuinely aimed at socialist transformation – and those of Hugh Gaitskell and the right's ideologist Tony Crosland, advocates of capitalist ameliora- tion who mounted the first unsuccessful effort to expunge the commitment to public ownership from the party's programme. The latter predominated within the PLP, while failing to make an impression at the polls against either Churchill or Macmillan. Bevan himself ultimately became reconciled to the most potent symbol of British imperial power, the possession of nuclear weapons.

The Wilson Sponge

Before the advent of 'Corbynism', a genuinely left-wing Labour government has only twice seemed a prospect. The first came with Harold Wilson in the sixties, the second at the zenith of the movement associated with Tony Benn in 1980–82. Wilson was originally from the softer end of the party's left-wing. He defeated the definitely right-wing George Brown to become party Leader in 1963 following Gaitskell's sudden death (not, as it turned out, the work of the KGB, as it was rumoured at the time). Labour narrowly won the 1964 general election and another in 1966 more handsomely, on a mandate to modernise Britain economically and socially. To some extent Wilson was successful in the latter– it was on his watch that abortion became legally available, homosexuality was decriminalized and racial discrimination outlawed in some respects. However, the Treasury frustrated his attempt to challenge its dominion in economic policy, which soon became little more than an exercise in crisis management. The government prepared the way for its own defeat by launching the first post-war legal attempt to curb trade unionism. The trade union movement was strong enough to see off the 'In Place of Strife' proposals, but the political damage was done. Meanwhile the radical youth were alienated by Wilson's political support for the Vietnam War (although, wiser than Blair, he refrained from obliging Washington to the extent of dispatching troops to the conflict). Labour's membership imploded, turning many local parties into hollow shells by the time the Tories regained power under Edward Heath in 1970.

Like Wilson before him, Heath was compelled to tack and trim in the face of rising working-class strength. A new surge of trade union militancy across a range of industries was headlined by two miners' strikes and the occupation of the UCS shipyard on the Clyde. Leading sections of the ruling establishment began to fear they were losing their grip, and that the country stood on the brink. When Wilson returned to Downing Street in 1974, Labour's left wing appeared to be better placed than ever before. Figures like Michael Foot and a freshly radicalised Tony Benn played key roles in a cabinet formally committed, despite a wafer-thin parliamentary majority, to extending the gains of 1945 through public ownership, allied to a broad Bennite economic strategy oriented towards socialism, which has been described, not wrongly, 'as a crowning moment of Labourite anti-capitalist thought'.[20] Certainly, Corbynism never went as far.

Tony Benn's diaries record the gradual extinction of these hopes.[21] Labour militancy was temporarily subdued as Wilson ensnared the unions in a 'social contract' with government, trading wage restraint for social reforms that proved increasingly chimerical (the first steps towards statutory equal pay for women being an exception). Inside the cabinet, Benn was demoted by Wilson after losing the referendum on British membership in the Common Market. He then lost the struggle, if not the argument, with Wilson's successor in Number 10, James Callaghan, who took the IMF debt crisis of 1976 as the spur for retrenchment, appeasement of the City and embrace of the market economics that later came to be called, in its various mutations, monetarism, Thatcherism and neoliberalism.[22] The moment of radical social democracy's greatest influence in government had passed, but Benn would carry on his fight for Labour socialism on the Opposition benches.

Benn was, in my view, the most formidable leader the Labour left ever had. He moved to the left rather than the right as he aged, becoming more consistent and principled than Bevan, more worldly wise than Lansbury and more experienced than Corbyn. A parliamentarian, of course, but a radical one, he became more invested in extra-parliamentary movements from the days of the UCS occupation onwards, deploying formidable oratory in their support. Backed by a powerful left in the constituencies and, critically, in many unions, giving him at times majority support on Labour's executive, Benn stood at the head of an assembly of forces not seen since the aftermath of the First World War, and not repeated to this day. Those forces do not in some cases exist today, but the Bennite coalition is nearer to a template for the future than the Corbynite.

From Benn to Corbyn, via Blair

At least it was clear, in the wake of the 1979 defeat, that there would be no advance to socialism by electing Labour governments that conducted themselves as they had in the past. Labour would have to have a different relationship to the wider party and movement if it was to transform society. Ministers would have to answer to members and implement the policies determined by the party, rather than falling into the grip of civil servants and powerful establishment interests, moneyed and military, from the moment they entered office. This was the critical insight at the heart of the movement associated with Benn which briefly came to dominate Labour politics in the early years of the Thatcher government. As well as drawing up a radical programme to meet Britain's economic and social crisis from the left, it also proposed constitutional reforms for the party itself.[23] In the febrile atmosphere of the early eighties, with the trade union movement as yet undefeated on the industrial field, Bennism secured significant rulebook and policy advances, enough to allow for the hope that the next Labour government would indeed be different.

Jeremy Corbyn himself – and John McDonnell and Diane Abbott, among others – emerged as a metropolitan subset within the Benn movement.[24] The most representative figure in this milieu was Ken Livingstone, leader of the Greater London Council. Sweeping away an encrusted old guard in one constituency party after another, the new metropolitan left identified new priorities, emphasizing antiracism, women's liberation, anti-imperialism and an enhanced individualism. The differences with the more traditional Labour left can be overplayed. The 'old left' were scarcely strangers to anticolonial and antiracist campaigning, nor were the 'new left' indifferent to trade unionism and its imperatives. Still, Livingstone et al. unarguably brought a sharper edge to questions of equality, as well as an ability – at their best – to speak to an increasingly diversified social base, recalibrating the representation of class in British politics. Their ability to speak to and for other industrial communities was a different matter: Livingstone's personal popularity diminished notably the further one got from London. This was a problem that would resurface during Corbyn's leadership with, it is fair to say, a vengeance.

Compared to the Corbyn movement, which attempted to pick up some of its threads, Bennism was in a position of some strength. In the early eighties the socialist left remained a force, in Britain and internationally. The Soviet Union still existed as an alternative system, and the European Union was seen for what it is – a construct of capitalist authority – rather than celebrated for the cosmopolitan liberalism that it sugared this pill with. Britain's trade unions were strong, and were heavily influenced by the left.

Benn himself was a politician who had extensive government experience and was an outstanding orator. Had the left secured government, it would have been ready: it had policies and a perspective. But it was met with the united, full-force resistance of Labour's right wing, the media and the Establishment, in a manner prefiguring the onslaught that Corbyn would endure. Four senior Labour figures from the Wilson and Callaghan years founded the breakaway Social Democratic Party, which split the anti-Tory vote. Together with the impact of the Falklands War, which salvaged Thatcher's popularity, this defection on the Labour right saw Michael Foot heavily defeated in the 1983 general election, setting the stage for an internal counter-revolution which led, by stages, to New Labour.

Defeat in the political field was swiftly followed by industrial defeat, most significantly in the epic miners' strike. Thatcher's ruthless deployment of the state apparatus against the workers' movement – the police and courts in the first rank – illustrate the reserves of capitalist power which have to be overcome for socialism to become a serious possibility. The passivity throughout the miners' dispute of Labour's new leader, Lord (as he then wasn't) Kinnock, anxious to restore the party's conformist credentials after the Benn episode, illustrated the other great prop on which the country's bourgeois order rests. Soft reformism and the British state closed ranks.

These setbacks were mirrored in many other countries. In the late eighties, 'actually existing socialism' ceased to actually exist as the 1917 process ran its course. Thereafter the whole issue of roads to socialism, and whether Labour could be a vehicle for it, became a preoccupation of the politically marginalised. Clause Four, which had come into Labour's story with the Soviet Union, not coincidentally went out with it. Under New Labour there was not even the slightest pretence that capitalism was to be challenged or society transformed. Tony Blair barely mentioned the word 'socialism'. New Labour made the management of capitalism the explicit summit of its ambitions, and a deregulated, *laissez-faire* capitalism at that.

The fact that New Labour was initially established by something akin to a coup within the party by a remarkably small number of politicians – Blair, Brown, Mandelson – and that it was explicitly non-socialist, has led some to the view that it was an aberrant departure from the party's history. This is only partly true. There is also some veracity in Blair's assertion that New Labour was advancing the party's traditional values through modern methods – provided it is understood that those traditional values have been broadly about the management and reform of capitalism, and that the methods Blair employed were those suited to an age when social democracy had, almost universally, abandoned its previous tools of public ownership, demand management and relatively high levels of taxation. The real novelty of New Labour was its loving embrace of a highly deregulated City of London, and its concomitant indifference to widening social inequality and core working-class concerns such the availability of affordable housing. Traditional values were falling by the wayside as well.

The New Labour record is well known, and resentment within the party membership at its pandering to the rich and its foreign aggressions fertilized the soil for the Corbyn insurrection. Although these were years when socialism was most definitely *off* the agenda, Corbynism was nevertheless incubating. Its roots lay within the old Labour tradition of ethical socialism and more immediately in the broad Benn movement, with its opposition to racism and imperialism and its openness to social movements outside and alongside the classical organisations of the British working class. Between the ages of Benn and Corbyn there was no socialism, but there were socialists. A great economic crisis was required to bring them blinking into the sunlight of a world in which suddenly capitalism could not convincingly claim that it had all the answers anymore. In that world, Corbyn and his supporters inherited the ambivalent century-old legacy of Labour, radicals at the helm of one of the most historically conservative products of the international working-class movement.

2
Context of Crisis, Crisis of Context

'We Are All Socialists Now', US magazine *Newsweek* solemnly advised in the midst of the bankers' crash unleashed in 2008, as governments shovelled endless billions of taxpayers' money into the financial system in a bid to keep its private monopolies – the culprits for the crisis – solvent.[1] Of course, it wasn't true. *Newsweek* was describing Operation Rescue Capitalism, not the transition to a better way of organising society, much as that was what was needed and what millions desired. But at least it reinstated as a possibility what had been for a generation unthinkable – an alternative, *pace* Margaret Thatcher.

The perennial questions – what was a socialist society, and how could it be attained? – remained, and were if anything still more acute. Both the perspective – socialism – and the agency charged with introducing it – the working class – could not be picked up in the twenty-first century just where they had been discarded twenty-five years earlier. Socialism in its two main variants, Soviet Communist and West European social democratic, had either collapsed or run out of political road in the 1980s. Capitalist globalisation, the emergency of climate change and the internal challenges of feminism, anti-racism and a renewed emphasis on the individual had reconfigured the problems which socialism had to solve if it was to maintain its viability. They posed questions to which it had yet to give a worked-out answer.

Likewise, a politics which assumed that the heavy lifting of social change (whether at the ballot box, on the streets or in the factories) would be undertaken by an organised working class with a high degree of internal cohesion and common class referents, itself at the cutting edge of economic and technical development, looked threadbare. In the generation intervening between social-ism's disappearance as an imminent possibility and its reappear-ance as a desirable option, there had been no shortage of critiques of the consequences of neoliberalism, capitalist globalisation and the 'Washington Consensus'. But these critiques dissolved into vagueness when they concluded, at the point when a plausible alternative to unbridled capitalist power was needed.

So if socialism re-emerged as a political subject in a context of capitalist crisis, it did so also in a context of its own crisis. New Labour, of course, gave up the search entirely and on principle, but it was aberrant only in the intense degree of its relaxation about the filthy rich, to cite Peter Mandelson.[2] All this is by way of saying that if there are ideal circumstances for a resurgence of a move-ment for socialism, they were not those pertaining in 2015 when Jeremy Corbyn was elected to Labour's leadership.

Much has been written about the changes in the working class associated primarily with the decline of heavy and manufacturing industry, as major employers of labour at least, and the concomi-tant erosion of those mass-based class organisations which stood upon that industrial foundation. It is, however, an error to imagine that a change in one class could leave the others unmarked. Such social formations can only exist in a mutual inter-relationship. Globalised capitalism has wrought great changes in middle-class expectations as well, as the fears of older generations – of super-session in the scheme of things by the organised working class – have been supplanted by the difficulties of maintaining living standards, of job insecurity against which university degrees afford no protection, and of the difficulties of their children in finding an affordable place to live.

The simultaneous erosion of the traditional bases of imperialist social democracy and of the hegemonic project of the ruling class, developments which both Thatcher and Blair expedited without willing them, has created greater space for political phenomena which would have seemed implausible not so long ago. Corbynism found its scope in that setting of unsettlement, where new drivers of egalitarianism, among the socially disenfranchised urban young in particular, to some extent supplanted the old, rooted in a power-ful movement of organised labour. The post-2010 austerity programme imposed to save capitalism could only exacerbate these trends.

Corbynism's ascendancy owed nothing to any great shift in parliamentary opinion – he was imposed upon the PLP by external circumstance. This was one of its historically unique aspects – the perspective of a 'parliamentary road' without and to a certain extent against parliamentarism and parliamentarians. Corbyn was the first Labour Party Leader to be more oriented towards the demonstration, the mass protest and (where they could be found) the picket line, than towards the green benches of the House of Commons (this is true of John McDonnell as well). He came to office as the living embodiment of the politics of mass protest, of resistance to austerity and war. This was one of the two factors which made Jeremy Corbyn so entirely unacceptable to mainstream social democracy – he was not one of them, not beholden to their procedures, rituals and priorities. The other was his anti-imperialism, which we take up in the next chapter.

War, Slump and Resistance

The emblematic mass movement of this century remains the anti-war movement from 2001 onwards, which reached its mobilising apex in February 2003, when around 2 million people were brought onto the streets to oppose the Iraq War and Britain's participation in it. Most of the elements of what became the Corbyn coalition came together there for the first time – the 'old left', students and school students, trade unionists, ethnic minorities (Muslims especially), radical liberals and pacifists, and more.[3]

Stop the War established that the left had the capacity to extend its political reach deep into society, including into the multitudinous ranks of the generally non-political, given a significant issue and appropriate tactics. The movement was a dry run for what became 'Corbynism' a decade later in terms of the new elements mobilised into political action and of the translation of mass extra-parliamentary action into pressure on politicians. Corbyn's prominent personal role in the movement was clearly relevant to his later ascension to the party leadership.

The crash of 2008, the return of the Tories to office in a coalition with the Liberal Democrats and the subsequent imposition of swingeing reductions in social expenditure and other public goods (allied to tax cuts for the better off) generated a further wave of mass protest. Students were first in the field, with the increase in university tuition fees inspiring massive demonstrations which included besieging the Tory Party headquarters in London. The anger was at least in part the consequence of Liberal Democrat Leader Nick Clegg's particularly lurid betrayal of his election promises on this issue: he had pledged to scrap rather than treble the charges.

The trade union movement too found a taste – and a capacity – for mass demonstrations, both directly against austerity and in support of its resistance to government attacks on public sector pensions, the latter also leading to the biggest strike action seen for many years. This was unfortunately not developed by most of the unions involved. The People's Assembly, a broad coalition of trade unionists and campaigning groups, carried forward the mass demonstration tactic throughout the five years of the Cameron-Clegg coalition.

More unconventional campaigns developed as well. UK Uncut highlighted tax avoidance by big corporations. Its method was high-profile store occupations and other stunts which leveraged the direct action of a small number of people into big media coverage. This naming and shaming of the greediest big businesses, who had learned nothing from their collective humiliation in 2008, was eventually brought to an end by police threats to UK Uncut's activists.

The Occupy movement, travelling east across the Atlantic, also foregrounded the grotesque inequalities engendered by thirty years of neoliberalism. The chosen means was the symbolic occupation of significant public spaces, in Britain's case outside St Paul's Cathedral, where a sizeable encampment was established, open to all. Occupy did not have a programme or clear set of demands (nor any recognisable leadership) but it did have an idea that became a slogan – 'we are the 99%'. This could be objected to on the grounds of a substantial oversimplification of the class structure in contemporary society, but as a way of dramatising the point about global inequality and its refraction within each country, it was striking.

The riots that originated in London in summer 2011 but then spread swiftly to many other parts of the country are part of this picture. These were not strictly against austerity, which had scarcely started to bite; but nor were they apolitical (or even simply criminal), as much of the left seemed to view them. The trigger, as so often in the past, was the police killing of a black person.[4] In Hackney and Nottingham the riots had a sharp antipolice focus. Rioters in Battersea chanted 'you are rich, we are poor', as they both confronted police and looted shops. For twenty-four hours, the Metropolitan Police appeared to lose control of London. The episode concluded (outside the courtrooms at least, wherein Keir Starmer's prosecutors were seeking condign retribution) with urban gentrifiers in Battersea and Hackney turning out to clear up the detritus of the disturbances. This represented one part of Labour's metropolitan coalition – the part suitable for photo-ops – literally shaking its brooms at another.

So there was a stew of discontent simmering in austerity Britain from the start. Its extent and impact should not be exaggerated – none of it succeeded in changing the political weather to the required extent. However, it was sufficient to indicate that the possibilities of mass resistance to the consequences of capitalism had not disappeared under the ruins of a declining trade union movement and a Labour Party that had embraced the main tenets of neoliberalism. Nor had the capacity for tactical innovation been lost, even if there remained a lack of clarity on objectives beyond the immediate and insufficient mobilising muscle. These movements against austerity, including among those who played little or no part in regular politics, constituted another of the foundational elements of 'Corbynism'.

New Labour's Lingering Death

Little of this apparently registered with the Labour Party in parliament. In May 2010 its share of the vote had fallen to just 29 per cent, the second worst in its post-war history, and only 6 percentage points ahead of the Liberal Democrats. Only 8,609,000 voters chose Labour. It bears repeating that these figures are markedly worse than they were in 2019. The 'red wall' was already looking shaky in many places. A 'blue Labour' tendency arose to address the growing evidence of estrangement from Labour within sections of the working-class electorate. Red-white-and-blue Labour would have been more apt, as it wrung its class politics through the mangle of community, patriotism and moral conservatism. Since these were not values especially offended by Tony Blair – who, metropolitan as he may have been, could scarcely have been more exuberantly flag-waving – the diagnosis was at least largely misplaced.

At the same time, Labour's membership had dropped to well under 200,000, less than half what it had been in the first years of Blair's leadership. Iraq was undoubtedly the big problem here, but beyond that, Labour seemed an organisation bereft of purpose and ideas, let alone idealism. Corbyn, McDonnell, Abbott and a handful of others (many of them getting on in years) continued their dogged advocacy of radical social democracy in Parliament, unevenly and intermittently buttressed by support from affiliated trade unions, but their efforts attracted little attention from their parliamentary colleagues or the mainstream media.

Trade union votes in the party's baroque electoral college had ensured the election of Ed Miliband, who represented the most left-wing edge of the now-defeated New Labour project of Blair, Brown and Mandelson. Certainly he was the more radical of the Miliband brothers – older sibling David was the candidate of undiluted Blairism.[5] Thus began a hesitant shuffle away from the priorities of New Labour. The new Leader seemed to wish to embark on a more radical agenda, learning the lessons of the deregulation and indulgence of high finance which had helped precipitate the 2008 crash. However, the majority of the Parliamentary Labour Party remained apparently unshaken in its commitment to the market economy, privatisation, balanced budgets, low tax on big business and the rest of the ideological paraphernalia of the post–Clause Four ideological dispensation. It would go no further than conceding the case for somewhat tougher regulation than had been practised by New Labour in office. Strong in numbers, potent in their factional malice and resolute in their belief that they were led by the wrong Miliband, the Blairite element in the PLP cast a long shadow over Miliband's tentative efforts to chart a modified course. Nor can Blair's supporters be blamed for everything – the impeccably Brownite Ed Balls, Miliband's second choice as shadow chancellor, promoted when the feckless Alan Johnson bailed, helped keep him tethered to Treasury priorities of balancing the budget, at the expense of welfare if necessary. Miliband's personal preferences notwithstanding, his Labour Party remained largely imprisoned by a status quo that was, in the world beyond Westminster and Whitehall, increasingly rejected. His Labour became lost in a no-man's land, offering enough of a break with the politics of the past to enrage the *Daily Mail* and the *Telegraph* into seeing resurgent Bolshevism, but not enough of a difference to actually attract any new voters to the party's side.

Alternatives Lacking

If Labour looked unattractive, alternatives to it appeared still worse. Throughout the New Labour years, one initiative after another was taken to form a party in opposition to Labour, once the latter had abandoned any pretence of working for socialism. None of them got any serious traction other than, briefly and locally, Respect, which benefitted from being led by an experienced politician (George Galloway) and from close association with a powerful mass movement (Stop the War). Nevertheless, their votes in elections ranged from the poor to the entirely risible, sometimes being less favoured by the electorate than explicitly silly parties seeking to memorialise Elvis Presley or champion the interests of dogs. The role of the first-past-the-post electoral system played a part in this sorry record – where proportional representation was applied, in the Scottish Parliament, for example, the far left briefly did somewhat better, before being terminally overcome by a sex scandal involving its leading personality, Tommy Sheridan. But it cannot be the whole story. The disengagement of the left from the concerns of most of the people most of the time, over a prolonged period, is the greater part of that story. Sectarianism, outsized personalities and a tendency to get bogged down in disputes concerning events long ago make up much of the balance.[6]

The picture sketched here of the left in the years immediately before 2015 is of a decent amount of oppositional energy crackling around, a paucity of strategic vision and a lack of serviceable organisational vehicles for its ambitions, all in an environment where its arguments could at least expect a hearing. In turning to parliamentary politics, it remained facing a more-or-less solid wall of elite commitment to the Thatcher-Blair settlement combining free markets, lightly regulated corporate power and aggressive Atlanticism, modulated only by an intermittently applied social liberalism.

The 2015 general election painted all Labour's weaknesses on an unforgiving canvas. Ed Miliband secured an anaemic improvement on the 2010 vote, but lost seats as Labour's Scottish redoubts were swept away in a nationalist landslide which saw the Scottish National Party (SNP) win fifty-six out of fifty-nine Scottish constituencies. Here was the first 'red wall' being blown apart through the replacement of class by a different political alignment, and it was nothing to do with Brexit or Jeremy Corbyn. Elsewhere, there was growing evidence of Nigel Farage's UKIP eating into Labour's vote in many of its traditional strongholds. This was to prove to be a gateway drug to full Toryism four years later. The Green Party too made progress, albeit more modest, among the young and the liberal. Ed Miliband had ended up pleasing nobody, with Labour's vote fragmenting in every possible direction. Many Labour voters apparently wanted change, but not the rather tepid change Labour was proposing. The election terminated his leadership, with the prevailing assumption among the pundit classes now being that Labour would revert to full-blown Blairism, since there seemed no other vibrant possibility on offer. That is not what happened, of course.

The left had only tattered sails to raise to catch the post-election breeze. The advent of 'Corbynism' was a phenomenon it had scarcely anticipated. Nevertheless, it was a left which Corbyn's ascent was able, *mirabli dictu*, to unite. As historically fissiparous as it was contemporaneously enfeebled, it rallied all the forces it had, old and new, to make the most of the surprising opportunity. The old argument about the utility of the Labour Party was at least suspended, talk of new parties was stilled, and the Labour-sceptics gladly shared the same trenches as the Labour-foreverists on the left. Enthusiasm for the most part conquered time-honoured doctrinal disputes. No one with even a passing interest in the British left could fail to be astonished at this development, nor have been surprised when some of the familiar divisions started to reappear.

It was this precariously united left, gathered in support of a parliamentary leading group unprepared for leadership and with inadequate social weight in the country as a whole, which had the chance to re-pose the question of socialism in Britain. Even from the present perspective of defeat, it seems astonishing not that it failed, but that the failure did not come much harder and much sooner.

3
Radicalism without a Route Map

When Jeremy Corbyn threw his hat in the ring for the succession to Ed Miliband, his appeal was largely oppositional. He was against austerity, and had been against the Iraq War: positions that demarcated him from Labour's recent past and from his rivals for the leadership. He was against dissimulation, against trimming or hedging one's bets – qualities that emerged from the very first leadership debate, held in marginal Nuneaton, and which the other candidates, marinated in Westminster bubble-speak and New Labour triangulation, could not emulate: straight-talking, honest politics.

One of Corbyn's greatest personal and political strengths was his determination to act as a tribune for the poorest – the homeless, the destitute and impoverished, the migrant worker, those struggling with mental health conditions, the disabled. The plight of all these people had been worsened by the savage spending cuts imposed by the Cameron coalition after 2010. Corbyn had fought against these depredations in the streets and in Parliament, challenging Labour's own wee timorous opposition to the Tory-Liberal Democrat measures. Miliband had been anxious not to over-alarm Blairites in the PLP, which was not a concern for Corbyn. The Labour frontbench's non-opposition attained its apogee immediately after the 2015 defeat, when acting leader Harriet Harman whipped Labour MPs to abstain on a Tory welfare bill mandating further cuts – all in the interests of financial responsibility. This undoubtedly benefitted Corbyn's campaign, since he rebelled against the whip (as he often did) to oppose the Tory measures, while his leadership rivals meekly accepted that the poor might have to pay a price to demonstrate Labour's market rectitude. By this stage, party members had had enough of such equivocations. His setting out an alternative was both right in principle and politically timely.

Corbyn did not, of course, have a ready-made programme for government, nor worked-out policy proposals for most issues. He had his instincts and life-long convictions – necessary, but not sufficient. The stock of socialist ideas had not been refreshed, the prospect of a socialist government in Westminster having appeared so remote. No Keynes or Beveridge, no Crosland or Benn, had been tilling the political soil in readiness for a left-wing Leader of the Labour Party. This was not a unique shortcoming of the Labour left: Corbyn's success in the leadership race was in part a consequence of the nullity of his opponents, who lacked two ideas to rub together. But Burnham, Cooper and Kendall sought power to keep things largely as they were, which is the easier route. The Corbyn Project needed more than this. Before delving into the story of how that project fared – its highs and its lows – it might be helpful to draw out the two things that perhaps more than anything made 'Corbynism' what it was: a comparatively radical economic offer, and its hostility to militarism.

Napkin-omics

I was contacted by the director of Corbyn's leadership campaign, Simon Fletcher, on 20 July 2015.[1] The campaign was accelerating; Corbyn's popularity and plausibility were growing daily. Fletcher asked me for urgent suggestions for a speech on the economy which candidate Corbyn was to make a couple of days hence. I was on holiday at the time, walking along Hadrian's Wall with my wife Anna and two friends from Stop the War, Lindsey German and John Rees. We discharged our mandate in a pub called The Crown that evening, drafting an economic programme on a napkin, which I retain. The gist was conveyed to Fletcher the next day in the more conventional format of a text message. Straight from the napkin:

JC needs to have a wealth-creation agenda so he is not only the candidate of welfare. Free-market wealth creation has failed so we need an imaginative interventionism to get Britain producing. We have wasted seven years since the crash – seven lean years – where growth has been anaemic or non-existent and we have become a low-wage low-skill economy. Ideas: a productivity programme that rewards investment rather than speculation; taxing manufacturing and financial firms at different rates. Britain is in a Tory development trap – low wages mean no incentive on bosses to invest. Raise living wage, public ownership of rail and energy to secure infrastructure, massive state investment in housing – homes, not market bubbles. End the Casino Economy by making finance work for the economy. Set up a National Investment Bank to drive innovation and high-tech investment.

The napkin indicated that the new movement around Jeremy Corbyn would need to develop an economic strategy that was more than simply opposition to austerity. Corbyn's rapport with the poor needed to be complemented by an 'offer' to the larger sections of working people not on the breadline, but who were troubled by the prospects for themselves and their children under Tory rule. More profoundly, this was a challenge to rearticulate the argument, unmade for a generation at least, that socialism could allow for the more dynamic development of the economy than capitalism. This meant overturning the entrenched 'common sense' that while the left had the heart, the right had the wallet; that the former could be trusted with wealth distribution but only the latter with wealth creation. Hence the emphasis on investment, productivity and a creative tax policy. All that together did not amount to socialism, of course – several more pub napkins would have been required to extend the perspective that far – but it did indicate a more classically social democratic approach that reversed New Labour's laissez-faire outlook and replaced it with something that was radical, especially by the standard of political options shrunk by the decades of neoliberal consensus.

Fleshing out a policy offer proved to be a slow-burn process, however. The ferment of ideas sparked by 'Corbynism' was slow to . . . ferment. The Corbyn leadership itself was overwhelmed by the daily political agenda. Parliamentarism is designed not to permit space for strategic thinking, as the remarkable lack of important political works written by politicians illustrates. John McDonnell did sign up some blue-chip economic advisors, but most found reasons to bail out as soon as the political wind turned adverse. I recall making an impassioned plea at the April 2017 *Historical Materialism* conference for our academic supporters to start getting their hands dirty. Jon Trickett and I subsequently tried to pull together some advisory groups, but this got bogged down in a bureaucratic 'preparing for government' programme run by LOTO. Of course, prior to the June 2017 general election, few took seriously the idea that Labour might actually need a programme for government. Andrew Fisher, director of policy, did a good job on the manifesto, which was more or less pitch-perfect (see chapter 4).[2] Afterwards, the pace quickened. The irrepressible Mark Perryman produced a volume of essays trying to flesh out our agenda, while new thinkers like Novara Media's Aaron Bastani and economist Grace Blakeley did some fermenting of their own.[3]

McDonnell Gives a Lead

Of course, the task of carrying economic policy forward fell largely to John McDonnell. His appointment as shadow chancellor in September 2015 had been made easier by the decision of the incumbent, Chris Leslie, not to serve under Corbyn, thus setting Leslie on a road which took him out of the shadow cabinet, the Labour Party and parliament in short order. Leslie is now a lobbyist for debt collectors. Unite and other unions opposed McDonnell being named his replacement. We were wrong to do so. There was a concern that giving McDonnell the Treasury brief would be seen as a sectarian signal and make it harder to win PLP support for the new leadership. We urged that he become shadow business secretary instead. The unions' arguments more or less reversed reality. In fact, PLP backing – or even toleration – of Corbyn was not attainable, and his first shadow cabinet proved to be considerably over-inclusive, stuffed with people who had no intention of making a constructive contribution. This was appeasement without a purpose.

McDonnell proved to be an outstanding shadow chancellor. He gradually assembled a serious economic plan for a radical Labour government, putting economic flesh on the bare bones of 'Corbynism' through a focus on the productive economy and socialist wealth creation. He also sponsored the development of the Green New Deal, a significant synthesis of new progressive political thinking. McDonnell's presence at the heart of policy-making, and at Corbyn's side, was clearly essential. As for our preferred alternative for shadow chancellor, Angela Eagle . . . that would not have worked, so much is clear.[4] It was not the last misjudgement made while we grappled with opportunities few had prepared for. The construction of a Corbyn front bench was not something that had been extensively game-planned.

The most serious criticism that can be made of McDonnell's overall strategy was his gratuitous ruling out of exchange controls to stop capital flight in a January 2019 interview with the *Financial Times*.[5] That was a mistake at several levels. It failed to recognise that a degree of delinkage between global capitalism and a radical government set on economic transformation would be unavoidable, if the government were to work. To allow capital to move freely would simply put that government at the mercy of speculators who would start a run on the pound at the first sign of discomfort, destabilising Labour's economic strategy from the outset. It was also an act of political disarmament, a signal that Labour would not meet City resistance to the implementation of its programme by escalation – curbing the City's powers – but would instead be prepared to back down if it could not persuade high finance to be reasonable. This logic had the potential to constrict even a tax-and-spend, anti-austerity government, as plenty of experiences elsewhere – and indeed Britain's own social democratic history – have shown. Of course, delinkage from international capitalism would not prove cost-free, in either the short- or long term. But it would have been democratically defensible if the City – unpopular since 2008 at least – attempted to force an elected government to abandon its mandate. Pre-emptively discarding the most potent weapon against such sabotage sent a signal that even a Corbyn government would not cross red lines drawn by global markets.

The capital controls issue underlines that the Corbyn project was not about seeking to immediately break with capitalism per se, nor was it situated in a framework of class struggle. It instead articulated a desire to end austerity and reduce inequality: traditional social democratic objectives which social democracy had, in Britain and elsewhere, largely abandoned. Of course, what 'Corbynism' did offer was radical enough to earn it the enmity of all those invested in the status quo, in the labour movement and without, in part because the elite could have had no confidence in how a Corbyn government *would* respond in the event of a real or manufactured crisis. It's impossible to know whether McDonnell would have been as accommodating to finance capital as his charm offensive in the City was intended to suggest. His programme represented a rupture with the norms of governance that had prevailed for the preceding forty years. Democracy would be given scope to push back against big business, workers re-empowered against their employers. Meeting social needs would drive key areas of government policy. It would have been a start.

Corbyn's Anti-imperialism

If Corbynomics was regarded as a provocation by the authorities, Corbyn's other distinctive agenda – his anti-imperialism – moved them to transports of rage. It struck not just at their interests but their very identity, for reasons rooted deep in Britain's past. The historic use of systemic coercion to ensure the transfer of wealth from the oppressed peoples of Asia, Africa, Latin America and the Middle East to the metropolitan centres – with a fraction of the proceeds being used to help create welfare provision and allow for higher wages at home – is the underlying premise of reformist socialism, and it has helped integrate working-class opinion into de facto toleration of capitalism. The ideological underpinnings of racial superiority, or a special British mission, has been an articulation of this. The words of 'Land of Hope and Glory' are peculiarly well-suited to a regime of capital accumulation: 'Wider still, and wider, shall thy bounds be set/God, who made thee mighty, make thee mightier yet!'

The expansion of democratic rights in Britain more or less kept pace with the extension of the Empire. It would be an oversimplification to say that every broadening of the franchise from the Second Reform Act through to the end of the First World War was accompanied by a new accession of colonial territories to the mother country, but there is a correlation. If the struggle of the British peoples won democracy from the Establishment, it was the strength afforded by the formal and informal Empire that made the concession bearable to the ruling elite. From Bevin's determination to preserve the Empire after 1945 down to Blair's enthusiastic support for the disastrous aggression against Iraq, Labour's record in office bears witness to its overriding loyalty to the system that accorded British working people, however impoverished, economic and political advantages denied to those the Empire ruled over, or those that imperialism subordinates today.

It is important to remember three things that imperialism *is not*. First, it isn't over: imperialism has outlasted the formal possession of colonies and pertains as an organising dynamic of the international order to this day. Second, it isn't a policy, such as can easily be switched on and off. Rather, imperialism is a systemic issue shaping British society. And third, it isn't only about what happens 'over there', because imperialism also impacts on what happens at home – indeed, on what 'home' is. The neatest definition of imperialism was supplied by a British Marxist historian of these matters, Victor Kiernan, who described it as 'coercion exerted abroad, by one means or another, to extort profits above what simple commercial exchange can procure'.[6] To this day, British political economy is to a significant extent conditioned by the consequences of the country's century of global hegemony and its enduring central role in capitalist globalisation. It is commonplace to deplore the disproportionate power of the City of London in Britain's economy – a hypertrophied financial sector servicing global capital far more than domestic industry and shaping the British state's willingness to support intervention anywhere necessary and possible, the better to maintain a world of unimpeded capital flows, from which the City profits mightily.

Imperialism, then, is not a static phenomenon: formal colonies have been relegated to history. Capitalist globalisation has swept the world, modifying the political dynamics of the export of capital, and the justifications for military intervention by the great powers have moved with the times. 'Christian civilisation' and 'stopping the spread of Communism' are out; 'introducing democracy' and 'preserving human rights' are in. The mechanics – bombing, military occupation, regime change – are not so different, however.

From its earliest years, however, Labour has also been home to a dissident trend, supportive of the struggles of people around the world for independence and self-determination, and opposed to neocolonial wars – the tendency of Fenner Brockway and Tony Benn, for example.[7] That tendency has never been dominant when Labour is in government, or even particularly influential. Instead, bipartisan continuity of foreign policy has in practice involved Labour maintaining the main lines of Tory policy, with occasional ethical embellishments. British social democracy thereby effected a schematic division which grips many of its supporters, including some on the left, to this day: that domestic and foreign policies exist in different watertight compartments, and so one can be a radical in domestic policy without addressing the international situation or Britain's privileged and often aggressive place within it. Nationalisations and nurseries are fine, but don't mention NATO or nukes.

Jeremy Corbyn not only stood in the anti-imperialist tradition, it was one of the main focuses of his political work since entering parliament in 1983 – he was known as the 'foreign secretary of the left'. This above all outraged the Establishment and its echo chamber on the right of the Parliamentary Labour Party. The PLP majority would not die in a ditch to keep the water industry in private hands, but the alliance with Washington, the right and capacity to intervene militarily wherever necessary, and the solidarity of NATO – those were different matters. There was nothing in 'Corbynism' more threatening than its anti-war campaigning and refusal to automatically assume the alignment of popular interests with those of the British state on international issues. There is also nothing on which recent history has, from Iraq to Libya to Afghanistan, supplied it with a more resounding vindication.

Corbyn had been attacked from his earliest years in the Commons because he turned a sympathetic ear to the cause for which the Irish Republican Army fought, a position that did him no harm at all in his Islington North constituency – anyone who spent any time in the Archway Tavern in the 1970s could attest to that. He spoke out against the great injustice done to the Chagos Islanders, evicted from their homelands to make way for a US military base by the Wilson government. Indeed, when he had the opportunity to meet President Obama in 2016, it was the first thing he raised. He strongly sympathised with the Palestinian cause, and reached out to organisations like Hamas and Hezbollah which have stood against Israeli occupation and expansionism.[8] He was famous for his anti-war campaigning and was deeply knowledge-able about progressive struggles around the world, in Latin America in particular. And he was a long-standing champion of the Campaign for Nuclear Disarmament and its demand for the scrapping of Britain's *soi-disant* independent deterrent, which is neither independent nor much of a deterrent, but is ruinously costly. All this led to him being simultaneously denounced as a pacifist and a terrorist sympathiser, consistency not being an issue for his critics.

The internal opposition to Corbyn's international agenda manifested itself from the start. On 26 November 2015, the Cameron government proposed a new campaign of bombing in Syria – this time against Islamic State, as opposed to 2013, when the putative target had been the Assad government. Much of the shadow cabinet rebelled against Corbyn's argument that a further military intervention in the Middle East was a bad idea, and that Britain should instead exert itself to bring the civil war in Syria to a negotiated end as a prerequisite for isolating ISIS. It was by this stage clear that the regime in Damascus, flush with Russian military support, was not going to be brought down. At McDonnell's urging, Corbyn did not impose a whip on the PLP – a step backward from Ed Miliband, who had whipped the 2013 vote. The cockeyed argument was that going to war was 'a matter of conscience', on which MPs should be accountable solely to their inner voices. Most Labour MPs did follow Corbyn's lead but others, including Deputy Leader Tom Watson, did not, and the Leader had to endure the embarrassment of shadow foreign secretary Hilary Benn making a barnstorming speech from the front bench in favour of the bombings.

In like vein, the biggest single policy rebellion against Corbyn's leadership came on 26 October 2016, when around 100 MPs refused to back a Labour motion to end arms sales to Saudi Arabia. The rebellion was a cynical attempt to undermine Corbyn and to prove fealty to imperial priorities in the Gulf at the expense of the suffering people of Yemen. The same loyalty to imperialism on Labour's backbenches found its hooligan voice on the day that the endlessly delayed Chilcot Report into the Iraq War was finally published. As Jeremy Corbyn spoke in the House of Commons an enraged Ian Austin shouted, 'You're a disgrace.'9 Corbyn, on the other hand, took the opportunity of the report's publication to deliver on the commitment he had made in his leadership election campaign to apologise to the Iraqi and British people on behalf of the Labour Party for the aggression against Iraq in 2003, a Labour government initiative, of course. This he did before an audience that included Iraqi representatives, leaders of the Stop the War

Coalition and British soldiers who had been sent to fight in that criminal and futile adventure. A journalist once asked me what had been my proudest moment during the Corbyn leadership. That was it, neck-and-neck perhaps with his response to the Manchester bombing during the 2017 general election campaign, which established that our international outlook was popular as well as right.

Practical Corbynism in the World

Translating that outlook into a new foreign policy was obviously going to be challenging. This was an area in which Corbyn gave a strong personal lead, albeit not one always followed by the relevant members of the shadow cabinet. At a meeting of his strategic team in November 2018, Corbyn led with a clear exposition of what he wanted in this field of policy. There was to be an 'end to the consensus on foreign policy since World War Two', and no more wars of intervention.[10] Security was 'not about weaponry but about instability, climate change and cyberattacks', among other issues. Britain would remain a NATO member under his leadership 'despite scepticism', but would 'push a human-rights agenda'. It would 'reach out' to Russia, 'without backing away from human-rights issues'. 'Human rights, peace and democracy' would be our parameters for dealings with the world, including in trade arrangements. Saudi Arabia was cited here as a target for tightening up. The Department for International Development would be strengthened, but there would be no Ministry of Peace, which Corbyn felt would be gimmicky. Nor would he press for unilateral nuclear disarmament by scrapping Trident, preferring to 'move the debate forward on a global ban on nuclear weapons'. This was a concession, but one substantially vitiated by the scarcely concealed fact that Corbyn would never order Trident's use. (Moral considerations aside, no party Leader has ever explained under what circumstances 'pushing the button' might make whatever situation Britain was in anything other than substantially worse.) Finally, he pledged to continue to stay engaged with the Party of European Socialists after Brexit, while also reaching out to broader forces, like the Brazilian Workers Party.

Working with Jennifer Larbie, the international officer in LOTO, I produced a strategy paper early in 2019 to carry forward the foreign policy proposals, noting that

> we need to do more to outline what we mean by Labour's new approach, and win still greater public support for our main proposals. Amongst other things, we need to be clear as to how Labour's approach enhances our security. This in turn means a united front bench commitment (particularly in the most relevant portfolios) behind a new international radicalism . . . the simultaneous rise of China economically and the sort of authoritarian nationalism embodied by Trump politically are making the existing consensus unsustainable quite independently of anything our party says or does.[11]

The paper thus addressed a particular blind spot – China.

> Far more serious work and thinking needs to be developed as to how a Labour government would relate to China given its growing international importance economically, the potential of the Belt and Road Initiative and its . . . counter-hegemonic role on the one hand, and the concerns about the abuse of its Muslim population in Xinjiang, and other human rights issues, on the other.

There was never the debate about China within the Corbyn team that its importance demanded. The paper concluded by enjoining the front bench teams for foreign affairs and defence to 'ensure there are workable strategies for advancing this agenda when in office. Civil service recalcitrance may be anticipated'.

The paper's conclusion indicated that the shadow ministers leading in these areas, Emily Thornberry and Nia Griffiths, were not exactly signed up to Corbyn's worldview.[12] Preparations for introducing a new approach when in government were desultory at best, although a roundtable discussion with a range of experts on different aspects of foreign affairs in 2018 tried to put together a workable plan for pursuing our objectives. The idea of a reshuffle that would address the front bench problem – the most favoured version had Diane Abbott and Thornberry swapping posts – was one of those interminable issues that was never resolved. Reshuffles were not altogether a forte for Corbyn's office.

Although there was a pragmatic recognition that neither NATO withdrawal nor unilateral nuclear disarmament were on the immediate agenda – not least because there wasn't the slightest chance of securing a parliamentary majority on either matter – a Corbyn government would have aimed at disengaging Britain from the US-led hegemonic project to focus instead on dispute resolution, de-escalation of conflicts and the reallocation of resources to poverty alleviation. It would have been a friend, rather than the sworn enemy, to movements for liberation and social justice around the world. Over a longer term it would have reduced the power of the City of London and curbed the arms trade, two drivers of neo-imperial policy. It would have taken arms conversion seriously, and it would not have assumed that Britain has the right or the responsibility to intervene militarily willy-nilly. Such a foreign policy would have been a historic development and, I believe, a popular one, both in Britain and abroad.[13] In view of the record of New Labour in office, such a reorientation could scarcely fail to be an improvement for both the British people and the rest of the world alike.

Opposition to austerity, a new place for Britain in the world, an end to neoliberalism, a return to state intervention in the economy, a healed society and honest politics: that was the basic promise of Corbyn. Many of the ten points on which he successfully stood for leader in 2015 – growth, not austerity; action on climate change; public ownership of the railways and the energy utilities; a fully funded NHS – have indeed become, as he was to tell the 2017 Labour Party conference, the new common sense.

It is perfectly true that this platform – McDonnell's economic strategy allied to a slightly diluted Corbynist anti-imperialism – was no more than a programme for a revived and radicalised social democracy, buttressed by expanded scope for politics beyond parliament. It was not socialism by a long chalk. It would, however, have created circumstances in which the connection of the one to the other, of reforms today and systemic change tomorrow, could be explored anew. It was also a platform for something else: hope, in a country becoming increasingly hopeless. A conviction that democracy had to be about genuine choices, not repackaged variants of the same old, same old. Corbynism's transformative capacity was never tested in practice, but it opened up new spaces.

4
2017: Oh, Jeremy Corbyn

> Conference, against all predictions in June we won the biggest
> increase in the Labour vote since 1945 and achieved Labour's best
> vote for a generation. It's a result which has put the Tories on
> notice and Labour on the threshold of power.

Thus Jeremy Corbyn addressing the Labour Party annual conference in September 2017, to a rapturous reception, after Labour had
succeeded in wiping out the Tory government's majority in the
general election four months previously.

Against all predictions indeed. On my first day working on
Labour's election campaign that year, I was sagely advised by
Patrick Heneghan, the party's executive director for elections and
campaigns, that the struggle we were just embarking on would
avail little. 'All elections end up within two or three per cent of
where they start out', he told me.

Heneghan was merely channelling the conventional wisdom,
which was that for all the huffing and puffing general election
campaigns barely moved the dial of voters' preferences, which
preceding years had already set. Had he been right, Corbynism

was heading for calamity. When Theresa May had called the election, three years earlier than required and in defiance of her own commitments to do no such thing, she was more than 20 per cent ahead in the opinion polls. Labour trailed at around a 25 per cent vote share. On Heneghan's calculation, Labour would lose safe seats hand over fist and would see its number of MPs shrivel to well below 200. That would at least have had the merit, from the perspective of the Labour HQ panjandrums, of bringing the Corbyn experiment to a swift termination and putting the insurgent left firmly back in its box.

What actually happened was very different. Labour's share of the vote rose from 30 per cent in 2015 to 40 per cent, the biggest increase since that secured in 1945, when the base line was a general election ten years earlier, rather than two, and with a world war in between. That 40 per cent was more than the share achieved not only by Ed Miliband in 2015, but also Gordon Brown in 2010 and Tony Blair in 2005. In terms of absolute number of votes, Corbyn's Labour of 2017 outpolled Blair's of 2001 (when a landslide Commons majority was nevertheless retained) by more than 2 million. Perhaps the most staggering fact is that Corbyn won more votes *in England* than Tony Blair secured in his 1997 pomp, or ever.[1]

Lesson One: The conventional wisdom is conventional not because it is wise, but because it serves to keep us stupid.

This result needs remembering, precisely because so many are so keen to forget it – the media pundits who misjudged the whole election and Labour's right wing above all. They joined Theresa May as the big losers of the 2017 election. Rather than Heneghan's anticipated losses, Labour added thirty seats to its total, sufficient to deny the Tories an overall majority. Labour's advance was secured despite a hurricane of press abuse, a campaign scarred by two major terrorist attacks, and the cynical defeatism of parts of the party apparatus and indeed some of the Labour MPs who ended up beneficiaries of the Corbyn bounce. Of course, it was not enough – the Tory vote increased too, by nearly 6 per cent over 2015 (something often forgotten by Theresa May's Tory critics), and the Conservatives remained comfortably the largest party in the Commons.[2] A diminished May was able to cobble together a governing arrangement with the Democratic Unionist Party of Northern Ireland. Nevertheless, for a campaign which began with Theresa May set fair to implement the injunction from the *Daily Mail* to 'crush the saboteurs', to end with the 'saboteurs' so defiantly uncrushed was a decent achievement.[3] It showed the potential of radical social democracy.

This result and the eight months or so that followed it represented peak 'Corbynism'. Many of the arguments deployed so vituperatively against Corbyn in the media and the PLP over the previous two years were briefly stilled. It was a moment when, in the words of John Stuart Mill, 'The fundamental doctrines which were assumed as incontestable by former generations are again put on trial', or, as Daniel Finkelstein put it more prosaically in *The Times*, Labour had taken politics 'to the left and won votes rather than lost them. It is hard to argue now that such a platform is a loser'.[4] Had another snap general election been held, as seemed plausible given the inconclusive outcome in June, a Labour victory under Jeremy Corbyn would have been a likelihood.

Today, this is all bittersweet. The election result – product of a progressive remaking of Labour's politics turbocharged by the efforts of tens of thousands of activists – provided the platform for a further advance that never occurred. It proved to be a precursor not to great new possibilities but to a great unravelling. However, if that unravelling is replete with lessons that the left needs to examine, so too is the 2017 election, when over 40 per cent of the electorate was won to support a left-wing programme for government breaking with the main tenets of neoliberalism – something that had sat outside the bounds of the possible, according to the prevailing consensus, for more than thirty years.

The Campaign

We were surprised to be even fighting a general election campaign. When Corbyn had ascended to the top job in 2015, the next general election was meant to be five years away – an assumption fortified (mistakenly) by David Cameron's introduction of the Fixed-Term Parliaments Act, which seemed to preclude snap elections. We had no five-year plan when we started out, and it seemed quite possible that Corbyn's leadership would have ended before it could be tested in a general election. The Brexit referendum with its unscripted outcome, the defeat of the preposterous MPs' coup of 2016 and Tory duplicity all mandated otherwise. That a Conservative premier might lie was perhaps something we should have assumed – Boris Johnson has put the matter beyond doubt – but my recollection is that only Seumas Milne was consistent in urging us to assume that Cameron's postreferendum replacement Theresa May was being mendacious when she claimed she would go the five-year distance.

Barely a month before polling day local elections results were distinctly underwhelming for Labour. Opinion polls showed

Labour running behind the Tories even in ever-loyal Wales. I was visited in my Unite office by two leading left-wing commentators who insisted that the union should intervene immediately to avert catastrophe by securing Corbyn's replacement as leader. This plan was subject to a number of overwhelming practical objections, but in any case I advised my colleagues that the best thing to do was to hold firm, do the best we could for the cause and assess the results once they were in. Those who declined to panic would have a greater right to be heard in debates about the left's future when the smoke cleared. In the end, they both followed my advice.

Lesson Two: If things look bad, they will only get worse if you lose your nerve – any success presupposes resolution in pursuit of it.

I started working on the Labour campaign two weeks after the general election had been called, seconded full-time from my job at Unite. My arrival was greeted negatively in the capitalist press, I am happy to say. I even received the distinction of an editorial in *The Times* devoted to attacking me, which is a decent accolade. I was described as 'a longstanding supporter of the dictatorship of the proletariat', which was not as inaccurate as some other things written about me then and subsequently.[5]

My brief was, in part, to try to harmonise the efforts of Corbyn's own staff, decamped to party HQ for the campaign, with those of the party apparatus. The two were deeply estranged on political grounds and working in isolation from each other. In particular, there was a view among Corbyn's team – only too well-founded, as it subsequently proved – that the party staff under General Secretary Iain McNicol were less than fully on board. It was felt that my experience of managing Unite, an organisation with 1,300 employees, allied to my close association with Corbyn and some of his key operatives, including Communications Director Seumas Milne and his deputy Steve Howell, would assist in getting things done.[6] Managerial experience was at a premium among the Corbyn team. My authority was doubtless reinforced by the fact that I represented Unite – political philistines tend to respect money and power as much as they are indifferent to ideas, and Unite embodied money and power more than anything else in Labour's universe. Indeed, in the early weeks of the campaign it was funding Labour almost single-handedly. The philistines made nice, to my face at least. As the campaign developed my role extended into other areas, including strategy, communications and some speech-writing. It was an all-hands-on-deck few weeks, with enthusiasm in a common cause more than compensating for the absence of the management structures and punctilious decision-making I was more used to.

Regarding the result as in the bag, the Tories fought an awful campaign, exposing the inadequacies of May as a politician. She appeared averse to human contact and incapable of unscripted speech. The Tory manifesto was a dud, majoring on a 'dementia tax' plan to pay for social care which, while perhaps an honest attempt to grapple with a major problem, was a political liability. The Liberal Democrats, too, were obligingly inept, and were incapable of moving on from the issue as to whether their leader, Tim Farron, a Christian of fundamentalist disposition, did or did not regard gay sex as sinful. Farron was incapable of clarifying his thoughts, or more likely of articulating his feelings. Attempts to introduce other subjects, as when he revealed that his teenage bedroom wall had been adorned with a poster of Margaret Thatcher, did not particularly assist a party still struggling to escape from the odium of its coalition with the Conservatives.

Some assert that it was these blessings from Labour's opponents that accounted for our success. They certainly didn't hurt, but the argument is implausible. The surprising ineptitude of the Tories did not stop them registering a healthy increase in their vote; while the Liberal Democrats would still have been stymied by their engagement in austerity politics and their sensational dishonesty over tuition fees even had their campaign not been so fatuous. Theories that people voted Labour because they knew it wouldn't win have even less to recommend them. Voting for a party because you are certain it won't succeed is a motivation that gets very few people to the polling station. These are some of the theories peddled by those unwilling to examine the real sources of Labour's electoral renaissance. The professional politicians of the PLP and their ideological camp followers could not face up to the scale of their misreading of the popular mood. That is why, for Labour, 2017 has become the forgotten election.

Lesson Three: The left must remember its achievements, because our opponents won't.

That is not to say that many Corbynistas (this author included) were not surprised by the eventual result, which was above the top end of our more optimistic projections. I spent a fairly miserable two hours on election day in a hotel basement room in Victoria with Corbyn and his wife, Laura Alvarez, Seumas Milne, Karie Murphy and Andrew Fisher discussing responses to the possible outcomes expected that night. Luckily for my reputation I did produce a scenario for a hung Parliament in which event, I told Jeremy, his leadership would be safe. The other possibilities I outlined were bleaker.

How was relative success snatched from the jaws of absolute disaster? Immediately the election had concluded I was asked to produce a paper summarising the strengths and weaknesses of Labour's campaign, which was sent to the political leadership and the main figures at party headquarters. It is still my perspective, and is set out in the appendix.

Clearly some of that immediate analysis, which mixes political judgements with tactical, almost managerial, assessments, reads over-optimistically today. But a few of the points bear elaboration on account of their strategic importance.

Manifesto and Manchester

Above all, Labour offered the sort of genuine alternative in the election which had long since been excluded from mainstream political discourse. There was clear pink river separating Corbyn's Labour not just from the Tories, but also from the balance-the-books, free-the-markets positioning of New Labour, which had persisted in diluted form under Ed Miliband and Ed Balls.

The radicalism of the 2017 manifesto was well judged. It committed Labour to public ownership of the railways and the water and energy utilities, as well as Royal Mail. Taxes on the better-off (those earning over £80,000 a year) would rise, as would corporation tax, but fairly modestly. There would be a 'fat cat' levy on companies paying inflated salaries, and tax avoidance would be tackled. Welfare benefits would be unfrozen and the hated bedroom tax scrapped. University tuition fees would be abolished.

Much of the battery of Tory anti–trade union legislation, which had so shifted workplace power further towards the capitalists, would be scrapped and the scourge of zero-hour contracts ended.

A new National Investment Bank would help drive inward investment, including in manufacturing and in poorer regions. Labour also committed to building at least 100,000 units of social housing per year to tackle the gross shortage of affordable homes.

This was a programme compatible with the survival of capitalism but not with its prevailing neoliberal incarnation. The priorities of the market would no longer be imposed on society. Democracy would be given scope to push back against big business. Workers would be empowered as against their employers. Meeting social needs would drive key areas of government policy. The finance-capital priorities of the Treasury would be subordinated to those of the wider economy.

Ironically, the manifesto was weakest in the area where Corbyn's personal commitments were most passionate. The renewal of the Trident nuclear weapons system was reaffirmed, and there was even a pledge to meet the NATO military spending target of 2 per cent of GDP. Accompanying these was a sincere commitment to multilateral nuclear disarmament, but even centre-right governments pay lip service to that. In the field of foreign and defence policy, there was no sharp break from Labour's past.

For that, events were to play their part.

Even before the Manchester terrorist bombing on 22 May, Corbyn had made a campaign speech as good as saying he would never order the use of nuclear weapons, would withdraw British troops from Russia's borders, and halt British intervention in the Syrian civil war – indeed, would disengage from the whole regime change 'war on terror'. No part of this message was proving unpopular.

However, the outrage in Manchester brought the whole issue of Britain's wars of intervention in the Middle East and South Asia far higher up the political agenda. Campaigning was suspended immediately after the attack, and there was debate as to how Labour should respond – beyond the obvious condemnation of the terrorist and his actions – when politics resumed. It was Corbyn's own view, buttressed by Seumas Milne and myself in particular, that this was not the moment to resile from our long-held conviction that what happened 'over here' – however criminal or even barbaric – was connected with what Britain has done 'over there'. It was an unsought opportunity to engage the British people in a mature conversation about the consequences of British foreign policy under both parties. My own view was that there was little point in having Jeremy as Labour's Leader if at this critical moment we turned our back on the convictions we had so long campaigned for.

So, once again, 'conventional wisdom' went out of the window. Some were uneasy about this – not that they disagreed with the argument, but they felt it was risky and that it would be safer to stick with the usual orthodoxies in responding to the attack. Others held much worse opinions, of course. Labour staffers were later revealed in the leaked GLU report to have regarded Corbyn's position as disgusting, with one asserting that 'normal people' 'blame immigration' for terrorism, a reminder that 'Labour racism' is far from being an oxymoron. Corbyn was not that sort of normal, and he was determined to state the truth – that the 'war on terror' had failed in its stated objectives and had indeed contributed to the fact that such atrocities were still occurring in British cities. Milne and I drafted much of the speech in my Unite office, with Corbyn and Fisher improving it in an adjacent room. The key passages from the speech were these:

We will also change what we do abroad. Many experts, including professionals in our intelligence and security services, have pointed to the connections between wars our government has supported or fought in other countries, such as Libya, and terrorism here at home. That assessment in no way reduces the guilt of those who attack our children ... But an informed understanding of the causes of terrorism is an essential part of an effective response that will protect the security of our people, that fights rather than fuels terrorism ... but we must be brave enough to admit the war on terror is simply not working.

Naturally the Tories immediately presented his speech as an attempt to blame Britain for the terror attack. That was false, since Corbyn blamed nobody but the perpetrator, but more significantly it was a falsehood that failed in its purpose. Instant polling showed a big majority of the public agreed with the thrust of our argument, and the Tory line of denunciation was swiftly abandoned. There is a point here, especially important when we are endlessly advised that to regain working-class support Labour must wrap itself in the flag and mindlessly parrot the national security agenda as defined by the authors of the calamitous wars in Iraq, Afghanistan and Libya. We don't need to. People are perfectly capable of reflecting on the experiences of war this century and drawing rational conclusions. Nor do they believe the British government should be issued with a moral blank cheque for its actions abroad. The success of Corbyn's response to the Manchester atrocity was a measure of the embedding of the arguments of the Stop the War Coalition in the political culture of the country.

Lesson Four: A crisis is the moment to assert your values, not dilute them.

The Brexit Bullet

Theresa May framed the 2017 election as a Brexit poll, in which the Tories would assemble most of the 52 per cent Leave majority in the referendum behind her plan for a hard Brexit. The fact that UKIP, which secured 13 per cent of the vote in the 2015 election, had lost its *raison d'être* with the 2016 vote for Brexit made a Tory landslide seem like a plausible prospect. If those votes were all or mostly to return to the Conservative mothership, then all was over bar the shouting.

Labour's positioning on the issue was key to averting that outcome. We wanted to frame the election as being about social justice and Labour's positive agenda for transformation. In turn, that depended on dodging the Brexit bullet. The referendum result had divided much of Labour's vote – particularly in northern constituencies outside the large cities – from the party's member-ship, which heavily supported staying in the EU. The manifesto put it clearly: 'Labour accepts the referendum result and a Labour government will put the national interest first. We will prioritise jobs and living standards, build a close new relationship with the EU, protect workers' rights and environmental standards, provide certainty to EU nationals and give a meaningful role to Parliament throughout negotiations. We will end Theresa May's reckless approach to Brexit, and seek to unite the country around a Brexit deal that works for every community in Britain.' Further: 'Freedom of movement will end when we leave the European Union.'

This position stood on the democratic principle that the refer-endum result must be honoured and that, while the terms of Britain's departure from the EU were a legitimate matter for dispute, the fact of it was not. This reassured the many Leave voters in Labour seats (the majority of the electorate in most such seats) that the party was not going to seek to reverse the referendum result. They were assumed to be mostly fairly indifferent to the nuances between 'soft' and 'hard' Brexits, except concerning the free movement of labour. Labour made it clear that since this was exclusively an EU mandate (along with the free movement of capital, goods and services) it was a right that would lapse with Britain's exit from the EU, to be replaced by whatever migration policy Labour wanted to adopt. At the same time, there were strong commitments to the rights of EU nationals already living in Britain and to continued cooperation with our neighbouring countries.

Manifestly, this policy worked in terms of holding together the Labour coalition. It allowed Labour to move on to other, more unifying and fruitful, issues. An internal paper delimiting our strategy was even less equivocal than the manifesto: 'This election is about Britain not Brexit. Brexit is settled. The issue is how we protect jobs and living standards and build a fairer Britain after Brexit.'[7] As my report to the leadership on the campaign indicated, there was evidence that some of the ex-UKIP vote returned to Labour – a minority, but crucial in terms of holding seats in Leave-voting areas.

Some seek to frame the election differently. Peter Mandelson, still struggling to come to terms with the 2017 result and keen to avoid acknowledging any sort of success by the left or Jeremy Corbyn, argues that

> 2017 of course was a Brexit election. It was like a rerun of the referendum the year before, when the Leave half of the country lined up solidly with the Tories, and indeed increased the Tories' vote

share, and the Remain vote quit the Lib Dems and swung around behind Labour, raising our vote share too. That's what that was about. It wasn't a vote for socialism. It was actually a vote for Remain.[8]

Mandelson is wrong on every point. There was no movement of Liberal Democrats to Labour overall – the Liberal Democrats polled only fractionally worse than they had two years earlier. The source of Labour's 10 percentage point leap in vote share cannot be found there. The more objective British Electoral Study, after crawling over every nook and crevice of the polling data, concluded that:

> the main reason that Labour gained so much in the campaign at the expense of the other parties is the strong performance of Jeremy Corbyn, especially relative to Theresa May . . . Labour's election campaign allowed them to reach deeper into the pool of Euro-scepticism than they had in April.[9]

This allowed Labour to register substantial gains in vote share in what were to become the famous 'red wall' seats, which were then lost two years later. Indeed, most estimates conclude that nearly 4 million of Labour's 2017 voters had chosen Leave in the EU referendum – around a third of Labour's total vote.[10] Our general election script had spelt it out: 'This election is not a re-run of the EU referendum. The decision to leave the EU has already been taken by the British people.' Clear enough. As Ed Miliband subsequently observed, 'There is a danger that people want to write their own version of history which is most convenient. For some, 2017 was a rather inconvenient election.'[11]

Essentially, we did not allow the electorate to become polarised around the Leave/Remain axis and made it easier for those who shared Labour's economic and social perspective but wanted to leave the EU to vote for Labour. There is a lesson here in terms of handling the supposed 'culture war' divisions cleaving the working class. I can recall no resistance to our Brexit strategy either among the political leadership or within the HQ hierarchy. The contrast with 2019 could not be starker or more painful.

Lesson Five: Class politics should define our political battleground – play on Tory territory and you are losing from the outset.

Bureaucratic Betrayal?

An inspiring aspect of the 2017 election campaign was the active engagement of so many people working for a Labour victory. Labour's membership had soared under Corbyn's leadership to the point where it was the largest party on the left anywhere in Europe. When Theresa May flung down the gauntlet, there was a mass movement waiting to pick it up. Aided by benign spring weather, tens of thousands of people flung themselves into the campaign, canvassing, leafletting, organising rallies and other events, and flooding social media with Labour messages. They were not, *pace* Lord Mandelson, seized by a fit of 'remainia', but were mobilised by Corbyn's message of hope and change. In its closing weeks, the campaign acquired an evangelical flavour, driven above all by the itinerant Corbyn's programme of mass rallies around the country.

Were these activists – and, indeed, all Labour voters – betrayed? This question arises from the unofficial publication in April 2020 of a report prepared for the then general secretary of the party, Jennie

Formby. The report was designed to assemble all material relating to the work of the party's Governance and Legal Unit in handling anti-Semitism cases and to be submitted to the Equality & Human Rights Commission as part of Labour's evidence to the inquiry that the EHRC was conducting into it. In the course of researching the report, staff came across a mass of messages left on the party's servers that had been exchanged between senior and middle-rank party officials. Some of these were included in the report as evidence for its contention that handling anti-Semitism cases had been complicated by factional considerations, including by the faction opposed to Jeremy Corbyn's leadership.[12]

The messages are replete with racism, misogyny and generally abusive remarks made by party officials regarding Labour politicians (Diane Abbott in particular) and other staff or activists regarded as being on the left. They speak to the reactionary opinions of too many Labour employees, and to the rotten political culture which New Labour had baked into the apparatus as it decayed politically, a culture at odds not just with Corbynism but with even the most minimal traditions of social democratic decency, not to mention contemporary standards for organisational management. As a window into the inner world of New Labour's bureaucratic residuum, the report did an invaluable service.

It also revealed that some workers at party HQ on 2017 election night were crushed by disappointment when the BBC exit poll revealed that the country was heading for a hung Parliament, and that the expected destruction of the Labour left would have to be put on hold at very least. A safe space was established for them to grieve in – the general secretary's office no less.[13]

More significant, however, was the evidence that Iain McNicol had permitted the diversion of financial resources to a secret project, organised behind the backs of the party and campaign leadership, to provide funding to constituencies held by MPs beloved of the party's right wing who were not on the agreed list for HQ support – direct mailing to voters and social media promotion. According to the evidence, a special unit was set up in a separate building, Ergon House, to manage these resources, which may have amounted to around £135,000.[14]

To understand the significance of this, we must divert into the strictly specialist subject of seat targeting in an election campaign. This is the process determining which constituencies should have their campaigns resourced from the party's central funds, within the spending limits laid down by law. It can be a fraught matter, since it involves choices. Funding direct mail, for example, cannot be extended to all Labour candidates, at least without the spend on each falling to levels where it could not make a difference. Relevant seats are divided into two categories – 'defensive' ones, where Labour already holds the constituency but might be at risk of defeat, and 'offensive' seats, those held by other parties (mainly Tories in England) which Labour might hope to gain.

At the outset of the 2017 campaign, HQ officials led by McNicol and Patrick Heneghan were fighting an exclusively defensive campaign. All money was being targeted at supporting existing members of the PLP. This strategy flowed naturally from their reading of the polls and their assumption that the best Labour could hope for was damage limitation. Having already conceded the election to the Tories, their priority was to preserve as much of the right-wing/New Labour element in the PLP as possible – a basis for the return of Labour to 'common sense', they probably thought.

My first role upon joining the campaign in May was to prevail on McNicol and Heneghan to adopt a more offensive strategy and redirect resources to, at a minimum, enough campaigns in Tory-held seats to allow Labour to secure a potential parliamentary majority of one. To do otherwise would be to demoralise our campaign from the beginning, since it was more-or-less certain that this defeatist plan would leak to the media – as everything in Labour HQ did. We had to be in it to win it. Steve Howell had already been at work, in the name of the elected party leader, on securing a reorientation and with my additional support this now happened – in theory. Heneghan was obviously unconvinced, and remained keen to preserve his original target list.

McNicol and Heneghan said they would go along with what they had been told to do. During the campaign, Howell and I would frequently laugh that we had absolutely no idea, nor way of finding out, whether what had just been agreed in a meeting would be actually implemented. The apparatus held all the means of carrying out decisions (or not) in their hands. Our suspicions were well founded, but they were not really a laughing matter. If the revelations included in the GLU report are to be credited, McNicol went behind the backs of the party NEC, the party Leader, the campaign co-chairs and the elected party treasurer to divert funds to some of the seats that they felt needed resourcing, on the grounds that their removal from the original list had been a 'factional' move by Corbyn's team.[15] It should be said that where a particular candidate sat on the left–right spectrum was never a factor in our decisions on resource allocation. We were bound to look only at a seat's winability, or the extent to which it might be in danger, based on polling, canvassing evidence and so on.

Had these funds been allocated to the seats in which we were pushing to topple Tory incumbents in the final couple of weeks – seats which had not seemed marginal at the start of the campaign, long-shot seats now coming into prospect – could Labour have won? In my view it is possible but unlikely. The £135,000 allegedly siphoned off to the covert operation would have had to be absolutely precisely targeted on the right seats, since the total sum would have had a much smaller impact spread across a larger number of constituencies. Steve Howell, however, who has gone into this matter in the finest detail, since targeting was an area for which he had executive responsibility in 2017, thinks it is possible and his arguments should be given a hearing:

> Had we had the £135,000 that had apparently gone to the Ergon House operation, we could have added further 35 seats to the list for that final mailing. Would it have made a difference? As it turned out, of the 12 seats we did add, we won eight . . . and of the 35 seats we couldn't afford to add, we won 14 anyway. But we missed out on a further seven of those 35 seats by narrow margins – an average of only 451 votes. Any marketeer will tell you that a direct mail campaign normally has a success rate of 3% to 5% – and 3% of a mailing to 15,000 voters is 450.[16]

Eight was the magic number of additional seats required to deprive the Tories of the possibility of forming a governing majority with the Democratic Unionists. Of course, even with the extra eight seats, a Corbyn government would hardly have been a shoo-in. Given the Establishment's hatred and fear of such an administration, some other arrangement, including a minority Tory government, would seem a more likely outcome. But enough counterfactuals. The hard fact is that, if the evidence in the GLU report proves to be true, the Ergon House project was an unprincipled and dishonest manoeuvre, powered by political misjudgement.[17]

I do not know if McNicol and Heneghan and the rest of the Labour HQ hierarchy wanted Labour to lose in 2017. From my own dealings with them I think it improbable, although the hostility of some of the staffers immediately below them in the hierarchy was brazen. What united them all was a deep conviction that Labour was going to be defeated catastrophically and that the best they could do was try and mitigate the consequences, particularly with regard to their political allies. For what it is worth, I do not think they were working to sabotage Labour's campaign. They were instead imprisoned by their own pessimism and New Labour groupthink, but this did not stop Labour taking its share of the poll from 30 per cent to 40. The advance owed little to their efforts, but to imagine that such a vast leap forward could have been still greater without them is, on balance, an improbability. Had the entire Labour apparatus been fighting energetically and enthusiastically for a Corbyn victory from the moment of his election as leader – that is a different matter.

Lesson Six: If you can't verify, don't trust. But while they may indeed be against you, it's still in our own hands.

Weaknesses Exposed

Cracks were immediately apparent in the electoral edifice Labour erected in June 2017. For one thing, and almost decisively, six seats were lost to the Tories – five on the day, and one just slightly earlier in a by-election. They were all in traditional Labour areas in the Midlands and the North, most dramatically in the former mining seat of Mansfield, held by Labour since 1923. In these and all Labour's 'red wall' seats, the party's vote and its share of the poll both rose, sometimes considerably, and often to the highest levels since 2001, something Corbyn's critics were unwilling to acknowledge.[18] However, the consolidation of most of the ex-UKIP vote around the Tories, driven by the Brexit issue above all, flipped the six constituencies and made several more start to look marginal. In these areas – and there are many of them – working-class support for Labour, while refreshed, was looking increasingly conditional.

Another disappointment was the anaemic recovery in Scotland. Labour's haul went up from a humiliating one seat in 2015 to a merely derisory seven in 2017. The increase in the Labour vote in Scotland was only 2.8 percentage points, as against the 10-percentage point rise Britain-wide. The SNP's overpowering electoral hegemony, established despite its defeat in the 2014 independence referendum, was dented but far from dismantled. Many seats, in and around Glasgow particularly, were within a whisker of being won by Labour (and might indeed have been won had the campaign run for another week, as the wind blew briskly in our sails), but this was less due to Labour advancing than to the SNP losing votes to the Tories in seats the latter could never hope to win. Here was another warning: once politics reconfigures around an alternative identity to class – in this case the nationalist/unionist polarisation – it does not swing back swiftly or easily.

The campaign also highlighted endemic weaknesses in the Corbyn team in terms of strategic thinking and integrated planning. All those I worked with had great political and personal qualities and shared a fierce commitment to socialism, but only Jon Trickett found it easy to think and plan in longer-term, strategic frameworks.

The disjuncture between strategy and tactics was to become acute in relation to Brexit, the rock on which our hopes foundered.

Shortly after the campaign, Seumas Milne and I produced a paper on how to carry our position forward. Its conclusion was the obvious one. Labour needed to aim to increase its 40 per cent share of the vote to around 45 per cent to be sure of a majority. As the document put it,

> The extension of our vote needs to focus on those three areas where we made less progress than average in 2017, especially a) the working class in the north and east midlands . . . Although our vote rose significantly in these areas, the disproportionate shift of UKIP support to the Tories cut majorities and sometimes lost seats . . . it must be noted that our problem in these constituencies has been building up since 1997 . . . b) older people . . . our very serious deficit here requires some analysis, given the Tory attack on pensioners and social care, and our own positive offer on these matters. A possible factor is that these voters trusted the Tories to 'deliver Brexit' more than Labour, and that this over-rode other considerations . . . c) Scotland . . .[19]

Taking this analysis seriously would have mandated one thing above all – maintaining our position on Brexit, which was clearly key to enhancing support amongst the older and those in 'left-behind' industrial communities. As we know, that is not what happened. In practice, our tactics became oriented towards other groups entirely.

Scotland was clearly different, but there the problem was less policy on Brexit than how to modulate our position on Scotland's constitutional future, so that Labour was not confined to a three-way fight over the unionist half of the electorate, leaving the SNP vote effectively unchallenged over the rest. Polling indicated that this, rather than Brexit, was the key issue for most Scottish voters, although they were entwined.[20]

All this notwithstanding, the Corbyn project emerged from its first great electoral test firmly camped on the high ground. Following the terrible Grenfell fire a few days after the election, when Corbyn's compassionate response to a social crime again contrasted vividly with Theresa May's apparent empathy deficit, the party was in a clear polling lead. For the most part, the PLP was stunned into acquiescence in Corbyn's leadership after a campaign which had plumped up their majorities nicely for the most part. The hateful media pundits were not lost for words, but appeared lost for influence.

Of course, the old saw that you're never as vulnerable as when you're riding high was shortly to become fully operative. The frittering away of the gains achieved began before long. But for now we could bask in a measure of achievement. As Corbyn told the party conference that September:

It is often said that elections can only be won from the centre ground. And in a way that's not wrong – so long as it's clear that the political centre of gravity isn't fixed or unmovable, nor is it where the establishment pundits like to think it is. It shifts as people's expectations and experiences change and political space is opened up. Today's centre ground is certainly not where it was twenty or thirty years ago.

A new consensus is emerging from the great economic crash and the years of austerity, when people started to find political voice for their hopes for something different and better. 2017 may be the year when politics finally caught up with the crash of 2008 – because we offered people a clear choice.

We need to build a still broader consensus around the priorities we set in the election, making the case for both compassion and collective aspiration. This is the real centre of gravity of British politics. We are now the political mainstream. Our manifesto and our policies are popular because that is what most people in our country actually want, not what they're told they should want.

June 2017 had indeed been about the people not doing what they were told by the Establishment. The domination of the 'extreme centre' was threatened – and it did not take this lying down.[21]

5

Corbynism versus Labourism

Many of the obstacles in the way of advancing to a socialist society are obvious – the capitalist class, the state power it wields, the media it owns, the democratic routines it manipulates, the ideological presuppositions it determines (the natural order of commodity production, above all), the international alliances it contracts, the social habits it inculcates and much more.

However, the first rank of obstacles must include the Labour Party itself. Its century-long record was sketched in chapter 1, and it is scarcely encouraging for those looking to it as an instrument – *the* instrument in some perspectives – of social transformation. This history is not accidental, nor is it the product of nefarious misleaders bent on betrayal. The latter do feature, of course, but they are more symptom than cause. The roots of the problem lie in the impact of imperialism, and its accompanying reformism, on working-class political expression and the supremacy of parliamentarism buttressed by bureaucracy in its counsels. Those factors have made Labour, created as the party of the masses, also and at the same time a party of the state, integrated into the Establishment as a sort of auxiliary detachment. It has appeared more often as immovable object than irresistible force in the struggle for socialism in Britain.

The obstructive dynamic was operative in spades from the moment Jeremy Corbyn was elected Leader. The sharpest attacks on him came from within. The Establishment relied first of all on the Labour Party itself to rid the body politic of this turbulent preacher.

Parliamentarism and Its Problems

Pride of place must here be given to the Parliamentary Labour Party (PLP). In its majority, it fought the party's elected Leader from the outset, displaying little to no regard to the choice of the party's membership. Many of the party's elected representatives – the men and women whose support would be required to sustain a Labour government – denied the legitimacy of Corbyn's mandate as soon as it had been secured. This ferocious and unprecedented resistance of Labour's MPs to the party's preference as Leader overshadowed everything.

Several members of the shadow cabinet declared that they would refuse to serve under Corbyn, some going so far as to announce their resignations even as he was making his acceptance speech after the leadership election result was announced. He was faced with a wall of undisguised contempt and hostility at the weekly meetings of the PLP from the start, a raging of the entitled that sometimes seemed to teeter on the edge of physical violence directed against the Leader and his staff and supporters. Most Labour MPs considered it their bounden obligation to bring this aberrant leadership to an end as swiftly as possible, with abuse and intimidation acceptable weapons.

As we have seen, a significant minority, led by Deputy Leader Tom Watson, rebelled against Corbyn's opposition to bombing Syria at the end of 2015, in a calculated attempt at humiliating him.[1] The proceedings of shadow cabinet meetings were leaked to the media in nearly real time. Working hand-in-glove with the hostile journalists of the lobby, no trick was missed in trying to create a climate that would lead to Corbyn's speedy defenestration. This culminated in June 2016, just ten months after he was elected, when 80 per cent of the PLP voted no confidence in Corbyn, thereby precipitating a further leadership election for which, it transpired, the plotters were significantly less well prepared than the leadership itself and the movement supportive of it.

No Leader of the Labour Party in its history has been treated thus. The PLP set itself outside, apart from and *above* the rest of the party through a wholesale rejection of the Leader chosen by an electoral system which, when adopted two years previously, commanded near-universal assent (indeed, it had been blessed by Tony Blair himself in a rare endorsement of a Miliband initiative).[2] There was no pause for reflection as to why such a rank outsider as Corbyn had bested by a very considerable margin all the candidates offered up by the once all-conquering but now degraded New Labour dispensation. Instead, there was the implicit – and sometimes explicit – invocation of superior political wisdom and superior constitutional authority on the part of the party's elected MPs, sufficient to justify the imposition of their own judgement as to what was acceptable for Labour come what may.

Motives

The anti-Corbyn majority among Labour MPs were informed by different, if overlapping, political concerns. For a large number, the antipathy was based overwhelmingly on opposition to Corbyn's policies and programmes – his campaigning against imperialist war, his disregard for neoliberal economic orthodoxies (including austerity), his willingness to champion concepts long discarded by mainstream politics, like public ownership and tax increases on business and the rich. All this was anathema to New Labour, and their resistance to the new leadership was determined by their whole outlook, supportive of the capitalist system and the imperialist world order as it was and is. As Blair himself said, even if Corbyn's policies proved popular, they should still be rejected by right-thinking party members.[3]

For the rest of the party's MPs – probably the larger number – the issue was electability rather than programme. The PLP is full of decent men and women, rooted in their communities and sometimes the broader labour movement, who have nevertheless drunk deep and over-long at the poisoned well of conventional wisdom. They were convinced that Corbyn could only be an epic vote-loser. Had they believed otherwise they might have jogged along obligingly enough – as indeed they did in the months after the June 2017 election surprise. Fear for their seats and careers (or, more generously, the future of the party as an electoral force) rather than deep-seated ideological commitment to the decaying bromides of Blairism motivated their unhappiness with Corbyn. They were ready to be as social democratic as opinion polling allowed, but saw the new leadership as being several steps beyond that golden mean.

The PLP as it stood in 2015 had been shaped by a generation of New Labour hegemony within the party. Under the Blair leadership it was almost impossible for a candidate from the left to be adopted in a winnable seat. Those socialist MPs that Blair inherited upon assuming the leadership he tended to leave be, but vacancies were almost invariably filled by his supporters, leaving the Campaign Group of Labour MPs to slowly wither on the vine for want of reinforcements. Seats were divided up on an informal patronage system among New Labour grandees, with Gordon Brown and Peter Mandelson, as well as Number Ten, enjoying opportunities to place their supporters in safe Labour constituencies. Ed Miliband, when Leader, tended to wind down the central interference in selections for favoured sons and daughters, leaving it to local parties to make their choices unimpeded (the fiasco of his intervention in the Falkirk selection in Scotland being a disastrous exception). But the damage was done, and reversing it could only be a slow and protracted process, given the difficulties in replacing a sitting Labour MP in any circumstances other than their voluntary departure or electoral rejection.

'Clause One Socialism'

What is, or should be, the PLP's role in relation to the wider labour movement? The conventional view was clearly propounded by Lord Neil Kinnock, as set out in chapter 1 – Labour was, and must be, a party of parliamentary supremacy in which, therefore, parliamentarians must be supreme.

Kinnock connected two ideas, obviously linked but also distinct, in his little homily. The first is that the road to socialism could only lie through Parliament, and the winning of a parliamentary majority. The second is that therefore parliamentarians should have an enhanced and special role in determining the direction of the party, including who should serve as its Leader. Both proposals are questionable, and united in the Kinnock formulation, their weaknesses are compounded. However, Kinnock was on to something – Labour is pre-eminently a parliamentary party. Throughout, it has sought to operate strictly within the confines of the country's conservative constitutional arrangements, which in its periods of office have in turn generally been left very much as they were found in all essentials (devolved administrations in Scotland and Wales aside).

However, from its inception Labour has been a parliamentary party with a difference. The Tory and Liberal Parties emerged as court cliques, developed into parliamentary factions promoting distinct interests, and only became mass organisations in the country under the impulsion of the expansion of the suffrage (most successfully in the case of the Tories), whereas Labour developed elsewhere. It was rooted within society, and then sought to secure parliamentary expression for the interest that called it into being, organised labour. The traditional sequence – Parliament to country, elite to masses – was reversed. Labour had no need to adapt its form to democracy, since it was a product of it. The Tory Party was the Church of England in secular power, the party of Baldwin's 'hard-faced men' in business, of the imperial overlord and the Rear Admiral. It extended its reach into the masses of the middle classes and the professionals and beyond, including to the worker deferential to a social hierarchy sanctified by tradition and apparent successes. It created a mass political basis for an Establishment which hitherto had found little requirement for such a thing and had rested instead on coercion, commerce and Christianity. Labour began in the actual mines and mills, and specifically in the organisations formed to promote the immediate economic interests of the miner and millhand, the trade unions. Advancing that cause came to require parliamentary representation, for which the Liberal Party, the party of the mill-owner, was unreliable. Socialism, as known, had nothing to do with it, although socialists of a variety of hues circled as moths around the trade union flame in the early Labour Party. The aim of the Labour Party was initially to place trade unionists in Parliament – products of the movement and answerable to it.

That accountability was the first target of the Establishment. Diluting or even removing the responsibility of elected Labour MPs to the wider movement outside was the price of Labour's respectability. All MPs are expected to answer to the electorate in their constituencies at election time, of course, but in the meantime should answer only to their consciences and the Crown, and not necessarily in that order. Such is the essence of 'parliamentary sovereignty' – it sits in opposition to popular sovereignty and control. Decades later Arthur Scargill, then leader of the Yorkshire area of the National Union of Mineworkers (NUM), was threatened with being called to the bar of the House of Commons for his impertinence in suggesting that Labour MPs representing the Yorkshire coalfield, and sponsored by his union, should in turn be obliged to carry forward the policies advanced by the NUM. This outrage was condemned by a *Labour* MP, George Cunningham, in the House in 1975.[4] Cunningham displayed his own developed sense of parliamentary privilege by presenting himself successfully for re-election in Islington as a Labour candidate in 1979, before leaving the party to sit as an independent MP and then moving on to join the breakaway Social Democratic Party without in the least violating constitutional propriety, since it was only to his own sense of the appropriate, rather than to a democratic labour organisation, that he was obliged to present an account.

So Labour moved speedily towards what is now known as 'Clause 1 socialism', as embodied in the party's rule book: 'Its purpose is to organise and maintain in Parliament and in the country a political Labour Party.' Note the order of priority. The party thus constituted shall 'give effect, as far as may be practicable, to the principles from time to time approved by Party conference'. Alas, what the conference has held to be desirable or even urgent has very much proved to be not parliamentary-practicable down the years. The question of the proper relationship of the PLP to the wider party has been answered in practice – near-complete autonomy. The party can formulate whatsoever policy it likes, but its decisions can never be more than advisory. The parliamentary leadership alone determines what may be implemented and what discarded, whether it is as government or official opposition, answering to a phantom 'national interest' of which the movement from which it springs is a subordinate fraction. Never was this truer than under New Labour, when Blair made it a point of honour to demonstratively ignore any resolution passed by party conference which did not correspond to his own intentions.

For most of Labour's history, the Leader of the party was explicitly and first of all the leader of the PLP, elected solely by Labour MPs. The last so chosen was Michael Foot in 1980, following the resignation of Jim Callaghan. The seven leaders (as of 2021) chosen subsequently have emerged either from an electoral college of somewhat convoluted composition and procedure, or more recently from a direct vote of members, associated trade unionists and supporters. None of this has changed the essence of the balance of authority at all. It was on that assumption of time-honoured supremacy that the PLP rose up in 2015 and 2016 against a Leader imposed on them by scandalous intrusion of the outside world.

This was the consequence of treating MPs as a caste, raised above and insulated from the movement which created and sustains the party and sends them to the House of Commons. Indeed, the PLP's links with the wider movement have radically diminished in recent decades, and it is particularly unrepresentative of manual workers nowadays. This caste is invested with superior responsibilities, for the exercise of which the MP must depend on his/her own judgement, even if that sensitive plant can generally find expression only under the impulse of the party whip, as cracked by the Leader.

There is no path towards socialism which does not include addressing this issue of the supremacy of the Parliamentary Labour Party. That is why the failure of the 2016 coup was of such significance. For the first time, the membership of the party and the wider movement imposed its will on the MPs. Parliamentary resignations and votes of no confidence counted for nothing. Here was a dramatic rebalancing of authority which should resonate for the future.

The defeat of the coup was a near-run thing. Iain McNicol and the party apparatus did their best to assist the PLP, providing inaccurate legal advice to the NEC that Corbyn would need to secure fifty-plus nominations from MPs to secure a place on the ballot paper, which he would not have been able to do.[5] The effect of this would have been to remove the Leader without the members having a chance to vote on the matter. The decisive vote on the NEC was decreed to be taken by secret ballot in order to give the representatives of unions and other bodies the possibility of

breaking their mandates from their organisations. The manoeuvres failed, and Corbyn's place on the ballot was ratified in the
courts when the NEC decision was challenged. McNicol felt no
obligation to resign, which astonished nobody.

The left was brittle as well. While Corbyn remained firm as
waves of shadow cabinet members – eventually including nearly
all the 'soft left' – resigned, many of his allies did not. At the height
of the coup, I took calls in my Unite office from prominent left-
wingers urging that he stand down in favour of John McDonnell,
or Emily Thornberry, or Clive Lewis, or anyone or no one. They
all believed that his leadership was dead because MPs had withdrawn their blessing. They were all wrong. Unite did not waver in
its backing for Corbyn. On his return from a union conference in
the USA, happening as the coup unfolded, Len McCluskey
dismissed all talk of capitulation. Our view was that if Corbyn was
to be forced out of his hard-won office it would be better by far if
it were by decision of the members rather than by capitulating to
the clique in the Commons. The decision of the members proved
to be quite otherwise.

The Imperative of Reform

Would it hurt if the way Labour MPs voted was determined instead
by the policy of the party, as agreed by an executive representing
all elements of the movement? It seems undeniable that every
single Labour government in history would have left behind a
more profound record of social reform and played a more progressive and pacific role in world affairs had it been thus. Take the New
Labour government of Blair and Brown. Had it implemented
policy adopted by the party at its conferences, it would have

renationalised the railways, restored the right of trade unions to take solidarity action, funded council house building and held company directors responsible for health and safety breaches. It would not have embarked on the Private Finance Initiative, transferring public wealth into private pockets. It is also scarcely conceivable that it would have joined in the cataclysmic invasion of Iraq. Would not Labour-in-government have had a better record had it been guided in its policy by Labour-at-large?

Whatever sterling individual qualities a particular MP may have – and let us allow that a great many are conscientious in cultivating their constituents and are attentive to their concerns – they are there solely because of the Labour Party. Any other candidate advanced by the party would get more-or-less the same vote on polling day. Yet the Labour candidate in the moment of their success slips the control of the party and enters into a compact with the state instead. Some resist the cloying embrace of the Establishment and retain a strong connection to their socialist principles, the labour movement or even just the trade union with which they have been particularly associated. But they have never yet constituted a PLP majority, nor set its direction. Still less was that the case after the prolonged neoliberal hegemony of the Blair years.

The answer the left of the party has given to this problem has long been to demand mandatory reselection of Labour MPs. Under this procedure, every Labour MP would, in the course of each Parliament, have to submit themselves to their local party for re-endorsement. If a Constituency Labour Party is dissatisfied with their parliamentary representative they could choose another as their candidate for the next election, whereupon the incumbent would be expected to retire gracefully from the scene. Sometimes this is called 'open selection'. It has a lot to recommend it – an MP would be obliged to pay close regard to the views of their constituency party on issues which come before Parliament, for fear of losing their tenure. It could counter-balance safe-seat complacency by introducing an element of accountability separate from that of a general election.

It is also a problematic solution. Certainly, it is no panacea. When it was official Labour procedure in the 1980s, mandatory reselection did little to shift the balance of the PLP which, indeed, moved to the right throughout the period. What it *did* do was turbo-charge the breakaway organised by the Social Democratic 'gang of four' in 1982 by drawing to them MPs who might otherwise have stayed with Labour but for fear that their local parties were about to terminate their political careers.

Mandatory reselection became an issue again when Corbyn was elected on a platform which included a radical democratisation of the party. Scepticism as to whether the antagonisms it would generate with an always-febrile PLP were worth the bother led to a split in the Corbyn-supporting coalition at the 2018 party conference, to a certain extent pitting affiliated trade unions against left activists in constituencies, always an unhappy situation but by no means a novel one. In the end a tepid compromise was agreed, making it easier for local parties to 'trigger' a reselection process but falling short of making it automatic. In a sense it was a pointless argument – the new 'trigger' procedures were activated in a few constituency parties but did not lead to the replacement of a single Labour MP once the matter was put to a local vote.[6]

New thinking on this question would not hurt. The flaws in the mandatory reselection approach, even though the demand has attained totemic status among Labour progressives, are serious.

Above all, it deflects a collective problem – the relationship of the PLP to the wider movement – onto consideration of the individual merits of particular MPs. The latter is, exceptional cases aside, a dead end. It devolves responsibility for policing an MP's political performance from the party as a whole onto particular constituency parties. The results are bound to be invidious. Stalwart MPs who champion the party's policies could still fall foul of their local party (or cliques within it) for secondary or parochial reasons. Conversely, MPs who oppose the programme adopted by the party but nevertheless cultivate a good reputation in their constituency are unlikely to be threatened. It would be a lottery in which political considerations play no more than a part. Transforming the character of the PLP by such means would be the work of a lifetime at least.

It also unsurprisingly invokes the most spirited resistance from most MPs, who fear a distraction at best or their expulsion from the Commons at worst. Doubtless, such a system would bed down and become normalised over time. That was time Jeremy Corbyn never had.

A Collective Approach

More importantly, there is a different way to address the problem, one which does not devolve the solution onto 630 constituency parties each acting individually and which cuts to the heart of the disease of parliamentarism.

Recognise first that Parliament is a part of the labour movement's work and an obviously important one, but it is not the whole of it, nor are Labour parliamentary representatives the whole of the party. They are the section of the party delegated to work in Parliament to forward those of its objectives that require legislation and the formation of a government. They answer to the whole. In practice this means answering to the National Executive Committee of the party. This body already includes, in admittedly somewhat arbitrary proportions, representatives of affiliated trade unions, individual members in the constituencies, MPs, local government, youth, BAME members and so on. Its structure and make-up could doubtless be improved, and it could be chosen by a more uniform and comprehensible system of voting than at present. However, the biggest change needed is in its mandate, which has for many years excluded any significant role in policy-making, and none at all in the supervision of the party's parliamentary work. This has long been effectively delegated to the Leader and his staff, mostly based alongside the Leader in the House of Commons. The Corbyn leadership did not change this unsatisfactory state of affairs, although it would have liked to.[7]

Why should the NEC, representing the whole party, not direct the work of Labour MPs – not perhaps on every detail, but on the main matters of policy? Parliamentary sovereignty would not be compromised thereby, only the isolation of MPs, alone with the Whip and their scruples, from the movement to which they completely owe their position. Such accountability would be direct, open and democratic, unlike the clandestine, men's-club accountability of bourgeois politicians to big business, the City and the state apparatus which has pervaded parliamentary politics for so long. If it is unwieldy for the entire NEC to consider each matter, the work could be delegated to a permanent subcommittee of trade unionists and constituency representatives, charged with ensuring the fidelity of the PLP to party policy, as determined by the NEC within the lines laid down by annual conference.

This would then remove the focus from individual MPs (excepting only those cases where an MP wilfully votes or speaks against party policy) to the PLP as a collective. MPs would understand that they are delegates of the movement, and their constituents would know what, in voting for the Labour Party, they were going to get. Such a change would also emphasise that Labour is a national party with a centrally directed project of social change, and not a federation of constituencies, each exercising its powers of reselection in different and contradictory ways.

Corbyn's time as Leader did not allow for this debate. Instead, the issue of MPs' behaviour was addressed mainly through a re-run of 1980s debates on mandatory reselection. Just as the Jacobins of 1871 saw the Paris Commune as an opportunity to replay the greatest hits of 1793, so the debates of the early 1980s hung heavy over the Corbyn project, sometimes to the exclusion of a fresh approach.

The PLP remained for the most part recalcitrant opponents of what the Corbyn leadership was trying to achieve. Some of them went on to split from the party in 2019. Two of the most aggressively hostile – Ian Austin and John Woodcock – were rewarded with peerages by the Tory government for their efforts.

The conduct of people like these in the event of the formation of a Corbyn-led government, particularly one with a small Commons majority (the only sort that was ever likely) can easily be visualised. Just two Labour MPs stopped the first Wilson government, with its tiny majority, from nationalising the steel industry. The resistance to Corbyn delivering on his own manifesto would have been ferocious. It would be fair to assume that a significant element of the PLP would have formed an iron phalanx in defence of imperialism and the status quo and would, in extremis, have voted to bring down Corbyn altogether, could the right issue be identified. A group which would rebel in order to keep the Saudi regime supplied with arms as it attacks impoverished Yemen would not require very exacting criteria.

If the PLP constituted the core of the 'enemy within' – to repeat, despite whatever personal qualities many Labour MPs possess – it did not exhaust the category. Other detachments of this enemy operated under the cover provided by the parliamentary resistance. Without MPs champing at the bit to bring down the Corbyn leadership, these other elements would have lacked the legitimacy and the authority to attempt it for themselves. Parliamentarianism sanctifies any sin.

The Party Machine

The part played by Labour's full-time apparatus in the 2017 general election has already been touched upon. Their indifference, at best, to the party's prospects was characteristic of the attitudes pervading the permanent apparatus throughout. Moulded largely in the New Labour years, their hostility to Corbyn did not emerge from nowhere. The leaked report concerning the Governance and Legal Unit (GLU) on anti-Semitism exposes a hierarchy which had been scornful of Ed Miliband and even somewhat sceptical of Gordon Brown. Blair alone commanded their respect and the unconditional loyalty that they were paid to show Labour.

Their attitudes were therefore well to the right of the party membership, even before the 'Corbyn surge' and to some extent to the right of the country's centre of political gravity. The views expressed by some senior figures on issues from inequality to terrorism would sit more comfortably in the canteen room of an under-supervised police force than a social democratic organisation. Senior officials opined that MPs who supported Corbyn should be 'taken out and shot', that 'death by fire is too kind for LOTO', and wished death on particular activists.

It is small wonder that an apparatus designed to keep a restless party in line for Blair and the Blairites – who never sank deep roots in the membership, which over time they managed to reduce to historically low numbers – was ill adapted to Corbyn's vision of Labour as a renewed social movement, campaigning in communities all the year round, uniting with other progressive organisations, and a centre of political debate. More surprising is the fact that so little was done to change this situation over the years of Corbyn's leadership. Of course, the machine itself resisted change with a surly passivity throughout. It slow-walked the changes required to handle anti-Semitism mandated by Shami Chakrabarti in 2016. It resisted the introduction of community organisers to revive the party in areas – many of them then 'safe' Labour – where it had gone moribund. It made every change in personnel, procedure or policy an exercise in root canal surgery. This was the product as much of demotivation, leaving disgruntled apparatchiks merely pretending to work, as of planned political obstruction, a scenario which would endow the apparat with more wit and energy than it appeared to command.

Let one example stand for so many. The GLU report includes

an exchange between two Labour Party regional officials who were discussing Momentum's initiative to recruit their own regional organisers early in 2016. This development threatened the regional officials' control of the party at the grassroots, but one of them frankly admitted that Momentum's underpaid organisers would 'do the groundwork we cannot be arsed doing and they will engage the members in a way we cannot be fucked with. They are going to be so motivated.'[8]

Indeed, the only issue which could stir the functionaries from their torpor was the prospect of chasing down 'Trots', a category which in minds uniting malice with impenetrable political ignorance had nothing to do with actual Trotskyism and encompassed most of the party membership. This they did with vigour during the 2016 leadership election, finding exclusion of members rather than their recruitment the more congenial way to spend working time.

The National Executive

But the most salient resource HQ had in resisting any departure from Blair-era norms was the majority prevailing on the National Executive Committee until early 2018. Up to that point, the NEC, which had control over the party machine, was in its majority a coalition of the Corbyn-hostile with the Corbyn-sceptic, defiantly unrepresentative of the wider party, a disjuncture which could best be addressed by more democratic and less opaque forms of election. While the NEC was less flamboyantly oppositional than the PLP majority, it was hardly more accommodating to the elected Leader. Even the representatives of unions which had backed Corbyn, like Unison, were not reliably in his column.

Let me recount the story of my train journey back from the party conference in Liverpool in 2016. The train was only a few minutes out of Lime Street Station when I realised that in the seats immediately behind me were a member of the NEC – someone purportedly occupying the middle ground on that body – and a journalist from a Murdoch newspaper. They knew each other well enough to speak freely. The pair agreed that a young Corbyn-supporting NEC member was 'absolutely fucking mad', that support for Nelson Mandela was a 'liberal niche issue' and that right-wing MP John Spellar's control of Labour in the West Midlands was based 'on fear and it is wonderful to see.' All this straight from the NEC 'centre ground'.

Our loose-lipped NEC source added two things of some salience. The first was that if Corbyn did try to remove Iain McNicol from his post he would still lack the votes on the NEC to choose his successor. Our NEC friend was right. Corbyn could, in fact, have given the general secretary his marching orders at any point. However, the replacement would have been entirely in the gift of the NEC, and there was no chance that it would have chosen anyone proposed by the Leader. This circumstance did not change until pro-Corbyn members finally constituted a majority on the party's ruling body, at which point Corbyn – although it would be more accurate to say Karie Murphy – acted with dispatch, and McNicol was himself replaced, swaddled in the ermine he so craved. Only then could serious reform of the way the party worked begin.

The second insight the NEC member vouchsafed to Murdoch's man on the 16.15 from Liverpool was that Labour's real Leader was – Tom Watson. His address to the just-concluded conference – a highly combative performance which averred that 'capitalism is not the enemy' and avoided mentioning the newly re-elected Corbyn except once in a derisive rejoinder to a heckle – was the 'real Leader's speech', the voice from the seat behind me claimed.

Like most Labour MPs, Watson was quiescent after the great advances Labour made in 2017, a success to which he contributed nothing particularly notable. At conference 2017 his panegyric to New Labour and capitalism of a year earlier was replaced by a curious but apparently sincere tribute to Corbyn: 'I realised it's actually better to be loved than to be feared. And Jeremy has shown us that it's possible.'

Nevertheless, Watson managed to overcome the tug of love soon enough. According to Pogrund and Maguire, his staff assisted Sam Matthews in laundering attacks on LOTO staff (including the present author) into the media, a fairly astonishing circumstance.[9] More substantively, having urged pragmatic acceptance of the Brexit referendum result in its immediate aftermath, he later reinvented himself as an uber-Remainer. The 2016 Watson: 'We're never going to apologise for holding the government's feet to the fire. But nor we will ignore the democratic will of the British people. Unlike the Lib Dem Brexit Deniers, we believe in respecting the decision of the British people. To do any less is to fail to respect the British people themselves'.[10] And 2019 tricky Tom: 'The only way to break the Brexit deadlock once and for all is a public vote in a referendum . . . There is no such thing as a good Brexit deal, which is why I believe we should advocate for Remain.'[11] Probably there was more Corbynphobia than new-minted Europhilia behind this shift, which saw him unilaterally declare Labour a 'Remain party' at a time when it was trying to reach across the Brexit divide.

Changing the Party

Making Labour a more democratic and campaigning party was central to Jeremy Corbyn's agenda as Leader, as indeed it has been for all his political life. Nevertheless, achievements were negligible. Some of the reasons have already been indicated. Opposed by the majority of the PLP and obstructed (at least until 2018) by the party apparatus, the base for advance was slender, and was shrunk still further by the lack of active support in practice from three of the four largest affiliated unions: Unison, GMB and USDAW. The only secure foundation for changing Labour in a Corbynite direction would have been electoral success, Labour's *raison d'être*.

Some improvements were nevertheless secured. The policy sovereignty of the annual conference was restored, rescued from the byzantine procedures of the New Labour era which effectively concentrated all control in the hands of the leadership. Community organisers were ultimately appointed in an effort to revive Labour's profile as a campaigning force in many constituencies.[12] The democracy of the National Executive Committee was refined.

But the Labour Party post-Corbyn is not a radically different beast, at least in terms of its structures and modus operandi. The most significant change was in the membership, which nearly quadrupled as a result of recruits drawn in by Corbyn's vision and the possibility of the party actually becoming an agent of social change, a party that had at last learned from the disappointments (to use a term which would strike Iraqi people at least as wildly generous) of the Blair-Brown years. At the same time, some thousands of New Labour diehards resigned. In terms of its membership base, the party was renewed. This was a somewhat lopsided renewal. The new members were preponderantly drawn from among Labour's middle-class supporters. The largest increases in the size of constituency parties appeared to be in London and the south. I was surprised to find that there were very nearly as many Labour Party members in South East England as in the North

West in 2018, although the party then held more than six times as many parliamentary seats in the latter region. Greater London aside, the members were generally to be found where the electoral base – including most of the seats Labour could likely gain to secure victory – wasn't. As Panitch and Leys noted, Momentum too had a 'particularly weakness in the post-industrial regions where the need for engagement in class struggles, organising and education was most acute.'[13] This was a circumstance which certainly indirectly impacted on the Brexit debate.

The idea of turning Labour into a social movement, championed by Jeremy Corbyn himself, did not seem to fare much better, despite the influx of new blood. This concept was perhaps under-theorised. Labour's foundational purpose is the fighting and winning of elections. That was the reason for its creation. Other working-class requirements were catered for by other organisations. There is also no shortage of social movements, both broad and general, like the women's movement, or focussed campaigns, like Stop the War and Extinction Rebellion, or hybrids such as Black Lives Matter. It was unclear how a changed Labour Party would fit into that landscape.

The record does constitute something of a reality check to those who have based their strategic political objectives on the prospect of democratising and transforming the Labour Party. That is the position long and honourably championed by the Campaign for Labour Party Democracy and its most prominent advocate, Jon Lansman, since the 1970s.

Any consideration of the future of the Labour Party must give full weight to the apparent intractability of its structures and key personnel, and its resistance to change. The speed of its reversion to 'normal' after Corbyn's resignation as Leader has been striking.

As much as Corbynism indicated a potential, its failures outline the mountainous scale of the difficulties in making of Labour a serviceable instrument for socialism and anti-imperialism.

In the end, however, it was not PLP insurrection or activity by any of the other auxiliary detachments of the enemy within that brought Corbynism down as much as its own failure on what became a fundamental issue of democracy.

6

The Campaign against Corbynism

The work of arresting Corbynite socialism in its tracks was not left
to its internal opponents in the Labour Party alone, particularly
once it became clear that their unaided efforts might not be sufficient to stop the British people embracing radical change.

The Establishment felt menaced in a way that it had not done
since the 1980s. For thirty years the advent to office of either
governing party could be viewed with equanimity. The reserves of
extra-parliamentary power had not been called on for decisive
interventions since the defeat of the miners' strike in 1985, for the
most part. It turned out that they had not rusted from neglect.

Here we focus on three aspects which bore down hard on
Corbynism – the coercive arms of the state (or 'deep state', as it is
sometimes described); the media; and the anti-Semitism controversy. All contributed to Labour's defeat, although none should be
regarded as decisive set next to the vacillations and misjudgements
over Brexit. However, no perspective for attaining socialism can
neglect a review of these factors – one day they may be still more
consequential.

Spooks, Mutineers and Pall Mall Reactionaries

Richard Dearlove is a Pall Mall reactionary and a former head of MI6. In that capacity he was intimately involved in the decision to invade Iraq in pursuit of mythical weapons of mass destruction, and was criticised for it in the Chilcot Report. He wears it lightly, making himself generally available as a right-wing rentaquote on everything from Brexit to China to coronavirus.

At several points during Corbyn's leadership he hurried to give the security state's imprimatur to the campaign to ensure he never became prime minister. This from the 2019 general election campaign:

> Corbyn, Murray and Milne have at times each denigrated their own country and embraced the interests of its enemies and opponents. Their record is not in question . . . I spent 38 years in MI6, most of the time in the front line, working to counter the threat from the Soviet empire and the threat from terrorism. Labour and Conservative governments were both energetic in their commitment and determination to protect our national security.
>
> They never compromised in their pursuit of the national interest. They never disagreed about the importance of that struggle. It was not a party political issue. Changes of government raised no questions of allegiance. Today, that is no longer the case. Corbyn and his closest associates are compromised by their past. The political company they have kept has been authoritatively documented . . . It is important that every citizen understands who and what they would be voting for. When the issue is the protection of our national security, clearance to classified information would never be extended to anyone with Corbyn's background.[1]

The pregnant passage in that little diatribe – contributed to the *Mail on Sunday* – is the warning that, while previously a change of government 'raised no questions of allegiance', with Corbyn 'that is no longer the case'. Here is an eminent alumnus of the security services putting his thumb on the democratic scale in the most brazen way – telling the electorate who they should not vote for, and adding that if this advice is ignored there will be consequences. John McDonnell responded sharply at the time: 'I think he should spend his retirement in quiet contemplation of the role that he played with regard to the Iraq war where over half a million people were killed. He was strongly criticised as the head of an organisation whose intelligence took us into that war.'[2] Dearlove seemed more to be contemplating a retirement of intrigue and insurrection.

Dearlove's opposite number at the other pillar of the 'deep state' – MI5, the domestic security service – was not slacking in the struggle either. Stella Rimington, retired director-general of the service, was happy to share her thoughts on the Corbyn menace as well. She wandered down memory lane in 2017, telling a literary festival that 'I now see in Momentum some of the people we were looking at in the Trotskyite organisations in the 1980s', adding that 'their names are familiar, shall we say that much.' This was odd, since helpful media briefings directed the public towards Seumas Milne and myself as being Rimington's targets.[3] Both of us might take offence at being misdescribed as Trotskyists after more than forty years marching under another flag. The young Rimington had cut her teeth as a snooper spying on the Communist Party in Sussex in the 1970s, which as it happened is where and when I joined the party. I have never met her, but I feel we know each other well.

In warning of the essential illegitimacy of a Corbyn government were the former heads of the two services speaking for their successors in situ? It would be unlikely that the latter held wildly different opinions. Nor was the military missing in action. The former chief of the Defence Staff, Lord Richards, intervened in the 2017 election campaign to opine that 'Jeremy Corbyn, unlike many of his distinguished predecessors in the Labour Party from Clement Attlee through Denis Healey and beyond, has demonstrated why he should not be trusted with the ultimate responsibility of government – that of the nation's defence and security.'[4] Again a clear message – the top brass are fine with right-wing, imperialist, Labour but very much not fine with Corbyn's new approach to Britain in the world.

At least Richards put his name to his menaces. But all the resources of military intelligence and the security services have apparently failed to identify the 'senior serving general' who told the press shortly after Corbyn's election as Labour Leader – the very next week in fact – that the armed forces would take 'direct action' to stop a government formed by the new Leader:

You would face the very real prospect of an event which would be effectively a mutiny. Feelings are running very high within the armed forces. You would see a major break in convention with senior generals directly and publicly challenging Corbyn over vital important policy decisions such as Trident, pulling out of NATO and any plans to emasculate and shrink the size of the armed forces. The Army just wouldn't stand for it. The general staff would not allow a prime minister to jeopardise the security of this country and I think people would use whatever means possible, fair or foul to prevent that. You can't put a maverick in charge of a country's security.[5]

In that spirit, soldiers in the Parachute Regiment were filmed – in Kabul, at the fag end of British imperialism's fourth Afghan war – using a picture of Corbyn for their target practice. None were dismissed. With impeccable understatement the Labour Party complained that this constituted a 'breach of impartiality'.

Whether or not Corbyn was actually to be gunned down, the secretive senior general was clear – the army should in effect hold a veto over government policies, at least in areas it considered to be of sufficient importance, including the size of the armed forces. The 'convention' being breached here is properly named democracy. Threats are not action, of course, but even the public venting of such statements from the military and the security services constitutes a significant form of political intervention. They create an atmosphere in which the grand viziers of the state apparatus shape opinion and foment an anticipation of mayhem if their views are ignored. One analysis identified at least thirty-four separate stories attacking Corbyn placed in the media by sources in the security services.[6]

I was involved in a few. During the 2019 election campaign it was alleged that I had held regular meetings with an officer of Czechoslovak intelligence in the early 1980s, echoing an earlier smear that Corbyn himself had been on their payroll. I was supposed to be advising Prague on, among other things, the activities of the Monday Club, a group on the far right fringe of the Tories with which I had no contact and, as the *Morning Star*'s political correspondent at the time, absolutely no possibility of penetrating.[7] No less bizarre, the *Mail on Sunday* announced in 2018 that I had been barred as of June that year from entering Ukraine, a country I have never sought to visit in my life. They even illustrated the piece with a copy of the banning order. Those unable to read Cyrillic script would not have been aware that it was dated in September and did not mention my name at all. This coincided with news leaked from somewhere that, despite advising Corbyn for nearly a year at that point, I had still not been given a pass to enter the House of Commons due to 'vetting problems'.[8]

None of this was in fact terribly serious. But it did point to clear anti-Corbyn media activity within the security services. Who else could have advised the *Mail* of the banning order? The idea that the newspaper has its own sources in Kiev is risible. Who indeed might have suggested to the Ukrainian government that I be banned in the first place, ostensibly because of a speech I had made several years earlier? As I wrote in the *New Statesman* at the time:

> Call me sceptical if you must, but I do not see journalistic enter-prise behind the *Mail*'s sudden capacity to tease obscure informa-tion out of the SBU [Ukrainian security]. Someone else is doing the hard work – possibly someone being paid by the taxpayer . . . We are often told that the days of secret state political chicanery are long past and we must hope so. But sometimes you have to wonder . . .[9]

Naturally, scorn was poured on this speculation. Tom Watson was particularly vociferous in publicly discounting any talk of state opposition to Corbyn's Labour. However, after I had gone public I did get my Commons pass within a week – a charming security officer merely said I was an 'unusual case' that had required refer-ring upwards – although as far as I know I remain excluded from Ukraine.

Perhaps all this adds up to less than a conspiracy. But it must certainly constitute a warning. The point is not that Chris

Mullin's *Very British Coup* scenario *would* have materialised under a Corbyn government, but that it *could* have done. At the very least there would have been sustained, entrenched and menacing resistance to the government's foreign and defence policies. My opinion is that a coup, in the sense of overthrowing the government, would not have happened only because it would have been unnecessary. In office with only a small majority, dependent for survival on a largely hostile PLP, and with an element of the left uninterested in supporting a Corbynite foreign policy in any case, it is far more likely that a constitutional and parliamentary way would have been found to do the necessary, without involving all the complications that would ensue from an overt move against democracy.

But the question is begged by the reported remarks made by Mark Milley, the chief US military officer in the USA, when there was speculation about President Trump staging some form of coup to stay in power after his election defeat in 2020: 'They may try, but they're not going to fucking succeed . . . You can't do this without the military. You can't do this without the CIA and the FBI. We're the guys with the guns.'[10]

He was right. But what happens if the guys with the guns take a different view? Corbynism had no real answer to that, possibly because there is none within the framework of parliamentarism. Artillery trumps ethics in any game of political rock-paper-scissors, at least in the short term.

State Broadcaster and Fleet Street Fabians

The BBC's political editor, Laura Kuenssberg, given the opportunity to interview the radical socialist chosen to lead the Labour

Party a few days after his election, felt the public needed to know one thing above all – would Corbyn kneel before the Queen when he was inducted into the Privy Council? Not austerity, not nuclear weapons, not the future of Labour, but 'would he kneel?' was the matter she pressed as of prime consequence. It was an interview framed to demonise Corbyn around a matter of constitutional trivia which no voter (and probably not the Queen herself) could care less about. Even the right-wing pundit Dan Hodges said in effect, 'Give us a break.'[11]

Fast forward four years and here is the BBC's self-same political editor, at the climax of the general election campaign, tweeting that a Labour activist had punched a Tory staffer. It was an entirely false claim, allegedly emerging from a Tory source, which Kuenssberg had not bothered to check before retailing.[12]

Worse things were said about Corbyn in the media, and worse allegations made about Labour activists. *But this was the BBC,* and its most senior political journalist to boot, book-ending Corbyn's leadership with stories presenting the Leader and his supporters as anti-national, anti-democratic and violent. Kuenssberg has endured a good deal of social media abuse, much of it misogynistic, and that must be condemned without reservation. But it does not make her journalism objective. And this matters because it is the BBC – it is trusted far more as a source of news than the overtly partisan newspaper brands or, in fact, anyone else. A critical presentation on the BBC matters more than pages of smears in the *Mail* or the *Sun*, as the lopsided *Panorama* programme on Labour anti-Semitism by John Ware established.

And where the BBC went, much of the media followed, the *Daily Mail* inventions then in turn forming the agenda for the 'Today' programme on Radio Four, in a grisly symbiosis. As early as summer 2016 an academic study conducted by the London School of Economics found

> that Corbyn was thoroughly delegitimised as a political actor from the moment he became a prominent candidate and even more so after he was elected as party leader, with a strong mandate. This process of delegitimisation occurred in several ways: 1) through lack of or distortion of voice; 2) through ridicule, scorn and personal attacks; and 3) through association, mainly with terrorism.[13]

It might have been thought that the abuse meted out to Corbyn in the 2017 general election, including twelve pages of attacks on polling day in the *Daily Mail* alone represented peak Corbyn-baiting. But the insufficiency of the onslaught, evident from the results, demanded, and got, a redoubling of effort. 'Labour may have had a rough ride in the 2017 General Election, but it paled by comparison with the 2019 campaign', a Loughborough University study found. 'National newspaper print circulation is down by 25 per cent since the 2017 election, but negative coverage of Labour has more than doubled in this campaign. It is an interesting paradox'.[14] In the broadcast media the relatively benign coverage afforded Corbyn by the BBC in 2017 – a consequence of adherence to rules governing broadcasting balance during an election – was not replicated in 2019, when the threat he represented was taken more seriously.

The main lines of attack hewed closely, and not accidentally, to the imperatives of Corbyn's critics in the military and the securitocracy. He was a terrorist sympathiser, an unreliable pacifist, unpatriotic, weak, extreme, divisive, stupid, menacing and, ultimately, racist. Corbyn remarked that he himself 'would not like to live on the same street' as the man he read about.[15] The same methods were extended to John McDonnell and Diane Abbott, as well as advisors like Seumas Milne, and in a minor key, myself. The Labour Party was likewise presented as a home exclusively for thugs, fanatics, morons and anti-Semites.

It is perfectly true that all Labour leaders, with the singular exception of Tony Blair, have had to fight a degree of media headwind, and the Labour Party has never been the first choice for government of the sundry press barons (again, Murdoch's support for Blair was the revealing odd-one-out). Ed Miliband, remember, became all-but Bolshevik in the tabloid telling. Nevertheless, the onslaught on Corbyn and his Labour Party was of an unprecedented scope and vitriol. If it was all encapsulated in one place, it was in Tom Bower's biography of Corbyn, *Dangerous Hero*, a factlite and footnote-free construct of a fantasy Corbyn, a compound of every nightmare that has ever gripped the bourgeoisie about anyone, shot through with an implacable malice from beginning to end. Of the nine references to myself (naturally, Bower did not attempt to speak to me for the book), five are either entirely false or contain significant errors. To take just one example, the bilious Bower claims that Labour's 2017 manifesto was the work of 'three Communists' – Seumas Milne, Andrew Fisher and myself.[16] In fact the only one of the three who could actually be called Communist is the one who had nothing at all to do with drafting the manifesto (myself). The Conservative journalist of integrity Peter Oborne is one of those who have deconstructed Bower's work, concluding that it was 'not just intellectually dishonest, it is a farrago of falsehood and insinuation.'[17]

The capacity of the likes of Bower to shift the political dial is insufficient. They preach to the choir, to voters already on the edge of their seats with fear lest someone interfere with their water company dividends whilst simultaneously truckling with Muslims of dubious provenance. So special mention must be made of those media which carried the campaign against Corbynism into its heartlands – the *Guardian/Observer* and the *New Statesman*, spaces where the enemies without and within could conjoin and mingle. All these journals opposed Corbyn from the beginning. The *Guardian* backed Yvette Cooper for Leader in 2015, and pronounced Corbyn's leadership dead during the 2016 PLP coup. On both occasions, the paper was out of step with Labour members and most of its readers too. Its columnists – a college of centrists headed by Polly Toynbee and Jonathan Freedland – united to write off Labour's chances in the 2017 election in the most aggressive terms.[18] Even those columnists, like Marina Hyde, who had been most coruscating in dismissing the stale centrism of the Cameron-Clegg-Brown years found Corbyn beyond the pale. The paper's Sunday sister the *Observer* was even worse in that at least an occasional pro-Corbyn piece made it past the *Guardian*'s gate-keepers, but on Sundays opinion was exclusively a matter for Corbyn-haters Andrew Rawnsley, Will Hutton and Nick Cohen. No dissent percolated. Briefly stunned by their utter failure to anticipate anything like the 2017 election result, they recovered their (im)balance in plenty of time to resume the attack before the country next went to the polls. Their critique of Corbynism did not differ substantially from that of the Tory-supporting media, but with the added ingredient that this was the media heartland of 'remainia', so Corbyn's insufficient enthusiasm for reversing the 2016 referendum on EU membership exercised them as much as anything. Its 'Readers' editor was frequently called on to respond to an outraged readership objecting to the bias shown in the paper's comment section.

The *New Statesman* followed the same trajectory: dismissing Corbyn as an aberration taking Labour to electoral extinction at first, then a wobble back in the direction of giving the movement a hearing after June 2017, before resuming its initial editorial course, culminating in a portentious editorial declaring Corbyn unfit to be prime minister on the eve of the 2019 election. In short, it worked hard for the Tory victory it claimed not to desire.[19]

Here we meet the socialism in evening dress lounging in the drawing rooms of Engels's Victorian imagination. Take the *Guardian* and *New Statesman* as a study in the perils of Fabianism. They want – to some extent – the ends championed by Corbynism, but are entirely opposed to the means of attaining them. Polly Toynbee would do anything for the poor, as long as the poor refrain from doing anything for themselves. Social amelioration without systemic change is their hope, and disorder in pursuit of emancipation their deepest fear. As the media outworks of parliamentarism, they could not but dispute the legitimacy of a movement formed outside its precincts and reluctant to confine politics to the House of Commons order paper and the well-turned leader column. The pseudo-left media were the natural bedmates of the anti-Corbyn element in the PLP. Indeed, their critique of Corbyn synchronised comfortably with the MI5/general staff line of denunciation on most points.

Sometimes Corbyn's staff is criticised for not having developed better relations with the media. The odd opportunity was doubtless missed amidst the hurricane of attacks, but the criticism is unreasonable and unrealistic. The mass media, privately owned and state-run alike, are an integral part of the power structure in British society. Not only have they no interest in 'being fair' to a radical left-wing project, it would be against their nature. Even before one gets on to problems generated by the way political lobby journalists operate – a pack mindset enforcing a conformity of outlook; the liberal use of unnamed sources expressing opinions, not retailing secrets; a desire to stay 'in' with favoured sources, etc. – the fact that most newspapers are owned by extremely wealthy and reactionary tax exiles would determine the matter. There were very few journalists or mainstream outlets trying to even explain Corbynism, still less give it a sympathetic hearing. The *Financial Times* may be considered the exception here. As for the BBC, it is perpetually deferential to the powers that be. At the time of Corbyn's election its head of political programmes, Robbie Gibb, and its chief political interviewer, Andrew Neil, were both on the right (Gibb subsequently went to work for Theresa May), facts its present-day critics on the 'anti-woke' right neglect.

A new left-wing media did develop in these years – Novara Media and a revived *Tribune* magazine are examples, along with a profusion of digital initiatives, some more durable than others. They joined the stalwart *Morning Star* as key socialist communicators. Novara and *Tribune* are imaginative operations that carry forward the Corbynite critique of contemporary capitalism as well as promoting its anti-imperialist outlook. They are important cells for the regeneration of the left. Developing a new media infrastructure which can integrate the movement and communicate priorities is a better use of time and resources, and perhaps something the Corbyn leadership should have paid more attention to, as opposed to trying to charm or persuade the capitalist media, the resources of which should be distributed to a plurality of popular organisations in a socialist system.

The Anti-Semitism Controversy

The most systematic abuse of media power concerned the anti-Semitism issue, where an onslaught on Corbyn and Labour was developed, with little regard to fact and none to balance, by newspapers in some cases up to their necks in racism. This cannot be separated from the substance of the matter, but the media distortion of the actual position in the Labour Party was a story in itself, one that has been covered in some detail.[20]

It may be objected that consideration of the anti-Semitism crisis which swept Labour from 2015 to date should not be framed as the activity of enemies determined to obstruct a Corbyn government, as this belittles real concerns and reduces a complex question to a binary confrontation. Up to a point, this must be conceded. There are many strands to the question which stretch beyond the desire of the powerful to defeat Corbynism. Indeed, there were issues raised which it behoves the left to reflect upon, and which cannot be dismissed as simply the intrigues of our opponents. To do justice to all these considerations would require a book in itself.

However, there *was* a campaign against the Corbyn leadership, the full story of which has yet to be written. It drew on the full arsenal of anti-socialist media, including elements with scant interest in challenging racism and a lot in defeating Corbynism, and in the end it assumed the character of an unending witch-hunt directed against the left which is continuing full tilt as of late 2021. The immediate electoral damage may have been limited, although it surely reinforced the image of Jeremy Corbyn as a weak leader, given our inability to get on top of the issue. But the underlying harm done to the left may prove greater. The campaign sought to strike an ethical movement at the core of its identity, by associating it with the ethical abomination of anti-Semitism.

That is not to impute bad faith to all those organisations and individuals who challenged Labour on the issue, nor to deny that there were grounds for concern. However, when your cause is promoted by newspapers like the *Telegraph* and the *Mail*, papers which are not merely routinely racist in general but have been, in the recent past, explicitly anti-Semitic in particular, you can be sure that bad faith is playing its part.[21]

Anti-Semitism, a plastic and tentacular hatred which has attached itself to almost all modern political ideologies at one time or to some extent or other (not always excluding Zionism), is not unknown on the left. When the great German socialist pioneer August Bebel warned of anti-Semitism as the 'socialism of fools' he was not wasting words. There were such fools in Britain, including Henry Hyndman, the founder of the country's first Marxist organisation.[22] Jews in Britain were, in the years before and after the First World War in a position perhaps unique for a minority in being attacked from both above and below. Some socialists were fond of talking up the parasitism of 'Jewish capitalists', while some trade unionists were hostile to the immigration of poor Jews from the Tsarist Empire for the usual reasons poor immigrants are demonised – undermining wage rates and degrading social conditions generally. There were always those – a majority – who challenged the introduction of this admixture of racism into socialist ideology and practice, but the left's hands are not historically spotless.

The most common expression of contemporary anti-Semitism on the left is perhaps the holding of the Jewish community in Britain, or Jewish individuals, as responsible for the actions of the state of Israel. They are not. You can also find sometimes-inadvertent conspiracy theories regarding Jewish power and influence in business and the media, or which merely remove the word 'Jew' from a classic anti-Semitic trope and replace it with 'Israel' or 'Zionist', which is not really an improvement. The equation of Jews with money and avarice, probably the most deeply entrenched form of popular anti-Semitism of all, is occasionally promoted. It was suggested to a Labour MP in 2019 that she ought to reach out to the Jewish community in her constituency. 'There isn't one', she replied. 'There's no money in [name of constituency].' In fact, a minute's Googling identified three synagogues in her seat but, yes, that isn't the point.

Anti-Semitism did resurface in the Labour Party in recent years, and not just in its older home on the party's racist right. The absolute number of members crossing the line into anti-Semitism, particularly in comments relating to Israel, inflated with the rapid expansion of the party membership. The House of Commons Home Affairs Committee, a body with a Tory majority, could in late 2016 find 'no reliable, empirical evidence to support the notion that there is a higher prevalence of anti-Semitic attitudes within the Labour Party than any other political party', an opinion which could now get you suspended from Starmer's party.[23]

Nevertheless, those who campaign around these things focussed almost exclusively on the Labour Party in the years that followed, incongruously so since these were also years of violent outrages against Jewish communities by far-right terrorists in the USA and Islamist terrorists in Europe (never by groups or people on the left), and of pronounced anti-Semitic attitudes expressed by governments of the populist right.

Labour's Response

There were problems in addressing among the membership such anti-Semitism as existed. First, the machinery for handling disciplinary cases was cumbersome, inefficient and susceptible to factional manipulation, with unconscionable delays in processing cases the norm. Efforts to improve these procedures were made, but they were, proverbially, too little and too late. Second, there was an element among Corbyn's support – some of them Jewish themselves – which simply denied that the problem existed at all, since they had never experienced anything within the party which corresponded to the attacks being made. Third, prominent Corbyn supporters from Ken Livingstone through to Chris Williamson made self-publicising interventions which were unhelpful and sometimes indefensible. Ken Livingstone's assertion that Hitler was 'supporting Zionism before he went mad and ended up killing six million Jews' was offensive and ahistorical, although perhaps not more so than Benjamin Netanyahu's claim, while Israeli prime minister, that Hitler had been put up to the Holocaust by the Grand Mufti of Jerusalem.[24]

Let us take a look at Jeremy Corbyn's personal record. In 1990 he signed a Commons motion condemning the rise of anti-Semitism. In 2002 he personally helped clean a synagogue in his constituency after an anti-Semitic attack. In 2004 he condemned the French government for trying to ban the Jewish kippah in schools, one of a series of reinforcements French secularism has brought to institutional racism. In 2006 he condemned offensive remarks by singer Bryan Ferry. In 2006, too, he condemned a Holocaust cartoon competition run by an Iranian magazine.

In 2009, Corbyn condemned anti-Semitism on social media and the same year praised the heroism of British Jews in the Holocaust. In 2010 he urged the government to give Yemeni Jews refugee status in Britain; 2011 saw him condemn the anti-Semitism of John Galliano. In 2012 he denounced the sale of Nazi memorabilia and condemned anti-Semitic incidents at a football tournament in Poland. In 2013 he condemned (unlike the Board of Deputies) the anti-Semitic attacks on Ed Miliband, and in 2014 he praised the work of the Holocaust Memorial Trust. In 2015 he helped organise a counter-demonstration to a planned march targeting Jewish residents in Golders Green, north London.

In view of all the above, it is amazing that the question of Corbyn's alleged anti-Semitism should even be asked. Is this the record of a Streicher or a Bandera, or is Jeremy Corbyn actually the most hostile-to-Jew-hatred anti-Semite in history? Clearly it does not settle the matter. But the fact that this litany is simply ignored, treated as if it had never taken place, testifies to the malicious nature of much of the personal criticism of Corbyn and the imputation to him of racist views that he in fact abominates.

Nevertheless, the case against Corbyn must be considered, foundational to the whole 'Labour is anti-Semitic' narrative as it was. That case has been set out in many places – perhaps most comprehensively by Deborah Lipstadt, victorious legal foe of Holocaust denier David Irving, and Julia Neuberger, a London rabbi.[25] For a Twitter-sized litany, there is Dave Rich of the Community Security Trust.[26] Between them they cover a terrain which is by now familiar – the mural, the Hamas/Hizbollah 'friends' remark, the various associates who had said and done questionable things, the Tunis wreath-laying, the foreword to the book on imperialism and the 'irony' remarks. It is not necessary here to engage in a point-by-point rebuttal – that was done at the time and the responses are out there for those who are concerned. Some of the issues were clearly matters of guilt-by-association (with people who had made anti-Semitic remarks in other contexts and occasions) and some, while arguably ill-judged, were not anti-Semitic except by the most luxuriant definition – yes, Corbyn signed a Commons motion calling for the renaming of Holocaust Memorial Day, but the same motion was signed at the time by Tories, Liberal Democrats, Plaid and SDLP MPs and impeccable Labour right-wingers. The remark at a fraught public meeting that 'Zionists' alleged to have been disruptive at a previous event lacked a sense of English irony 'despite having lived here all their lives' does not read well, but it scarcely sustains former Chief Rabbi Jonathan Sacks's claim that it was the most racist speech in public life since Powell's 'rivers of blood' address in 1968, a comment which can only make sense as a measure of Sacks's ignorance of or indifference towards the torrent of racism directed at British people of Black and Asian heritage over the last half-century.[27]

The great majority of the charge sheet relates to incidents in some way or other connected to the Palestinian cause. A fringe of supporters of the Palestinian people's struggle for self-determination trade in anti-Semitic ideas and idioms. Like any other great cause, it can lure one into rhetorical excesses. I myself regret telling a rally outside the Israeli Embassy protesting the 2012 attack on Gaza that 'every dead Palestinian child is a nail in Israel's coffin' – defensible in point of fact, but at risk of playing into Jewish child-killer tropes. But the anti-Semites are a small element in the movement, desperately sought out by hostile media to be highlighted on every solidarity protest the better to besmirch the cause.

The venom of the attacks took a toll on Corbyn, there is no doubt. Jeremy became reluctant to give them the slightest legitimacy by engaging with them, an essentially political attack was treated as a personal slight, and he succumbed to passivity on a question which was doing us moral damage. Speeches were not made, initiatives not taken, outreach was limited, proactive political strategy was absent and concerned staff were marginalised. Every attack on the issue seemed to catch us unprepared. Emily Thornberry remarked that 'when people accused Jeremy of being an anti-Semite, he was so upset, and as a result found it difficult to deal with the problem. He hasn't dealt with it properly, but to call him anti-Semitic is wrong.'[28]

A better way of handling the question was advocated. Let me quote from the note of a telephone conversation between Corbyn and Labour-supporting Jewish academic Tony Klug in April 2018, as the crisis was coming to the boil once more. The abbreviated note of Klug's advice reads:

> Need to get ahead of the curve quickly rather than playing (non-achievable) catch up. Three interlinked underlying verities: a. Rising a-s, including on left, LP and wider society. Is a real issue. B. Is independent of but exacerbated by Isr-Pal conflict. C. There are people out to get JC – to discredit him personally and/or LP.
>
> Action needed to address all 3 verities simultaneously and put JC on front foot . . . So need for different strategy, comprising *an integral action package to be publicly announced* . . .

Klug's recommendations included 'read riot act to the left about reality of a-s in their midst, to recognize it, expose it and root it out, and stop using support for JC, or I-P issue, as excuse for peddling it. It is not support! Reiterate "socialism of fools". A-s is vile to all and not about hurting Jewish feelings'. He also suggested reaching out to Luciana Berger, the Labour MP who had endured torrents of anti-Semitic abuse and threats (how much from Labour Party members is disputed) and conducting greater education around the issue – 'most important as enabling people to under-stand these phenomena from the inside will ultimately be a lot more effective and equitable in every way than merely being told to obey rules handed down from on-high or being disciplined for failing to do so.'[29]

Unfortunately, Klug's recommendations largely went by the board, and the excellent speech he wrote for Corbyn to make on the subject went undelivered. Not only did we never get ahead of the curve, but the curve remained more or less over the horizon.

Israel–Palestine

However, the idea that another strategy could have ended the campaign against us is a fallacy. To start to assess this, we need to go back a little way. Consider these news items: A leading Jewish actor renounces her lifelong support for Labour in protest at its attitudes. Jewish support for Labour plunges to an historic low. The headlines are familiar – but they do not refer to Corbyn's Labour. They date from the period when Labour had its only Jewish Leader to date, Ed Miliband. Maureen Lipman's abandonment of her political party and the Jewish community's growing alienation from Labour happened on Miliband's watch and for the same reason – his decision to whip Labour MPs to support the recognition of a Palestinian state alongside Israel, Palestinian self-determination being some-thing that many of Israel's advocates – not to mention successive Israeli governments – find unacceptable, whatever hypocritical platitudes they mouth.[30]

As a result, the *Jewish Chronicle* reported, 69 per cent of Jewish voters decided to support the Tories, with only 22 per cent backing Labour. Seventy-three per cent of the *Jewish Chronicle* sample said attitudes towards Israel were either very or quite important in influencing their decision, and on that issue only 10 per cent supported Miliband's approach, while 65 per cent backed that of David Cameron. An accompanying article by journalist Marcus Dysch spelled out the lessons and the implications. 'Positioning himself as Israel's chief political critic during last summer's Gaza conflict and then backing unilateral Palestinian statehood . . . have holed Mr Miliband's relationship with the Jewish community below the waterline.' Labour anti-Semitism was not mentioned by Dysch at all.[31]

This illuminates important aspects to the controversy. First, Jewish voters had substantially abandoned Labour before the advent of Corbynism with no allegations of anti-Semitism being involved.[32] Second, their turn to the Tories was mainly about Israel and perceptions of its security. A pro-Palestine Labour Party was regarded as a threat by many Jewish voters in Britain – and by the Israeli state itself, apparently. An Al-Jazeera documentary broadcast in 2017 covertly filmed an official at Israel's London embassy, Shia Masot, offering then Labour MP Joan Ryan the use of a £1 million budget to take sympathetic MPs on trips to Israel.[33] Masot also attacked Jeremy Corbyn and spoke of 'taking down' a Tory minister at the Foreign Office viewed as critical of Israel. Masot left town in a hurry, almost as fast as the government started pretending nothing had occurred.[34] It would be naïve, however, to assume that was the end of the matter, any more than it was the start of it.

In fact, there could be no end to the matter, and the idea that the Corbyn leadership, even if it had handled the matter in a more sensitive and sophisticated way, could have secured one is wrong. Take the letter sent to Jennie Formby, Labour general secretary, in August 2018 by the Jewish Leadership Council and the Community Security Trust, two of the Jewish organisations which had spoken for the community in its relations with Labour, as a measure of the difficulty. The letter made clear that

> we do not believe that any real progress can be made in Labour's understanding of antisemitism, until those leading the Party undertake a deep cultural change in their attitude to the mainstream of the Jewish community, Zionism and Israel. This includes full appreciation of the fundamental religious and historical linkage between the Jewish people and the land of Israel.[35]

In other words, the price of peace would be a full capitulation by Labour to the Zionist argument over Israel/Palestine by endorsing what is in fact the *weakest* argument for Israel's existence, that which rests on religion and archaeology. That was not an aberration. All the Jewish organisations which engaged with Labour over this issue are campaigners for Israel. The Board of Deputies lists in its aims and purposes taking 'such appropriate action as lies within its power to advance Israel's security, welfare and standing.'[36] The Jewish Leadership Council includes in its mission ensuring a Jewish community in Britain 'confident in its support for Israel'. The Jewish Labour Movement, Labour's own Zionist affiliate, has as the first of its constitutional objects 'to maintain and promote Labour or Socialist Zionism as the movement for self-determination of the Jewish people within the state of Israel' and among its values promoting 'the centrality of Israel in Jewish life.'

There is no dispute that in taking this view these bodies, otherwise not necessarily very representative, speak for most Jewish people in Britain, who have some degree of identification with Israel, ranging from unconditional support under all circumstances to a loose affinity.[37] The JLC/CST letter called attention to 'the impact of the Holocaust and subsequent antisemitism upon mainstream Jewish support for Zionism and modern day Israel'. Indeed, a discussion of this issue that does not acknowledge the impact of the Holocaust on the balance of opinion between Zionism and other political identities among the surviving Jewish community, as some on the left tend to do, will be fruitless. We no longer live in the 1930s, when Communism and Zionism disputed for hegemony in the Jewish working class of London's East End.

Many of Labour's loudest critics have been clear that Israel is the issue. The sociologist David Hirsh, a leading opponent of the left, has written: 'Overt hatred of Jews violates the norms of respectable public discourse . . . antisemitism endures in more subtle ways, manifesting itself in the quality and intensity of hostility to Israel.'[38] Alan Johnson, an academic and editor at the Britain Israel Communications and Research Centre defined the problem that Labour faced as 'a programme to abolish Israel, a movement to boycott Israel and discourse to demonise Israel'. It was 'almost never old-fashioned Jew-hatred.'[39] It would be easy to argue that they are wrong in this emphasis, but this is what is apparently believed by those who prioritised campaigning against Labour anti-Semitism.

To assert that because the majority of an ethnic group take a particular view of an international political issue anyone disputing that view is therefore racist is a nonsensical position, albeit one which the Labour Party under Keir Starmer is hurtling towards. It is a device to delegitimise solidarity with the Palestinian people and criticism of Israel, however oppressive and right-wing the latter becomes. The view of Israel as a refuge for a people long victim of the most unspeakable outrages in history cannot be dismissed, and is the most compelling argument for the state's creation – post-Holocaust, many Jews did not want to leave their lives and security at the mercy of others. The alternative view, equally accurate, is of Israel as a project of settler colonialism sponsored and sustained by world imperialism and which conducts itself towards the indigenous people very much as colonial states have always done. Criminalising – or even ignoring – either position nullifies any hope of progress.

The massive investment of the media in the issue, having found the perfect means to morally delegitimise a politician and a movement trading heavily on decency and integrity, also helped turn it intractable. As with almost every aspect of Corbyn's leadership, efforts and initiatives to address the problem (such as they were) got almost no coverage. And, yes, the actual volume of complaints about the conduct of party members was wildly exaggerated, drawing on submissions by pop-up campaigns of dubious provenance.

The IHRA Quicksand

These threads came together in the debilitating controversy over the International Holocaust Remembrance Alliance (IHRA) definition of anti-Semitism.[40] The definition originated in the desire to create a tool which would permit the accurate monitoring of the scale of anti-Semitic incidents in Europe. One of its leading authors, Kenneth Stern, has stated that it was never intended to be used for disciplinary purposes, nor as a gold standard, definitive, description of the evil.[41] Indeed, its famous examples omit the most ubiquitous form of anti-Semitic discourse, that Jews are mean and avaricious. Instead, its examples focus heavily on Israel, which features in seven out of eleven cited. Some of those examples identify views that are surely anti-Semitic – 'holding Jews collectively responsible for actions of the state of Israel' or 'using the symbols and images associated with classic antisemitism (e.g., claims of Jews killing Jesus or blood libel) to characterize Israel or Israelis', for example.

For all the flaws in the IHRA examples, it was in my view inexpedient to make a fight over this issue in summer 2018, since it was patently unwinnable given the preceding inertia in its handling.[42] I thought that we should accept the definition and the examples (which were either fine or at least could be lived with) with one exception, where a line had to be drawn. This was the example which asserted that it was (or might in context be) anti-Semitic to deny 'the Jewish people their right to self-determination, e.g., by claiming that the existence of a State of Israel is a racist endeavour'. This formulation all but brands anti-Zionism as anti-Semitic, as many of Israel's apologists (including Starmer) are now anxious to establish. It also silences pro-Palestinian discourse, not to mention the views of Palestinians themselves, none of whom could be found to regard Israel, based on their own collective experience, as anything other than a 'racist endeavour'. This formulation is used to attempt to ban within Labour the widely held view that Israel has developed a form of apartheid. Unlike offensive comparisons of Israel with Nazi Germany, the apartheid comparison is very near the mark – as Human Rights Watch and a range of Israeli citizens and organisations have acknowledged.[43] As for Zionism as a colonial project – its founders boasted of it, at a time when colonialism was eminently respectable. And so Israel has carried on, as a racist endeavour quite independent of the subjective views of many Israelis and Israeli organisations.

That is not to deny that Zionisms other than as an imperial project were a historical possibility, nor that a different Israel/Palestine is a future possibility. It is present realities that must be faced, however. These have been well set out by former United Nations Secretary-General Ban Ki-moon:

> This is not a conflict between equals that can be resolved through . . . traditional conflict-resolution tools. The reality is very different: a powerful state is controlling another people through an open-ended occupation, settling its own people on the land in violation of international law and enforcing a legal regime of institutionalised discrimination. Calls for a return to unconditional bilateral talks every time there is a fresh flare-up in fighting will only serve to perpetuate the status quo if these root causes are not addressed. What has become increasingly clear in recent years is Israel's intent to maintain its structural domination and oppression of the Palestinian people through indefinite occupation. This gives the dual legal regimes imposed in Palestinian territories by Israel – together with the inhumane and abusive acts that are carried out against Palestinians – new significance, resulting in a situation that arguably constitutes apartheid.[44]

That is the justification for the Boycott, Divestment and Sanctions campaign which has so disturbed Israel and its international supporters. A Corbyn government would have remained committed to the two-state solution, the position which the Communist political tradition I have been part of has always advocated. Today, that looks forlorn to the point of implausibility, given the extent of Israeli settlement in the West Bank and the ascendancy of revisionist Zionism in Israeli politics, a local variant of the ethno-religious national populism now ubiquitous. What could supersede the present torment is ultimately a matter that can only be resolved by the peoples of Israel/Palestine, but Corbyn was surely correct in recognising the present enormous disparity in power between the Israeli state and the Palestinian people, a disparity which makes any serious negotiation unlikely to start, still less succeed. Redressing that power imbalance through international pressure and solidarity is not inimical to peace, but essential to it.

We blundered in trying to rewrite much of the IHRA examples rather than focussing on these core political issues, which would not have resolved the dispute with the Jewish communal leadership but would have at least drawn the lines of difference on comprehensible grounds. A less satisfactory alternative would have been to adopt the caveats agreed by the House of Commons Home Affairs Committee when it discussed the IHRA definition.[45] That is not to say that nothing was done to try and reframe the question, and to address the real concerns raised. A focus group participant quoted by Steve Rayson in *The Fall of the Red Wall* (2020) asked 'why couldn't he [Corbyn] say "Yes, we've got a problem and I'm dealing with it and I'm sorry." Why couldn't he say that?'[46] In fact, Corbyn said and did all those things. One effort was his article in the *Evening Standard* in April 2018, which I drafted:

We must strive to understand why anti-Semitism has surfaced in our party, which has always stood for equality for all and opposed racism and discrimination.

As I indicated in my letter last month to the Board of Deputies and the Jewish Leadership Council, there are two particular contemporary sources. First, individuals on the fringes of the movement of solidarity with the Palestinian people can stray into anti-Semitic views.

The struggle for justice for the Palestinian people and an end to their dispossession is a noble one – just as a genuine two-state solution is essential to lasting peace in the Middle East. But when criticism of or opposition to the Israeli government uses anti-Semitic ideas – attributing its injustices to Jewish identity, demanding that Jews in Britain or elsewhere answer for its conduct, or comparing Israel to the Nazis – then a line must be drawn.

Anti-Zionism is not in itself anti-Semitic and many Jews themselves are not Zionists. But there are also a very few who are drawn to the Palestinian question precisely because it affords an opportunity to express hostility to Jewish people in a 'respectable' setting. Our movement must not be a home for such individuals.

Second, there are people who have come to see capitalism and imperialism as the product of conspiracy by a small shadowy elite rather than a political, economic, legal and social system. That is only a step from hoary myths about 'Jewish bankers' and 'sinister global forces'.

These views do no service to the struggle for a just society. Instead, they reproduce the sort of scapegoating that we recognise when directed at ethnic or religious minorities.

Anti-Semitism was responsible for the worst crimes of the 20th century. According to a survey conducted last year by two leading

Jewish community organisations, anti-Semitic views are held by a minority in Britain, and are more likely to be found on the right of politics. But we did not look closely enough at ourselves.[47]

How much of these arguments were really internalised by our supporters is hard to assess – the overheated atmosphere on the issue precluded much empathy. The result was that as 2018 and 2019 went on, more and more Jewish allies were driven into agnosticism regarding the Corbyn leadership, while the agnostics turned hostile. As for the Board of Deputies and its associates, they basically severed all connection with the Labour Party and spurned concessions and even contact. In the end, opinion polls showed that fully 85 per cent of Jewish people in Britain believed that Labour had a problem with anti-Semitism, which was a pretty disastrous position, even if all allowances are made for the Israel issue and other contingent factors – including the shameful role of the *Jewish Chronicle*, which seemed to have abandoned all conventional professional decencies.[48] A lot of unnecessary pain was caused to many within the Jewish community.

Ironically, in view of the exceptional contribution made by generations of Jewish men and women to the socialist movement worldwide, socialism itself has now been branded with the iron of prejudice. The Labour MP Siobhan McDonagh, admittedly no oracle of political science, opined that anti-capitalism was anti-Semitic, while former Blair consigliere John McTernan suggested that any challenge to inequality crossed the line: 'Rhetoric about the 1 per cent and economic inequality has the same underlying theme – a small group of very rich people who cleverly manipulate others to defend their interests. So anti-capitalism masks and normalises anti-Semitism'.[49]

Indeed, Jewish socialists in particular have now become the focus of Starmer's purges. The very presence of non-Zionist Jews in public life, particularly among those defending Corbyn, has become somewhat unacceptable to the anti-Corbyn clique. David Hirsh has gone so far as to assert that the Corbyn-supporting Jewish Voice for Labour 'is at the *very vanguard* of the anti-Semitic movement in Britain. It is made up of people who have spent decades now mobilising and parading their identities in the service of antisemitism.'[50] Here, the idea of 'Jew' has become disconnected from any necessary ethnic or religious qualification and become a political construct, and anti-Semitism denotes not hatred of Jews per se but opposition to a particular ideological position. That is the same position which allows the government of Israel, for example, to ally with overt anti-Semites such as Hungarian premier Viktor Orbán or US president Trump.[51] Not only is anti-Zionism anti-Semitism, but also there is no anti-Semitism worth troubling about other than opposition to Israel. It would not seem that Jewish people worldwide are well served by this ideology.

If anti-Zionists are a minority of the Jewish community overall, they are a larger one among Jewish members of the Labour Party, mainly organised through Jewish Voice for Labour. JVL has had its weaknesses, including limited connections with the wider Jewish community. But its demonization by other Jewish organisations has become near-pathological. The legitimacy of JVL members as Jews has been negated, since their activity challenges the narrative of a monolithic community. As their exclusion from Labour mounts, often for alleged 'anti-Semitism', they find no friends among those who campaigned against Corbyn on this issue.[52] The Board of Deputies and Jewish Labour Movement are silent and the Chief Rabbi does a victory lap at the conference of the American-Israel Public Affairs Committee conference in New York, boasting of the anti-Corbyn unity in Britain's Jewish community. JVL's crime, according to Hirsh, which merits their expulsion from Labour, has been to 'sow confusion about what is, and what is not, anti-Semitic.'[53] The anti-Corbyn campaign has gone a long way towards imposing its own version of clarity on this question, but it has *not* achieved any reduction in anti-Semitic attitudes or outrages in contemporary Britain, as all the evidence cruelly shows. Perhaps this was not the main purpose. At a moment when anti-Semitism is escalating around the globe, including in its most violent manifestations, and when the broadest unity is needed against it, that is a tragedy.

7

Class and Culture:
The Brexit Blunder

Corbynism ultimately impaled itself on the issue of Britain's membership of the European Union. Other factors were at play in its eventual defeat, but the timing, scope and content of its demise were determined by the controversy over Brexit.

Corbyn's leadership was aborted because much of its constituency and cadre clung to the tapestry of illusions woven around the European Union – a bastion of neoliberal order that nevertheless is taken to be a combatant on the virtuous side of the great identity conflict which has secured an apparent purchase on political discourse.

Labour's particular route to perdition over Brexit was through a double failure on the issue of democracy. The first mistake, excusable perhaps but nonetheless erroneous, was to hitch its political perspectives to membership of this entirely non-democratic, if impeccably liberal, institution, whose *raison d'être* consists in reducing the range of socio-economic options available to national electorates. The second, inexcusably, was to seek to overturn the decision of a majority of the electorate to leave the EU, going along with every available device of parliamentary obstruction and endorsing every judicial manoeuvre to do so.

The story of the period between the relative electoral success of 2017 and the absolute failure of 2019 is an account of Labour's miserable migration from being an insurgent agent of radical change to becoming perceived as part of a stonewalling Establishment, besotted with constitutional arcana and parliamentary process, incapable of initiative on the issue that overshadowed all others. This was a process which drained Corbynism of its vitality as a politics that was different and, above all, responsive to the popular will.

This failure was not, however, by any means entirely the responsibility of the Corbyn leadership. It is well understood that the Brexit vote coalesced a long-maturing political reconfiguration which has ostensibly seen politics of culture and identity displace more traditional politics of class, although it would be truer to say that the latter have been repackaged rather than superseded. The same phenomenon has swept politics across much of the first-wave capitalist world, and 'Brexit' is the name of its British expression. The issue of EU membership therefore stood duty for wider concerns about a 'culture war' ranging over issues of history, race, immigration and values, the rise of ethno-nationalist authoritarianism in the aftermath of the 2008 crash, and the future of the left in countries where workers employed in basic industries constitute a small and shrinking minority and their institutions are much diminished, depleting the 'class for itself' as the socialist subject. The Brexit vote also gave the many people alienated from the status quo the opportunity to administer a kicking to the Establishment. Given the centrality of these matters to any prospect of socialism, we need to locate the debates in the Corbyn leadership of 2017–19 in that broader setting. It is not only the story of how the commanding position attained in June 2017 was squandered, but also of how left-wing social democracy tries to meet these new challenges.

Euroscepticism and Europhilia

David Cameron's Brexit referendum was designed to overcome a protracted crisis in and for the Conservative Party. Despite an admonition to his party to 'stop banging on about Europe', bang on its membership, disproportionately composed of elderly home counties reactionaries, certainly did. This reflected two traditional preoccupations of the right: the assertion of nationalism with a particular hostility to immigration, and the view that a Britain outside of the EU could embrace the free market with still less inhibition once tiresome Brussels regulations were cast off. The requirement to meld these attitudes with the interests of big business and the City – always preponderantly and unsurprisingly supportive of 'Europe' as constituted – proved increasingly challenging, especially to the sound of raucous tabloid Brussels-bashing. It was an argument that high finance and the big monopolies lost within the Tory Party, a sea-change in itself for British politics.

The labour movement had travelled in the opposite direction to the Tories. For the most part opposed to joining the Common Market in the 1970s, Harold Wilson's political acrobatics notwithstanding, it became enthusiastic about Brussels from the late 1980s. When then EU Commission President Jacques Delors charmed the TUC in 1988 with his vision of a 'social Europe', he was offering new life for the social democratic palliatives which were no longer on offer from Westminster governments. What became

Labour 'remainia' was in the first place the product of the defeats of the Thatcher period. The EU was the anaesthetic for the pain. Europhilia was embraced by a movement down on its luck, with its self-esteem ebbing. It was not a novel route to socialism but instead a means of discarding such an objective, which had come to seem unattainable, in favour of a saviour from on high who might deliver at least something palatable.

Phase two of Labour's mutation into an almost unconditionally pro-EU force in British politics was the New Labour government, which wrapped up the issue with its general support for ineluctable capitalist globalisation. Although Blair and Brown kept a wary eye on the Murdoch media and did not trumpet their EU commitment too loudly (which in any case they more than balanced with a militant Atlanticism), essentially they placed the European single market within the framework of their economic liberalism and championing of market-based decisions. Indeed, leaving broad areas of policy-making to inaccessible officials in Brussels was consistent with the general thrust of their economic management, which was to remove key decisions from democratic control, starting with the shifting of the power to set interest rates from the Chancellor to the Bank of England. The founders of neoliberal thinking had well understood the potential for conflict between capitalism and democracy – Hayek had liked the idea of a European federation for that reason. Now this position secured the acquiescence of the leaders of social democracy. As Wolfgang Streeck has noted, they had 'bought in to globalist doctrine. Third Way social democracy came to accept as a dogma that open markets in an integrated world economy was not just inevitable but outright desirable.'[1] The European Union was a key building block for that unconstrained global market.

Much of the left, critical of New Labour in other respects, went along with this for somewhat different reasons. Trade unions convinced themselves that single-market access was critical to defending employment in Britain, notwithstanding the actual loss of manufacturing jobs at a rate of about 100,000 each year under New Labour. For others, the EU's liberalism was more than enough compensation for its lack of democracy and baked-in pro-market orientation. Support for the EU became a symbol of a debased 'internationalism', and even its desiccated and imperme-able bureaucracy appeared preferable to clinging to the nation-state as a political actor. Most working people, however, took a different view, understanding the enduring truth of Nye Bevan's condemnation of the Common Market in 1957 as representing 'the disenfranchisement of the people and the enfranchisement of market forces'.[2]

At root, much of the left confounded liberalism with democ-racy, and this confusion was one of the underlying weaknesses which debilitated the Corbyn project. The European Union is liberal both in the classical sense of upholding the rights of private property against the state and of entrenching market relationships, and in the more modern meaning of supporting individual free-doms (including saliently the right to live and work anywhere within its borders) without gender, ethnic, religious or other forms of discrimination. Its 'internationalism' offers the free movement of people within the EU (but not into 'Fortress Europe' from the rest of the world), as well as mandating the free movement of capi-tal, goods and services. As Costas Lapavitsas has put it, 'The EU is neither a purveyor of "soft power" nor a benevolent and humani-tarian force. Rather, it is a hierarchical alliance of nation states that have created the institutional framework of a single market relentlessly promoting neoliberalism'.[3] This liberalism constitutes the hegemonic ideology of the capitalist class worldwide.

Liberalism with an additional bureaucratic patina of internationalism made it good enough, however, for many on the left, ignoring that the EU is no better than a parody of a democracy, governed by an opaque officialdom barely answerable to an impotent masquerade of a European parliament. Of course, the democratic nakedness of this position has long been concealed by talk of pan-European solidarity and 'remain and reform'. The former is, alas, no better than embryonic in most respects, since class politics have not really generated a European locus, and mass action remains usually national or occasionally genuinely international (as in the worldwide day of demonstrations against the Iraq War in 2003). As for reform of the EU's institutions and procedures, these have scarcely captured the popular imagination, in part for want of a shred of plausibility. There is no prospect of serious reform in the EU's purpose and functioning absent the election of Corbyn-type governments in all the decisive countries in Europe at the same time, and no democratic leverage with which to effect such a change in the meantime. 'Remain and rebel', as the slogan morphed in 2019, added only a layer of ultra-left infantilism. For millions of working-class voters, voting Leave *was* the rebellion.

These considerations did not impact much on the course of the 2016 referendum. Labour went into it more or less united on the same side as Cameron's government – for Remain. The left-wing critique of the European Union – that it would be easier to effect real social change outside than inside – did not have more than a marginal impact on the debate. The idea of quitting the EU as essentially a right-wing project, and moreover a pandering to racism, was consolidated through the leadership of the Leave campaign by Nigel Farage and Boris Johnson. This shaped the subsequent debate within the Corbyn leadership. The view that to do anything that might expedite giving effect to the referendum result was an unconscionable compromise with the racist right co-existed uneasily with the notion that, as a party committed to democracy, leave the EU we still must.

The Backward and the Enlightened

This debate was mapped onto a range of other cultural and psephological issues, which were already brewing into a crisis for the Labour Party, as they were for social democratic parties across Europe. This was a coal mine which did not want for canaries. In most of what became known as the 'red wall' seats the Labour vote had been in uninterrupted decline from 1997 to 2017, when a reversal of fortunes was engineered, as we have seen. Voters in these seats had moved first to abstention and then, in some cases, to support for UKIP. It seemed that only the weight of local tradition was stopping the Tories becoming the ultimate destination, should the latter only turn sufficiently populist.

Tradition turned out to be a wasting asset. Two points, deeply linked, can be generalised about the Labour-held seats which supported 'Leave'. First, they are mainly composed of communities which have *not* benefitted from capitalist globalisation by any metric. Their industries have disappeared or moved elsewhere, the standards of employment and living have stagnated at best, opportunities have shrunk and confidence in the future degraded. Second, the social infrastructure that made these seats solid for Labour for so long has also atrophied and in many cases vanished. The connections of work, union, community and party were what made so many areas 'heartlands', and these have largely dissolved. The sentiments engendered by such connections do not disappear overnight when a pit or shipyard shuts, but the clock starts running down. There is another side too – some of these seats have gained a new profile as well as seeing the old one decay. They have become dormitory areas for the nearest big conurbation, new housing drawing in commuters with different lifestyles and relationships to their community. Eventually an electoral impact will register, unless the labour movement is able to reconfigure itself to meet the new environment. The 2017 election showed that this can be done, but a survey of twentieth-century working-class political strongholds across Europe shows that it is by no means easy or automatic.

The support for Brexit in so many parts of the country was the first real breach in the English 'red wall' in that voters ignored the recommendation of the Labour Party to support Remain, a position endorsed by the great majority of the party's members and most trade union leaderships. The Scottish 'red wall' had already crumbled by this stage, likewise under the impact of a referendum that recalibrated political identities. Such a divergence between the party membership and its heartland voters would have been unlikely thirty years ago. It was a registration of an estrangement that had already occurred. The reasons for voting for Brexit were varied and doubtless complex. Those who have written on the matter often strain for monocausal explanations – for Danny Dorling and Sally Tomlinson it was nostalgia for the British Empire, while Maria Sobolewska and Robert Ford make growing popular hostility to immigration bear most of the weight.[4] Both surely played a part, particularly the latter. However, to attribute Farageist views to everyone concerned about the changes EU membership had allowed to impact on the labour market would be a misjudgement.

Following the European elections debacle in 2019, erstwhile Corbynite columnist (now a Starmer supporter) Paul Mason called for the departure of Ian Lavery, the only ex-miner left in Labour's higher ranks, as party chair, largely because he was part of the beleaguered respect-the-referendum element in the shadow cabinet.[5] In a speech at the same time, Mason bore in on ex-miners again:

> I'm done with people saying 'we can't lose the working class', a Lithuanian nurse is working class, an Afghan taxi driver is working class. An ex-miner sitting in the pub calling migrants cockroaches has not only no added human capital above the people I just mentioned but it's also not the person we are interested in.[6]

This choice of image was striking. Mason symbolically identified the people who needed ejecting from the Corbyn coalition with the coal miners who had been the party's staunchest supporters for near-on a century. In 2019 he was obliged to a dramatic extent, as ex-coalfield constituencies ejected themselves. The Lithuanian nurses and Afghan taxi drivers, working class and worthy of equal consideration as they undoubtedly are, proved an electorally inadequate substitute, as might have been anticipated. This was the logic of recalibrating Corbynism from a class movement to a culture/identity one.

With former mining communities apparently the front line in the culture war, and the metropolitan left placing itself on the other side of the barricades, I thought I should pay a last visit before Labour kissed them goodbye. In the company of the local MP, I went in 2019 to a community centre in a village between Doncaster and Wakefield, in a parliamentary constituency that has returned Labour MPs for a century, yet had voted nearly two-thirds for Brexit Party/Tories/UKIP in the European elections, to meet a group of former miners.

They did not oblige the Masonic stereotypes by fulminating into their beer about migrants. Instead they described the post-coal labour market in their communities. A brand-name retailer established a warehouse creating around a thousand jobs – but few if any were advertised in the local job centre. Instead the work was subcontracted to a labour agency which recruits exclusively in Poland. The same agency then secures vacant properties in the surrounding villages to accommodate the Polish workers at maximum capacity (and doubtless rent).

The jobs that were available paid little more than miners could earn forty years previously. Many working families depend on the foodbanks now as ubiquitous across the coalfield as the pits once were. Talking to ex-miners it seems clear that New Labour's biggest failure ('apart from Iraq', of course) was in labour market regulation. The surprise is that many on the left do not acknowledge this, as if super-exploited Poles are not as much victims of this labour market as unemployed British ex-miners. Labour market regulation and stronger trade unions, between them able to prevent undercutting, are an obvious solution but not an immediately available one, and not one that the more middle-class left showed much interest in exploring.

My interlocutors acknowledged Labour's challenge. 'It's a national party, Jeremy has to balance London and the North. People up here want the same things, they like Labour's policies.' No culture war there. I asked: When people around here voted for

Brexit what problem did they think they were solving? 'Everything', was the answer.[7]

Mason was right, however, to recall that numbers of working-class people have always held reactionary ideas on race, war, imperialism, welfare and more. That is unavoidable in a capitalist society which generates such an outlook organically, as apparent 'common sense', particularly in a culture long shaped by a legacy of world supremacy and exceptionalism. Sometimes the Labour Party itself was the vehicle for the transmission of these views, although capitalism's ideological apparatus has plenty of other resources in this respect. Had there not been such voters, the Tories would scarcely have won a general election in the twentieth century, when up to three-quarters of the electorate belonged to the working class. Mason's error was in the view that such voters should be *ignored*. It is surely correct to say that they should not be pandered to. However, ignoring a significant section of working-class opinion is not the way that the labour movement establishes hegemony over the class it emerges from, still less other parts of society. The former MP Ian Wrigglesworth, who was on the right of the Parliamentary Labour Party in the 1970s and joined the breakaway Social Democratic Party in 1981, understood this better. After the 2019 election, he addressed the loss of Labour votes in areas like the one he had once represented (on Teeside): 'Many of those traditional Labour voters often had extreme right-wing views, but voted Labour for longstanding class and cultural reasons.'[8]

This expresses both a good and a bad thing at once, a unity that has been central to Labour's electoral strength for generations past. It is obviously negative that some working-class people hold reactionary opinions. But it is good that they nevertheless support the organisations of their class, electorally and industrially. That is how the relatively more advanced sections of a class become hegemonic. Clearly the backward can infect the more advanced too – the record of Labour governments over racism or imperialist war is far from discouraging for voters with right-wing, 'socially conservative' views. In that tension the political struggle for socialism is waged. The incapacity of the labour movement to reproduce those 'class and cultural reasons' in a changed economic environment came home to roost in December 2019.

It became clear that most people were far more invested in their choice in the 2016 referendum, be it Leave or Remain, than they were in their choice of political party. That was not inevitable. As Sobolewska and Ford note, 'Traditional class and ideological conflicts were organised out of politics by New Labour's move to the centre ground', which led many 'to feel they were no longer being offered a meaningful choice.'[9] Brexit was a means of expressing opposition as much as expressing an identity, at least in many working-class areas. Two-thirds of working-class people voted Leave, as high a percentage as has ever voted Labour in the party's history.[10]

The cultural gap between the spokespeople for the Lithuanian nurses and the representatives of the Yorkshire ex-miners ran through the middle of our strategy meetings on Brexit, although no one present would have disowned either. The hegemonic potential of June 2017 fell down that gap.

One further anecdote speaks for itself. I was discussing the campaign for a second referendum with one of its strongest advocates, a Labour election candidate, in late 2018. She insisted that a second referendum could not simply be on whatever exit deal was eventually agreed, but should also include Remain as an option, on the grounds that around half the electorate wanted it. Well, I responded, a large part of the electorate would prefer to leave without a deal at all, so should that be included as an option? She paused before replying 'Well, perhaps. But I think *we have a duty of care.*' The royal Remainiac 'we' collides with the people.

The 2017 Opportunity

The idea that there was a silver bullet solution to Labour's Brexit problem is false. By 2019 there were no longer any remotely easy options left. It is my view that a chance to frame the question to the advantage of the Corbyn leadership existed in 2017. It was missed then and never recurred.

Others disagree. In 2021 John McDonnell was asked: 'In the summer of 2017, was an opportunity missed to definitively rule out a second referendum?' He replied:

> To make that call then was almost impossible, I think. Again, once you have been bloodied in a coup, you are very wary about making sure you are not going to do anything that gives anyone any excuse for a second coup. There was conspiracy after conspiracy. That was part of my problem. Half my life was spent on just survival, and keeping the show on the road, as well as trying to develop the overall economic policy and other elements of our policy programme.[11]

John is wrong there, although there was indeed 'conspiracy after conspiracy'. But in the summer of 2017, the Corbyn leadership was riding high, basking in the unexpected advances of the June general election. The Labour Party was at Corbyn's feet. At that point, uniquely during his leadership, the chance of a PLP-led coup was zero. It was a time when tough decisions could have been taken and made to stick. It was also a moment when the campaign for a further referendum to overturn the decision of 2016 was muted. Most Remainers set their sights no higher than securing a soft Brexit, leaving Britain aligned with the EU single market. It was then that the Corbyn leadership could have set out its own terms for handling the Brexit issue with minimal political cost.

There were several connected imperatives. First, to ensure that the Brexit issue was behind us before the next general election. Best by far to have left the EU and have the space to develop a more attractive post-Brexit prospectus for Britain than that offered by the Tories. Second, to consolidate and expand the electoral coalition we had pulled together. The weakest link here, at least in England and Wales, was older voters and those in post-industrial communities, preponderantly pro-Leave demographics. Third, we should exacerbate Tory divisions by promoting a Brexit that was bearable to all parts of our coalition while causing a crisis amid theirs. The hung Parliament was not only a problem for the Tories – it gave Labour new responsibilities to advance solutions, as well as new opportunities.

To that end I produced a proposal for the leadership group in October 2017 that sought to take advantage of what was already clear – May's incapacity to advance Brexit. Obtusely, she had not modified her strategy in the light of losing her parliamentary majority – she continued to seek an exit deal which would be acceptable to the Tory Party (and its DUP bedmates) alone. There was never more than the slightest chance of such an approach working, the more so since May's credibility and authority within her own party were by this stage shredded. I argued that we should propose 'a common "national" position' to the government over Brexit and 'take responsibility for delivering it in talks with Brussels.' I believed that such an approach could unite Labour, make the party look confident and government-ready and get us off the Brexit sidelines. 'It would mean that the balance of argument could shift from the course of the negotiations with the EU towards the contrasting visions for a post-Brexit Britain. Much better territory for us . . . We should demand that a jointly negotiated Brexit should be immediately followed by a general election to determine what sort of country a non-EU Britain should be.'

I acknowledged the risks of the proposal, above all of collaborating with the Tories in any shape or form, but I still believe it was on the right track and would have led to better outcomes than the approach actually followed. It may be that the negatives which would have followed reaching out to May would have been greater than I allowed for (even had she rejected the overture, as I anticipated). It might have been sufficient for the Corbyn leadership to have simply and categorically made it clear that under no circumstances would Labour countenance a re-run referendum, and emphasised that the *only* debate was on the terms of Britain's departure from the EU.

My plan had the explicit support of Jon Trickett at the time, and the private backing of others on the strategy group. It was shot down primarily due to the intransigent and colourfully expressed opposition of Diane Abbott. I make no complaint about that, in so far as Diane's objection to any form of Brexit was undoubtedly based on principle – mainly the fact that it was championed by racists and xenophobes and had become a right-wing project, considerations which had come, for her, to trump the Bennite position on the EU to which she had once adhered. Given her experiences, mirroring those of so many black people, she could not be challenged on that ground. Diane was, moreover, unfailingly loyal to Corbyn personally and never to my knowledge used this or any other issue to indulge in back-stage scheming. At any event, Jeremy himself showed no interest in discussing the matter further.

Nevertheless, a chance was missed to make the weather, be it through the initiative I proposed or another. This is now widely acknowledged. In his fascinating book on the end of the 'red wall', *Financial Times* journalist Sebastian Payne found both Ian Lavery and Alan Johnson, spanning the spectrum of Labour opinion, in basic agreement that 'the moment Theresa May lost her majority was Labour's opening. Had Jeremy Corbyn held his nose and done a deal with the Conservatives, Brexit would have been delivered on softer terms. As well as splitting the Tories . . . it would have likely gone some way to propping up parts of the red wall.' Johnson, the sternest critic of Corbynism, told Payne that the best chance for Labour to have held on to its Leave seats 'would have been supporting Theresa May's deal.' Even Peter Mandelson has conceded that 'we should have supported May's deal as the least harmful option.'[12] If there was a single moment when the 2019 election was lost, it was in autumn 2017.

Rather than taking that or any other initiative, the leadership fell victim to a complacent assumption that the government, neither strong nor stable as it was, was on the point of collapse, that Brexit would be the instrument of that disintegration, and that Labour simply needed to maintain a normal oppositional intransigence to be the beneficiary of this process. But the perspective adopted de facto underestimated the grim determination of the Establishment and the Tory Party to prevent a Corbyn government at all costs. That spectre, suddenly all too real after June

2017, gave the government and its supporters a higher degree of cohesion than they might otherwise have had, at least at that stage. Nor were the Democratic Unionist Party in the least likely to bring down the Tories, even over a Brexit deal disadvantageous to the status of the six counties in the UK, if the consequence was to be Corbynism enthroned. As one leading DUP politician put it to Labour peer Andrew Adonis (who repeated the story to me): 'We will never do anything to put Sinn Fein into Downing Street.' The memory of Corbyn's association with Gerry Adams seemed almost as fresh as that of the Battle of the Boyne.

Missing: A 'Labour Brexit'

One of the reasons advanced in discussion for Labour not being seen to do anything that would 'get Brexit done' was that this was not what party members wanted. This was a potent argument, given that Jeremy and all the leading figures around him had spent their political lifetimes arguing that the views of the membership should guide the actions of MPs. I am not sure the conclusion was right, however. It all depended on the question posed. If you were to ask Labour's individual members (union affiliates were far more nuanced) whether or not they wanted Britain to remain in the European Union, then clearly the answer would have been a resounding yes, a fact partly reflective of the already noted disproportionate skewing of the membership towards London geographically and the middle class sociologically. Yet if the question was 'Would you rather stay in the EU or see a Corbyn government in Britain?', then the vast weight of party opinion would have come down for the latter choice.

Misguided by this individual members-first precept, one mistake piled upon another. The democratic obligation to deliver on the referendum result was forgotten. The perceived opinions of the membership occluded those of the wider electorate, and the electoral impact of bending in one direction or another was subject to increasingly far-fetched assessments, of which Emily Thornberry's conviction that her Islington South seat was endangered unless Labour was 100 per cent Remain was but one symptom.[13] The voters we had agreed to target in order to expand our support were largely discarded in preference to appeasing our core support in metropolitan areas.

The argument was well summarised by James Schneider, a smart Momentum organiser who graduated to become one of Seumas Milne's key deputies:

> I think the failure is two-fold. One is to not build a democracy argument, because that would have been useful politically for a broader range of things, not just on Brexit. Secondly, to not develop within the party a 'respect the referendum' or pro-democracy type pressure group early on, to balance against the well-funded weight of push-polling and all the rest of it for the continuity 'remain' organisations.[14]

In this milieu it is scarcely surprising that Labour made barely the slightest effort to outline how a progressive social democratic government might be able to do desirable things outside the EU that it would not easily accomplish within it – state aid to industry, public procurement policy (to name two things which Boris Johnson later did in fact name), basically anything that interfered in the operation of the market. John McDonnell did float the possibility once or twice but fell silent on the issue. Taken together with the commitment to the free movement of capital, this started to leave a Corbyn government somewhat short of interventionist instruments beyond classical tax-and-spend, which was, in truth, the summit of the ambitions of some in the leadership team. Of course there were things which Labour members all wanted to preserve from the EU – employment standards, environmental regulations and a liberal immigration policy. There would have been nothing at all to stop a Corbyn government enacting all of that and, indeed, going further. The potential of sovereignty was not understood.

Competing papers were produced outlining the impact of EU membership on the implementation of our 2017 manifesto. Jon Trickett's analysis found that EU regulations would cramp our style considerably, while Andrew Fisher's saw no great difficulties arising from Brussels. While it is true that much of our plans may not have attracted EU opprobrium, and it is further true that a country with Britain's weight in the EU can get away with quite a lot in terms of rule-bending, it is also the case that the 2017 manifesto could not have been regarded as the limit to our plans. Sooner or later a project of social transformation would collide with the rules of an organisation committed to keeping things pretty much as they are. Denying that was to whitewash the EU's foundational commitment to capitalism. The resistance to this recognition within much of the Corbyn camp was as much down to cultural identification with the EU (or definite non-identification with its leading opponents) as to any measured assessment of its utility in assisting a socialist government in Britain.

Some opponents on the right were more acute, recalling the days when the Tories had backed the EEC precisely because it 'essentially precluded the kind of socialism which was still the aim of the Labour Party in the 1960s and 1970s'.[15] The *Telegraph*'s

Ambrose Evans-Pritchard asked the left, 'Why are you dying in a ditch to defend a system that is reactionary, deflationary, hostile to everything you stand for and certain to block your policies however large your electoral victory?' Thatcher's biographer Charles Moore wrote that 'a Corbyn government could be much more easily beaten down with Britain in the EU than outside it. His socialism-in-one-country would quickly fall foul of single market rules and be squashed by the Commission and the European Court of justice . . . His government would become an impotent protest.'[16] This was more realistic than the position taken by many of our supporters, which was that the EU was a blessing and that the politics of 'Lexit' were Neanderthal and unworkable.

I do not recall the relative papers ever being subjected to serious discussion at a strategy meeting. The Corbyn leadership never developed a method for debating and resolving strategic political disagreements. The upshot was that the case for a Labour Brexit – by which was meant the case for asserting that, the decision to leave having been made, Labour could give it a distinct and progressive focus – went unmade. A crabbed defensiveness was offered instead, allied to an unappealing list of six tests for agreeing an exit deal designed by Keir Starmer, which resonated with neither side of the debate.

A 'People's Vote'?

Labour's stasis over Brexit was one of the elements making for a vacuum, a larger one being the government's incapacity in advancing its own proposals to give effect to the referendum outcome. Into that vacuum the campaign for a second referendum developed, moving to centre stage, as many supporters of the EU felt their possibilities expand from 'make the best of it' to 'we can reverse Brexit'. For the first time ever, Britain had a pro-EU mass movement. If Labour offered no explicit encouragement of this before 2019, neither did it foreclose the option of staying in the EU. The fact that both within and outside Parliament the campaign for a second referendum – or 'People's Vote' in its more benign self-description – was directed by the enemies of Corbynism, and the proponents of the politics of the 'extreme centre' ought to have wised the leadership up to a greater extent than it did. The PV campaign was Blairite in inspiration and, to a large extent, in management. The sixty-odd Labour MPs already marked out as anti-Brexit diehards were nearly all from the anti-Corbyn right wing of the party, and these were the people with whom the PV campaign liaised most closely. These MPs were at least as interested in getting shot of the party Leader as they were in defeating Brexit. Some, in the words of Labour MP Caroline Flint, a one-time Blairite who nevertheless stuck out for respecting the referendum, perhaps felt 'losing seats in Doncaster and Grimsby was a price worth paying [to stay in the EU].'[17] Since Corbyn was clearly reluctant to frame his whole leadership around dying in the anti-Brexit ditch, pressure for a new referendum was pressure on him too – this was the one issue which could divide the Leader from his base, as his opponents did not fail to notice.

And indeed, many of the hundreds of thousands who demonstrated for a 'People's Vote' were part of the Corbyn coalition. These were the mainly metropolitan, socially liberal, better educated and generally more-advantaged part of the Labour vote. They reflected the prevailing opinion in London, most other major cities and in university towns – and they also constituted a chunk of the Labour vote in majority-Leave constituencies which the party had retained in the Midlands and the North in 2017. There was the electoral dilemma made flesh, on the move and speaking out.

The political challenge grew with every month as May failed to make progress with producing a Brexit deal that could command a Commons majority and Labour waited for a governmental collapse that did not occur. The capacity to maintain the unity of our 2017 electorate – let alone expand it – came under increasing strain. The mutual incomprehension between the adherents of the new Leave/Remain identities infected Corbynite counsels. In so far as there was a plan, it was to maintain a focus on the core, unifying, programme of economic and social changes. That was certainly Corbyn's personal approach – to craft a class message that would bridge the new divide. Even then there was an imbalance – it often seemed that when speaking to the Remain part of our electoral coalition, Labour used the language of values but instead addressed the 'left-behind' working class with a hard cash offer. Essentially, the thrust was to bribe the North into abandoning its commitment to Brexit. People do notice when they are being disrespected, it turns out.

What should we have done instead? Categorically rule out a second referendum, renew our pledge to respect the first, advance a Labour plan for its implementation which met at least some of the concerns of the country's large Remain minority, and champion a socialist vision of a post-Brexit Britain – using the absence of EU-mandated restraints to build a better society in contrast to the Tory offer of more deregulation and heightened xenophobia. The supervening prerequisite for getting the Corbyn message across was to get Brexit done first.

The Vice Closes

The Brexit vice – the gap between the Remain views of most Labour members and politicians, now reinforced by a powerful campaign across the country, and the Leave preferences of most working-class voters and indeed most voters of all types in the majority of Labour-held constituencies – began to close at the 2018 party conference. Debate on the whole issue had been averted by slightly disreputable procedural manoeuvres in 2017 but, basking as we were in the glow of the general election surge, few seemed to mind. This was not remotely repeatable in 2018. Carefully crafted formulae covering the circumstances under which the party might support a second referendum were canvassed. A clear problem was that in any such referendum the party would surely end up campaigning for Remain, if that option was included on the ballot. So however much it might be argued that a further vote was needed to 'break the deadlock' or 'ratify the deal', essentially it was a device to give Remain a second bite of the cherry, a chance to reverse the 2016 defeat which the panjandrums of Europhilia still found both incomprehensible and unacceptable.

Keir Starmer, already seeing the possibility of leveraging this issue into a leadership bid when a vacancy was declared, seized his moment, departing from the agreed script of his conference speech to assert that 'nobody is ruling out Remain' as an option – which was in fact what the party had been doing ever since 2016. He got a standing ovation from delegates, a circumstance which needs to be recalled by anyone arguing that Corbyn could have sanctioned him for his breach of discipline.[18] Corbyn himself, however, pointed in a different direction in his own conference address the next day, concluding: 'Let me also reach out to the Prime Minister, who is currently doing the negotiating. Brexit is about the future of our country and our vital interests. It is not about leadership squabbles or parliamentary posturing. If you deliver a deal that includes a customs union and no hard border in Ireland, if you protect jobs, people's rights at work and environmental and consumer standards – then we will support that sensible deal. A deal that would be backed by most of the business world and trade unions too. But if you can't negotiate that deal then you need to make way for a party that can.' This was not very different to what I had proposed a year earlier.

So Labour left its 2018 conference with three policy options: a further referendum, including the possibility of reversing the 2016 decision; negotiating its own Brexit deal; or supporting a May deal if the terms were acceptable. At the first strategy meeting after conference I suggested we clarify what terms of a deal we would find acceptable – in effect, asking what Jeremy had meant by his peroration on the subject.[19] No clarification came.

8

2019: The Road to Defeat

By spring 2019 the Corbyn leadership was in agony. Just two years after Corbynism had shocked every pundit in the country, rattled the powers-that-be and established what appeared to be a secure ascendancy within the Labour Party, it was unravelling. All the structural weaknesses in the project opened wide, all the streams of opposition to its aspirations came to a confluence in 2019. Its fate was all but sealed before the electoral coup de grâce at the end of the year. By then, Corbynism had already mortgaged its strongest political cards and divided both its electoral coalition and its core supportive networks, including the team at the very heart of the project.

Was this unavoidable, or was it contingent on mistakes made by the leadership, mistakes which different, smarter, people might not have made? We have already argued that the critical acts which boxed Corbynism in on Brexit above all had been acts of omission, acts not undertaken when the initiative was there to be seized in 2017. On Brexit, there were no longer good options available by 2019. It must also be remembered that the opposition of the Establishment and its epigones within the Labour Party was unremitting, vituperative and multifaceted – forget that, and one omits three-quarters at least of the picture. Corbyn's team enjoyed no possibility of taking any decision or having any discussion under any circumstances other than those of unremitting enemy fire. That is politics, of course, but the internal resistance to the leadership was entirely exceptional. There were also difficulties not of our making – paradoxically, one of these was the great weakness of the May government, which institutionalised paralysis on Brexit. This created a space for initiative which the Labour Party was incapable of taking – unlike, as it turned out, Boris Johnson.

The Regional Divide

A special Brexit strategy committee was established to navigate Labour through the shoals – as well as the regular strategy team, it added Starmer, shadow foreign secretary Emily Thornberry, shadow trade secretary Barry Gardiner and chief whip Nick Brown. The meetings were presided over, but not actually led, by Jeremy. Starmer was allowed to introduce the discussions, which focussed mainly on the upcoming parliamentary business – the series of debates on May's deal, the 'indicative votes', amendments and so on. Nevertheless, the meetings were sometimes the occasion for confrontation between Jon Trickett and Ian Lavery, supported by myself, and the north London Remain bloc of Starmer, Thornberry and Diane Abbott. That four of the leading politicians in the meeting (including Corbyn) represented adjacent constituencies in the metropolis (it would take about an hour to traverse all four on foot), and that these areas were centres of militant grassroots opposition to Brexit, certainly played a distorting part in proceedings. Lavery spoke emotionally of going to lay flowers on his mother's grave in his Northumberland constituency on Mothers' Day 2019 and being encountered by two retired miners who called him a traitor because of Labour's position on Brexit. Thornberry countered with tales of a Liberal Democrat Remain demonstration outside her constituency surgery in Islington South. It was this that convinced her she was now defending a marginal, which she wasn't (Lavery was, as it turned out).

A note I prepared in January 2019 summarised the case against a second referendum:

> Democracy: We pledged from the outset to respect the referendum result, voted for the triggering of Article 50 and put a commitment to negotiate a 'Brexit' in our 2017 manifesto. Embracing a new referendum negates that at a stroke and in effect commits us to fighting for a reversal of the 2016 vote . . . [W]e have consistently emphasised our commitment to bring people together around social and economic issues. A referendum on Brexit can only be divisive – it could condemn the country to months of campaigning around 'identity' issues in which a positive message would struggle to be heard. Moreover, given any outcome either way is likely to be close, it will entrench rather than supersede divisions and surely not bring closure . . . Party Unity: The individual membership may indeed want a second referendum, but there is little sense that this is their top priority. Nor will they want to be following Blair and Campbell, who are setting the terms for any 'remain' campaign . . .
>
> Electoral Impact: . . . we know that most of the seats we need to win voted 'Leave' in 2017 . . . Touring the left-behind areas telling them they were wrong in 2016 is unlikely to be helpful . . . Party

Message: Assuming that the Party campaigned for the 'remain' option, we would be essentially championing the status quo in a referendum, or be seen as such. The tone would be set by Blair, big business, the establishment and liberal elitism generally, and by others with no interest in seeing our project succeed (rather the contrary).

The paper acknowledged that there might be circumstances in which a second referendum would be unavoidable – essentially in the event of a Tory drive for a 'no deal' Brexit – but ended on what now reads a bit like an imploring note: 'It should be remembered that around three-quarters of the Party membership have joined for no purpose other than to support the present Leader, which gives him immense potential authority and capacity to win support for a decision – once it is made.' But 'once it is made' came to cover an ocean of political time.

Why did the arguments outlined above make little difference? The aroused views of the party membership, and of public opinion in constituencies like Islington North (always a factor for Jeremy) weighed heavy on the other side of the scales – opinion which, it must be acknowledged, appealed to progressive, or at least liberal, values on many points. Some of the leading politicians were strongly ideologically committed to the European Union, or could see advantages in appearing so. Others still convinced themselves that the real electoral threat to Corbynism came from the Liberal Democrats (and the Greens), and that expediting Brexit would lead to a haemorrhage of support in that direction. Finally, the need to minimise difficulties in the PLP was given perhaps excessive attention. That seemed to be the motivation not only of Chief Whip Brown but also of John McDonnell, who for a time said little at the Brexit strategy meetings but was clearly calculating the internal politics of the situation. His incremental move to the second referendum camp, liaising closely with Starmer and Alastair Campbell as he did so, proved decisive in shaping the party's eventual position. This was a sad irony, as he had been one of the few in the leadership who, after the 2016 vote, had been prepared to talk of the possibilities that a radical Labour government could exploit once outside the EU. However, his perception of the need to maintain party unity trumped those insights, and he influenced most of the younger Corbyn-supporting members of the shadow cabinet to abandon their initial scepticism about a second referendum. Ultimately he shifted Jeremy himself, somewhat I felt against the latter's better judgement. Since McDonnell and Abbott, his lifelong closest allies, were, for different reasons, on the same side on Brexit by this stage, the pressure on the Leader was intense. 'I can't go on like this, being contradicted,' he told one of the last Brexit strategy meetings.

The result was prolonged stasis. It was pretty evident that Corbynism's future depended on the Brexit issue being resolved before we next had to face the voters – it would be impossible to shunt the issue towards the margins of another election. That might allow voters to park their new-minted identities as Leavers or Remainers and focus once more on Labour's transformative social agenda and the problems it sought to address. The idea that a second referendum, returning perhaps a narrow majority for Remain, would have been accepted as legitimate by the losing side was a fantasy. So Parliament had to pass a deal. Labour stubbornly – and counterproductively – worked to ensure that it didn't. A different approach might not have secured a different outcome, in so far as May's agreement with the EU was so unpopular with her own supporters that no plausible amount of Labour assistance could have got it over the line, at least at first and second times of asking. But there was no serious effort put into promoting Labour's own Brexit plan and trying to negotiate some compromise around the issue. When May finally offered talks on a joint approach, nearly two years too late, it did not seem to be taken fully seriously on our side. I was not involved in those talks, but those who were from Labour's side were convinced that an agreement could have been reached, and that it could have secured parliamentary assent, had Labour been committed to reaching one.

Instead, the front bench was persuaded to rally behind the Kyle-Wilson amendment, named after its authors, Peter Kyle and Phil Wilson, two of the most hard-line anti-Corbyn critics in the PLP. This mandated that May's deal should be put to a confirmatory referendum. There was never more than the smallest chance of it passing, given near-unanimous Tory opposition to a further plebiscite and resistance from a significant minority of the PLP, including some on the right who were, nevertheless, attuned to their constituents' opinions. Much of this manoeuvring was ostensibly to 'take no-deal off the table'. In fact, the only way to have squelched 'no deal' was to have passed a deal. Britain eventually left the EU on much harsher terms that those spurned by Labour's Remainers early in 2019.

Change UK

The spectre of a split in the parliamentary party had hung over Corbynism from the outset. All the main players in the Corbyn leadership could remember the Social Democratic Party breakaway of 1982 and how it had assisted Thatcher to re-election, pulling the rug out from under Benn's movement in the process.

The tragedy of the SDP found its echo nearly forty years later in the farce of what became Change UK. That it was a fiasco was not pre-ordained. Everyone around the leadership assumed that a PLP split would be the third roll of the dice by the Establishment to prevent Corbyn getting anywhere near Downing Street, after the failure of the 2016 coup and the electorate's disobliging conduct in the 2017 general election. The potential for a breakaway lay in the large Blairite minority of the PLP – perhaps fifty or sixty strong – who loathed the party's leadership and policies. Some of these wore their Labour loyalty very lightly indeed. A breakaway on that scale would have had a bracing cleansing effect on the party, but it would also surely have put election success out of reach. It was a debilitating irony that our chances of victory depended on making at least some effort to keep our internal enemies on board, a consequence of our parliamentary inheritance.

Of course, what happened in February 2019 fell well short of those apocalyptic predictions. Rather than 1982's 'Gang of Four', politicians with a high profile and substantial records in government, the original seven Labour MPs (shortly joined by three Tories and a couple more Labour defectors) who paraded themselves as, initially, the Independent Group before embarking on a bewildering odyssey of name changes of which Change UK is the best remembered, were a collection of mediocrities with nothing much to them beyond anti-Corbyn bile. The best known was Chukka Umunna, whose reputation in the media ran considerably ahead of both his actual achievements in politics and his base of support in the party. He sounded too much like the smooth City lawyer he had been and was to become again.

The only star available to the splitters was Luciana Berger, who attended the launch heavily pregnant with her second child to announce her departure from Labour, mainly over its (non-) handling of anti-Semitism. Berger had for a time evinced more sympathy for Corbyn than many others on the Labour right – they had a shared commitment to taking mental health seriously as a political issue. As a Jewish woman MP she attracted a vast amount of online abuse and threats, some of it serious enough to send the perpetrators to prison. That the party did not reach out to support her more is a rebuke to all of us, even if she was not altogether ignored as some have claimed. Her presence at the launch of the breakaway was mortifying and gave a moral dignity to an enterprise otherwise singularly deficient in that regard. Remarks concerning people with a 'funny tinge' made in a post-launch interview by Angela Smith MP, otherwise a campaigner for the private water industry, underlined that Change UK was not being forged out of the best and the brightest.

The electorate showed scant interest in the new party, and it began to disintegrate after failing to win any seats in the May 2019 European elections. Its problems included the screamingly obvious one of fighting against the Liberal Democrats on a more-or-less indistinguishable platform of vanilla centrism. The SDP had confronted the same problem in its day, and resolved it first by an alliance and then by full merger with the Liberals. That appeared to be beyond the wit of Umunna and gang, although more than half their parliamentary muster did individually head off towards the Liberal Democrats in the end.

Nevertheless, it can be argued that this footnote in British political history had an impact as intended. First, it sent LOTO into a tailspin. The leadership was desperately anxious not to do anything which might maximise the number of defectors to the new party, as for example by doing something decisive in relation to Brexit.

There was a further source of anxiety in the response of Tom Watson to the split – he set up his own group in the PLP called Future Britain, entirely ephemeral as it proved but appearing menacing at the time, which attracted the support of around 150 Labour MPs and peers. Was this the start of a new creeping coup designed to squeeze the life out of the leadership, under the direction of the newly minted Remainiac Watson? None of these developments assisted the quality of LOTO's strategic thinking – rather it turbo-charged the tendencies towards appeasement of our opponents at the expense of Corbynism's integrity, not to mention our fragile electoral coalition.

Moreover, Change UK was not really about establishing a new force in politics. It was about stopping Corbyn becoming prime minister. The rest was window dressing. And here it contributed. Labour's polling started heading downwards, underlining the adage about voters disliking divided parties. Gavin Shuker, the Luton MP, who served as a sort of Mikhail Suslov to Change UK during its brief lifespan, gave an upbeat assessment of its impact in 2020: 'People might ask me in 30 years "what did you achieve in your time in politics?" . . . I will be able to say I helped prevent Jeremy Corbyn from leading us through a huge national crisis. And to be honest, I'll take that.'[1]

The Beginning of the End

The writing was now on the wall. With sober understatement Daniel Finn wrote in *New Left Review* that 'the Corbyn project faces a number of obstacles that may prove unsurmountable'.[2] The toxins from Brexit were poisoning the whole enterprise. What had once been seen as an insurgency looked more and more like an insiders' conspiracy to block the implementation of the 2016 referendum decision. Mass campaigning was supplanted by parliamentary obfuscation and obstruction. Straight talking became speaking out of both sides of our mouths or even, for long periods, neither. The narrative of Corbyn as an incorrigible ditherer was set, although this issue would have been a challenge for any Labour leader. The PLP was sulky at best and, at worst, feared to be lining up behind the Deputy Leader in preparation for some sort of Brexit-excused putsch (Watson, as it turned out, was no more a politician for decisive proactive moves than Corbyn was). Worse still, the team around Corbyn was increasingly factionalised, in part as a result of different views on Brexit and in part down to exasperation with political drift across the board, as well as unresolved tensions between LOTO and McDonnell's office down the corridor, the details of which are Westminster ephemera.

The enthusiasms of 2017 were fading fast as political life shrunk to a single issue on which easy choices were no longer available, and on which Corbynism could not settle on a message. As Finn put it, 'The unrelenting focus on Brexit drained attention from the domestic reform programme that was the centrepiece of the Corbyn project.'[3] I recall being contacted by representatives of London's grime music scene – people who had given Corbyn unexpected and enthusiastic support in 2017, believing that at last they had found a politician who was different. What had happened, they asked – why was he no longer in touch? In part these links fell victim to an inertia and a lack of imagination which kept Corbyn within conventional political bounds, where he was not at his strongest, and in part to a growing risk aversion which saw unorthodoxy as pregnant with the possibility of mishap. And, indeed, an earlier behind-the-scenes *Vice* documentary had misfired (the scenes are there for a reason), so this caution was not entirely misplaced.

Jon Trickett and I prepared a paper for the leadership in March advocating a range of measures for stopping the drift:

> Over the last couple of weeks we have lost the initiative within the Party. The long-predicted breakaway by a number of right-wing MPs (not the last in all likelihood), the change of position on the EU referendum, the revival of the anti-semitism line of attack on the leadership, the suspension of Chris Williamson have all created a sense of malaise.
>
> It is essential that we now act quickly . . . The central problem we face is that the establishment hate and fear the advent of a left-wing Labour government . . . they retain the balance of advantage within the PLP, in which supporters of the Party's new direction remain a minority. The majority are either unpersuaded or deeply hostile . . .
>
> There needs to be a more proactive approach to the PLP, which is seething with people who not only have doubts about, or are opposed to, our project, but who see no prospect of preferment at present. Returning to our original aspiration of a broader-based shadow cabinet, without doing any injustice to comrades who have stuck with us through thick and thin, would be very helpful in taking the wind out of the [Deputy Leader's] sails.
>
> The Leader should therefore consider a reshuffle with these objectives in mind, as well as securing other political objectives thereby.

A reshuffle – the normal way to refresh a team and retake the initiative – was something Corbyn always refused to entertain, except when it was forced upon him, as it was on an epic scale by resignations during the 2016 coup. It meant taking tough personnel decisions, including disappointing some loyalists. Reaching out to people to the right of the leadership – essentially almost the whole PLP – would have been controversial. Ed Miliband was the name most frequently mentioned; whether he would have been interested I do not know. But nothing was done, so an obvious way to address PLP alienation was missed, and a number of underperformers remained around the shadow cabinet table, including those not very committed to Corbyn's perspective.

The anti-Semitism crisis rumbled on as well. Sam Matthews, the official responsible for handling complaints, had resigned from the party's employment the previous summer, secretly taking a large cache of emails with him. He now began leaking them to the media through the agency of Watson's office.[4] The most salient related to a period in March/April 2018 when he of his own unprompted volition (as far as I know) had begun emailing myself and others in LOTO soliciting our views on particular disciplinary cases, with details appended. My view at the time was that if LOTO failed to respond we would be damned for obstructing the expeditious handling of anti-Semitism cases. So I replied to Matthews in around fifteen such cases, in all but one agreeing with his recommendation. He gave every appearance of appreciating the assistance (which was no more than offering opinions, since I had no authority to direct the handling of these matters) and indeed he emailed his concurrence with the one dissenting view I proposed. He did not leak *that*, funnily enough.

Trickett and I therefore had to address the anti-Semitism issue in our paper:

The failure to get on top of it thus far has damaged the cohesion and morale of the Party from top to bottom. It is also being used to power the breakaway initiatives and trash the leadership's reputation for honesty and decency, something which most likely will have a long-term impact.

We all want to move on to the front foot on this issue as rapidly as possible. Attacks around anti-Semitism will not go away, since there is a lot invested in them politically. The factors that have stopped us doing so hitherto include:

- the undeniable incidence of anti-Semitic views being expressed, very largely on social media, by a small number of Party members;
- a disciplinary system hitherto incapable of processing complaints promptly and fairly;
- repeated clumsy and embarrassing interventions on the subject by supporters of the leadership;
- and – this is the most difficult issue – unresolved disputes as to what constitutes anti-Semitism leading to mixed or muffled messages from the leadership on the issue.

Further steps were advocated, including giving the general secretary the power to auto-exclude clear anti-Semites and broadening the range of Jewish supporters we could work with. 'The Leader needs to engage personally in tackling this issue, and should consider making a speech addressing Anti-Semitism on the left – not in an apologetic sense – as proposed by Tony Klug and others. The Party also needs to rebut strongly the argument that it is institutionally racist and/or anti-Semitic. That is a smear. Events should be organised highlighting the party's diversity and its commitment to equality, drawing on history and contemporary campaigns and practice . . .', we wrote.

Little of this was done. In particular, Jeremy continued to see the issue as an unjustified attack on himself. Any response along the lines suggested risked legitimising the narrative of Labour's and his own alleged anti-Semitism, in this view.

On Brexit, Trickett and I made a last plea for a positive Labour approach:

> Over the last week, foregrounding our intention to support a People's Vote at the next stage has caused fresh anxieties and splits, compounded by a rampant lack of message discipline on the part of some of those most closely involved. We have sold our positive agenda short – consistently.
>
> - AIM: Avoid being viewed as solely the remain party, take control of Brexit media narrative up to the meaningful vote with a focus on our alternative plan, gain support in shadow cabinet
> - PLAN: JC makes speech or statement ASAP announcing meetings with cross party MPs to try and find Brexit solution . . .
>
> Beyond this immediate initiative, we believe that a strong grip needs to be taken at Brexit sub-committee meetings. The agenda should be set by the Leader with the expression of his own views, and not by the shadow Brexit secretary. It is obviously important that his voice is heard (alongside others), but he should not be allowed to assume leadership on the question.

Again, this advice made no discernible difference. Rather than LOTO taking a grip on the Starmer-dominated Brexit meetings, they simply ended up ceasing to take place. The space for sensible discussion was shrinking as LOTO retreated, squabbling with itself, into the proverbial bunker.

The European Parliament Elections and Their Aftermath

Events therefore came to determine strategy rather than the other way around. May's failure to secure parliamentary passage for her Brexit deal meant that the public had to endure being summoned to vote in elections for the European Parliament, the assembly of a body Britain was supposed to have left by then. This was good news neither for the Tories nor Labour, the parties responsible for this deadlock. The vote was pointless except for purposes of protest. So the results were an even less reliable guide to general election intentions than usual. Nevertheless, the reaction to the disastrous results for the two main Westminster parties – 9 per cent of the poll for the Tories, 14 per cent for Labour – shaped what happened next.

The Tories looked at the 31 per cent secured by the Brexit Party and drew the obvious conclusion. They needed to get those votes back, which meant ditching the hapless May, two years after all the air went out of her premiership, replacing her with Boris Johnson and then negotiating a harder Brexit which could whip the rug out from under Farage's pop-up party and, by allying most Leave voters with those Remainers who would still vote Tory because of an overriding fear of socialism, secure a majority.

Labour, for its part, panicked at the nearly 20 per cent of the vote won by the Liberal Democrats, and the nearly 12 per cent who put the cross next to the Greens (who beat the Tories into fifth place), both fighting on intransigent Remain platforms. This was the final push that moved Labour into supporting a second referendum under all circumstances. The theory was that, just as the Tories were aiming to consolidate the Leave vote under their banner, so Labour should seek to mount a symmetrical operation for the Remain side of the divided country, lest the Liberal Democrats supplant us. This position – wrong, but not irrational – was amplified by fears of impending moves to unseat Corbyn as his coalition of inner-party support disintegrated. We have seen that Paul Mason felt that firing Ian Lavery as party chair (and Milne and Murphy from LOTO) would do the trick, as he converted – somewhat improbably, given his scepticism regarding free movement and his opposition to the EU's tormenting of the Greek people – into an ardent Remainer-at-all-costs.[5] The metropolitan liberal wing of Corbynism (not to be confused with its substantial working-class support in London and other cities) began to fragment and seek an alternative standard-bearer, a quest that ultimately alighted on Keir Starmer (from its own perspective with disappointing results, it can now be said).[6]

The thinking underpinning this flight to Remain was multiply flawed, however. First, it assumed that Labour could aggregate Brexit's opponents under its own banner as easily as the Tories could win back Leave voters from the Brexit Party. Farage's party was an insubstantial single-issue operation, despite its Euro-election success, without significant roots and lacking a stable core vote. That did not apply to the Liberal Democrats or the SNP, or even the Greens. These parties had their own loyal electorate, experience in local and national government and entrenched traditions. Together, they were always going to be good for 12 per cent of the national vote at least in a general election, whereas the Brexit Party could be squeezed to near zero. Nor could we assume Tory Remainers would come our way in significant numbers. To compensate, Labour needed Leave votes if we were to compete.

Second, there was the matter of seats in a first-past-the-post election. Here losses in voter numbers to the Liberal Democrats or

Greens were evidently not equivalent to defections to the Tories. Put bluntly, losing a million Remain votes might mean little in terms of seat losses. Most of those missing votes would have the effect of either shrinking monumental Labour majorities in big cities or of putting Labour even further out of contention in southern seats where it never had any realistic chance of winning. Losses to the Tories, on the other hand, would spell doom for a large number of sitting Labour MPs in Northern and Midland seats, as the loss of six constituencies in 2017 had shown. Not to mention that we were still fighting to form a government, which would have meant adding seats, not merely avoiding losing them. Those seats were preponderantly Leave in 2016.

I prepared an analysis of what the Euro-election results, with all the usual caveats, could mean in a general election, and sent it to the leadership. I looked at thirty-six Labour-held seats, plus four of the 2017 losses, in what is now known as the 'red wall' and aggregated all the votes cast in May for parties committed to Remain (Labour, Lib Dem and Green) and for those advocating Leave (Brexit Party, Tories, UKIP). The results were stark – the Remain share of the May electorate in these constituencies ranged from just 33 per cent in Hartlepool up to a still inferior 46 per cent in Sunderland. I wrote:

> The message from these figures is not terribly ambiguous. If Labour fights a General Election as a 'Remain' Party, and Brexit is the main issue in that election, we cannot expect to hold many of these seats. *The gap is simply too large* . . . We may be as many as fifty seats down IF we nail our colours to 'Remain'. There are simply not enough potential compensating gains among seats we do not already hold in London and other remain-leaning areas.

Sadly, I was right. Of the seats included in the survey, twenty-three were lost in December 2019, and one more has gone since.

Labour's sharp strategy director, Carl Shoben, concurred. His paper analysing the European elections and the local government results, presented to the shadow cabinet in June, concluded:

> It remains the case that there are more target and defensive seats in the Midlands and North of England which voted leave. The recent elections don't suggest any change to this basic arithmetic, given the geographical distribution of Leave and Remain voters. There is an evident risk that shifting to a more explicitly pro-Remain position would leave us vulnerable in seats we need to hold or win without enough potential seat gains in winnable Remain majority areas.[7]

The Drift towards Remain

We were now running into a mighty headwind of aroused liberalism – the huge demonstrations for a second referendum on the streets of London, the views of most Labour members, the opinions of the liberal/left media and the strongly Remain balance in the constituencies represented by the key figures in the Corbyn leadership. Against this was pitched only the mythic might of the 'four Ms' – Milne, Murphy, McCluskey and Murray – who believed that for reasons of both principle and electoral expediency Labour should stick with its 2017 pledge of respecting and implementing the referendum result to leave the European Union. Of the four Ms the most significant was Len McCluskey, because he spoke for Unite, Labour's largest affiliate and funder, and a union which had campaigned for Remain in 2016 but was nevertheless well aware of the views of its working-class membership, who believed firmly that Brexit had to happen. McCluskey went to see John McDonnell, sure that the latter must have access to some special electoral insight which would show that the second referendum course he was urging would lead to victory, in spite of the arguments I and others had adduced from the evidence. He returned disappointed – McDonnell's position was no more than that Labour's membership wanted Remain, and that without a committed army, Corbynism would be defeated. As conference 2019 showed, when the issue was framed as loyalty to Corbyn that sentiment trumped the importance of Remain for most of Labour's membership anyway. What they needed was a lead which, through the long summer, was what they did not get.

Instead, the months were punctuated by a rococo series of demarches which spoke only to a project disintegrating: the vitriolic resignation of Policy Director Andrew Fisher delivered to a wide audience by WhatsApp and therefore speedily leaked (incomprehensibly he was invited to work out his three-month notice rather than being asked to leave directly, having savaged his colleagues); the on-off attempt to deal with Tom Watson by suddenly abolishing the post of deputy leader; and most bizarre of all, the decision to fire the ever-loyal Chief of Staff Karie Murphy on the eve of the general election campaign at the instigation of John McDonnell and the former head of the civil service, Lord Bob Kerslake, then advising the Labour leadership. To add madness to misjudgement, the ill-used and badly bruised Murphy was then charged with running the election campaign under McDonnell's direction – an arrangement which both tried to make work as well as possible but which you would not find recommended in any HR handbook.[8]

There was an attempt to reorient Corbynism's campaigning focus in the new Johnsonian situation. A strategy paper prepared by myself, Seumas Milne and Steve Howell, optimistically headed 'Destination Labour Government', acknowledged that the 'Boris Johnson government has changed the game – in terms of positioning, policy, dividing lines, electoral calculations and election timing'. It urged that we 'prevent the election becoming another proxy referendum'. That hope was forlorn, since our practical policy for the entire preceding period had worked to foreclose that possibility. Whereas in 2017 we had dodged the Brexit bullet, we spent 2019 blindfolding ourselves and yelling 'shoot' at the electoral firing squad. And despite the paper's accurate acknowledgement that 'we cannot win as a full-on "remain" party . . . there are not enough remain voters in many of the marginal seats in England and Wales we have to take to win a majority', this insight had a diminishing grip on policy. The paper also accepted that 'we have to improve the standing of the Party Leader' and 'meet the "Jeremy or Boris" choice head on. We offer an honest, passionate, trustworthy and committed leader, who can bring communities together and is clearly determined to transform Britain in the interests of the many, not the few, and create a fairer country that works for all', as against 'a politician of proven incompetence . . . who cannot be trusted to deliver on his promises'.[9] That at least still reads well, although Jeremy's personal ratings remained abysmal.

On the broader political canvass, Corbynism's motor was now entirely caught in the weeds of parliamentarism. A positive vision for transforming society in an egalitarian direction was mortgaged to arcana around the proroguing of the Commons, with the party apparently cheering on the judicial dictation of political life. And, when the House was duly reconvened on the instruction of the Supreme Court, the assembled MPs offered no way out of the national impasse over Brexit, but immediately fell to abusing each other roundly, and then the next day debating whether the previous evening they had gone too far. If MPs had wanted to make Boris Johnson's case for him – that this was an incapacitated Parliament that had exceeded its useful lifespan – they could hardly have done better. Johnson had himself wrung a more amenable, if fraudulent and unstable, Brexit agreement out of Brussels before purging the Conservative benches of all MPs who stood in the way of its implementation, without regard to ancestry or past service. Labour, by contrast, stood for a range of negatives – no to May's deal, no to a joint deal, no to no deal, no to Johnson's deal; 'perhaps' only to a further referendum, without any clarity as to how that would bring the torment to an end.

When Johnson finally secured Commons approval for his withdrawal agreement, with the backing of nineteen Labour MPs, the front bench still stuck with its programme of obstruction, opposing the procedural motion that would have allowed it expedited parliamentary progress. Labour would have to face the public without Brexit having been delivered. With the Liberal Democrats and the SNP having committed to supporting an early general election, the die was cast.

The Manifesto Fudge

Labour spent most of 2019 trying to bridge its own divisions on Brexit and reconcile the conflicting imperatives within a Corbyn movement sliding into the grip of the 'culture wars' recalibrating politics across the world. It was not, unfortunately, time well spent. The party eventually committed to offering a second referendum on EU membership, which would give voters a choice between an as-yet unseen deal to be drawn up by a Labour government, and Remain.

Since any Labour deal would hew closely to the EU's single market, customs union and raft of labour, consumer and environmental standards, this was already basically a choice between variations on the status quo, which would leave a very large minority at least of the electorate disenfranchised before the campaign had even started, thereby meeting the Remainer imperative of excluding the possibility of a clear Brexit. That was not the worst of it, however. The Labour deal had still to be negotiated – that would presumably be the work of the Brexit secretary, the chancellor, the foreign secretary and the home secretary. If government office followed shadow appointments, those would be Keir Starmer, John McDonnell, Emily Thornberry and Diane Abbott, respectively. Yet each and every one of these leaders indicated publicly that in Labour's referendum they would advocate for Remain and against the deal they would just have struck with the EU. Corbyn himself eventually, and only under the pressure of the campaign, indicated that he would be neutral. Who in the government would actually champion the agreement it had itself negotiated in the putative second referendum? That was another question never really answered.

So up against Boris Johnson's 'get Brexit done' mantra, Labour offered a further delay while a different deal was negotiated, which would then be immediately repudiated by the people who had negotiated it in favour of a fresh campaign to sell the status quo to a public for whom all this had already gone on for quite long enough. To compound the absurdity, a special Labour Party conference would be held to determine its collective position – undoubtedly it, too, would reject the handiwork of Labour ministers and commit for Remain. It is doubtful if any major party has offered the British people a more preposterous policy on a great issue of public concern at a general election.

On the other major democratic question – Scotland's position in the United Kingdom – Labour likewise ended up on the wrong side of the issue. While the manifesto welcomed Welsh Labour's proposals for a renewed devolution settlement, the still more important section on Scotland was unremittingly negative. Scottish independence was opposed as 'economically devastating', and so also was a referendum on the issue, pledging that a Corbyn government, in its 'early years' whatever that meant, would reject any request from a Scottish government – regardless of mandate – to hold one. This was essentially the same as Johnson's policy, and quite different from the position proposed in the 'Destination Labour Government' strategy paper, which argued that 'if it is the will of the Scottish people, expressed in voting for parties in Scottish Parliament elections which demand such a vote, we should clearly not obstruct'. It was based on the hope that the economic benefits that would flow from a radical government in London would dissipate independence demands in Scotland. It offered no concession to the democratic view that, if an elected Scottish Parliament requested a further referendum, there was scant basis for rejecting one. Nor was there any proposal to recast the devolution settlement relating to Scotland. The blame for this obtuse position rested more with Scottish Labour, retreating into the Unionist trenches as it was, than with the Corbyn leadership, which could scarcely impose a more enlightened position on the Scottish party, but it was a recipe for losing even the limited parliamentary gains made in 2017, which is what happened.

The Election Campaign

With the Brexit policy albatross around our necks, the 2019 campaign was never likely to reproduce the focus on social change – and hence the optimism – of its 2017 precursor. Hope cannot be sucked out of the thin air of an election campaign if it is not in the atmosphere already. And hopeless better defined the national political mood by the end of 2019.

My return to work after a prolonged illness absence was also the first day of the campaign. I underachieved. On day one I drafted a message from Jeremy to the Jewish community, reaching out to rebuild bridges. It was put on hold on the grounds that we shouldn't proactively raise the issue (as if it wasn't going to come up in the course of the campaign) and eventually issued, heavily amended, in the name of campaign coordinator Andrew Gwynne MP several weeks later. And on the penultimate day I wrote a strong attack on Boris Johnson's character and competence for Corbyn to deliver which again went unheard, victim I assume of his reluctance ever to make personal attacks on others. In between, a plan to name Labour's Brexit negotiating team and populate it with people who might have credibility with Leave voters – Len McCluskey was willing to serve – was likewise vetoed. The attacks on Labour and on Corbyn through the campaign reprised those of 2017, but the prolonged vacillations over Brexit made the rebuttals of the earlier campaign – straight-talking, honest politician – less likely to stick. Voters were no longer seeing Corbyn for the first time, and while I believe the portrayal of him as a terrorist-loving anti-Semite spoke only to the already-convinced, the charge of dithering and weakness undoubtedly had new legs thanks to Brexit above all. This was to some extent unfair, since there was no easy way solve the problem by 2019, but the impression seemed ineradicable.

Despite the best efforts of John McDonnell, Seumas Milne and Karie Murphy, Labour's campaign struggled to recapture the enthusiasm of 2017, something not just attributable to the encroaching winter gloom. 'For the Many Not the Few' had been replaced, unwisely in hindsight, by 'Time for Real Change' as the slogan. The latter never caught the imagination.[10] It was, however, aimed at addressing a substantive problem. With Johnson, the Tories were offering change of their own, above and beyond getting Brexit done. They were moving away from a decade of austerity with a range of new spending commitments – NHS, infrastructure, the North generally – addressing the ills they had themselves created. Given the centrality of anti-austerity messaging to Corbyn and Labour's popularity, this created a conundrum. The answer chosen was to double down on Corbynism's transformational message with renewed radicalism to put clear red water between ourselves and the government. In my opinion, the ground for this had been insufficiently prepared, arguably within the party and certainly outside. The 2017 manifesto had tested the limits of a new radicalism with a mix of measures to tackle inequality, extend public ownership and end austerity. Two years on it did not necessarily need much revision. Delivering all of it, while untangling our Brexit policy, would have taken all the energies of the first two or three years of a Corbyn government. While it would certainly have proved necessary to go further, the timing and scope of such extended advance would need to have been dictated by events, including the nature of the opposition from the capitalist class.

Anyway, we had a range of new policies that lacked the necessary strong framing to make them look like a programme for government. And they emerged in a torrent during the campaign, without any necessary sense of priority, nor of their interlocking character. Together, they represented more than any government would have the bandwidth to deliver (not all resources are financial). The problems were compounded by a lack of coordination and an atmosphere of secrecy, a consequence of deteriorating personal relationships at the apex of the Corbyn project. No sooner had one promise been promoted than another emerged from the ether, leaving activists uncertain what they were supposed to be pushing on the doorsteps. Corbyn himself objected on one call to the deluge of policy – all of it worthy in itself – but he was unable to arrest it. What had gone in one end of the policy pipe was going to come out the other, come what may. Belated attempts to boil down our offer to five or six key pledges never really stuck – no sooner had the list been agreed than someone started talking about a commitment that was not on it.

Nor were the strategic arguments about our focus ever really resolved. Half the campaign leadership were mostly worried about losses to the Liberal Democrats, while the rest were focussed on our shaky 'red wall', where the main enemy was clearly the Tories. This confusion bled over into targeting, as in 2017. The list of seats to be resourced centrally had to be revised halfway through in order to devote more money to shaky Labour-held constituencies at the expense of targets that were moving out of reach. Activists, particularly in London, continued to flock in huge numbers to 'winnable' seats that really weren't, like Boris Johnson's Uxbridge, while erstwhile Labour strongholds in the North reported few canvassers turning out.[11] In part this was simply a function of geography – most people can only engage in election activity like canvassing near to where they live – but it highlighted the misalignment between those newly enthused by Corbynism's promise and the people Labour has traditionally relied on for much of its parliamentary majorities.

It was a misalignment that bled into many aspects of the campaign. Ten days out from polling day Corbyn went to Yorkshire, where problems were piling up in the ex-coalfield seats (four were lost in the end), visiting Leeds to launch . . . Labour's bicycling policy – worthy, but hardly the answer to the problems we were facing. On the final weekend a senior figure posted a WhatsApp message spreading alarm about the Liberal Democrat vote in Sunderland being a threat, showing how distant political perceptions were from reality. On polling day the Lib Dem vote inched up from an average of 2.8 per cent across the three Sunderland seats in 2017 to a still very modest 6.1 per cent, and the party finished fourth in each constituency.

The extent of the error is highlighted by an examination of the fifty-four seats lost by Labour in England and Wales. In only ten of them was the increase in the combined Liberal Democrat and Green vote greater than the margin of Tory victory. Even had a ruthless focus on the Lib Dems and Greens squeezed their vote back to the 2017 mark, with all their increment accruing to Labour instead, and without spurring additional defections to the Conservatives, it would have done no more than slightly mitigate the defeat. Facts are stubborn things, and Labour Remainers were particularly averse to these facts.

This misdirection of political energy was at the core of Labour's defeat. Some of it was, I believe, subjective – leading politicians and staff *wanted* Labour's hopes to rest on becoming as much a Remain party as possible, and fitted the facts around their preference, declaring the Liberal Democrats the main enemy in defiance of so much evidence. In fact, the Liberal Democrat campaign was almost as daft as it had been in 2017, majoring on the fact that their Leader, Jo Swinson, would be Britain's next prime minister (she lost her own seat as it transpired) and that a Liberal Democrat government would simply cancel Brexit by fiat, without troubling with a further public consultation.

The change was in the Tory campaign, which maintained a laser-like focus on the one message of 'Get Brexit Done', kept a grip on Johnson to avoid any embarrassments worse than hiding from a reporter in a fridge and pocketing another journalist's mobile phone – he ducked an interview with Andrew Neil, while Corbyn alas did not – and moved towards a public spending offer aimed at Labour constituencies. The slightly surreal nature of the campaign was underlined by the fact that it was the Tory Leader who pledged, however insincerely, to use Britain's departure from the EU to launch a 'buy British' public procurement strategy and to give greater state aid to industry, two fairly traditional social democratic positions which would be compromised by Labour's determination to align with EU single market rules as much as possible. The Tories were fighting on Labour's traditional territory of deploying the power of the nation-state for the amelioration of working-class lives, territory that Labour itself was, if not abandoning, at least perceived to be ambivalent about. That problem encapsulates in a nutshell the worldwide crisis of social democracy in the age of capitalist globalisation. Wolfgang Streeck puts it well, arguing that the Corbyn leadership made

a massive strategic blunder . . . underestimating the significance of national sovereignty for left politics under globalisation . . . the party never understood the depth of the determination of these voters to no

longer allow their national government to enlist 'Brussels' or international summit meetings or European courts or the 'world market' as
an excuse for refusing to protect their interests.[12]

Angie Rayner, one of the few in the shadow cabinet not to commit
to remain-at-all-costs, was pithier. Her constituents 'wanted one
thing done and it's not happened and they hate us all'.[13] Rayson
cites a 'life-long Labour voter' from Redcar arguing that 'Labour
stuck two fingers up at 17.4 million who voted to leave . . . They
were trying to weasel out of giving us Brexit . . . They were no
longer listening to the people.'[14] Polling cited by Deborah
Mattinson, now Keir Starmer's strategy chief, listed the main
reasons why 'red wall' voters shifted to the Tories: Corbyn was
cited by 75 per cent, Brexit by 73 per cent, lack of faith in Labour
promises by 62 per cent and the feeling that Labour now longer
represented people like them by 61 per cent. Those motivations are
evidently entwined. Leave voters had looked to Brexit as an opportunity to 'revitalise manufacturing industry and bring back jobs'.
They were nostalgic for the Labour Party of the past, and believed
that its position on Brexit was 'further evidence of it not being the
party that stood up for them anymore'.[15]

In terms of the popular vote, the scale of Labour's defeat of
December 2019 has been escalated from bad to historically disastrous by the same commentators and politicians who were caught
napping in 2017. In fact, there are four occasions when Labour has
polled a lower share of the vote since the Second World War: in
1983 (under Michael Foot), 1987 (Neil Kinnock), 2010 (Gordon
Brown) and 2015 (Ed Miliband). Moreover, Labour lost in 2019
while polling nearly 700,000 more votes than it did in 2005, Blair's
third victory. Then, Labour's 35 per cent share of the poll secured

355 parliamentary seats, while 2019's 32 per cent won just 202. Such are the vagaries of the electoral system. Labour continued to be overwhelmingly the first choice of the young. None of this can obscure the fact that the Tories secured a very large majority, but it should be borne in mind by those who would use the outcome to write off 'Corbynism' as an aberration to be cast aside forever.

However, the verdict on Corbyn was unforgiving – the statements issued by Labour's right wing had mostly been prepared for release on 8 June 2017 and had been marinating, unused, in their own malice ever since. The result represented politics returning to something more like normal as the political establishment understood it. Within the Corbyn movement, every faction and pundit read into the result the vindication of their own pre-election advice. Remainers continued to believe, with the conviction of a cargo cult, that an even stronger pro-EU position would have secured a better outcome. The evidence simply isn't there. All polls showed that the 2019 election was a verdict on the handling of Brexit since the previous one, and that Labour's decisive losses were amongst its critical minority of Leavers in long-standing industrial communities.[16] Above all, it seems that around 1.4 million Labour voters of 2017 simply did not bother to vote at all in 2019, their democratic enthusiasm suppressed.

Even as Corbynism reached the end of its road, Corbyn himself developed a much-ridiculed argument that Labour had nevertheless 'won the argument' over policy. This had more than a germ of truth, as the Coronavirus crisis showed, but that is a truth his successor is deaf to.

9

The Starmer Counter-revolution

There will be no requirement for a book on 'Starmerism'. There is only, as Jeremy Corbyn might say, opposition to socialism. Starmerism is the empty suit which Labour's right wing has nailed as its standard for the struggle to extirpate all traces of his predecessor and his influence within the party. Even Engels's capacious list of the varieties of English socialism had no category for that.

Starmer's election as Leader was an act of self-harm by the party membership. Even allowing for Starmer's deception in running on a 'Corbynism-with-competence' platform – embodied in ten policy points about which nothing has been heard since his victory – it should have been clear that a North London 'Remainiac' lawyer, one of the principal authors of the disastrous 2019 political strategy, was not the answer to the problems Labour faced. Doubling down on London-led liberalism would have been a bad idea even had it not been allied with aggression towards the left. His was a win for nothing more than conventional thinking, which is that the candidate liked by the media is the one who should be supported, and that looking 'prime ministerial' means choosing the man in a suit in preference to the four women candidates, who between them covered Labour's political spectrum.

Despite the deepest social crisis for generations, the Starmer front bench has had nothing interesting to say about anything. The pandemic has served as an excuse for inaction and inaudibility rather than a rationale for radicalism. Bromides drawn from the Blair-Cameron playbook, expatiated on at extraordinary length by Starmer in a Fabian essay endeavouring to explain himself, eighteen months into his tenure, constitute policy. Not the first vacuous politician, he broke new ground in taking such verbose care to expose the fact.[1] A powerful critique of a selfish, bungling, corrupt government is still awaited. Taking a 'national' approach to a class question, Starmer has largely given Johnson and the Tories a free pass in their catastrophic mishandling of coronavirus. As David Rosenberg points out, 'Sir Oswald Mosley once dreamed of "a government unencumbered by a daily opposition." Starmer has made Mosley's dream come true for the travesty of a human being that is the current Prime Minister.'[2]

A few who at one time loitered in the Corbyn camp – largely the same people who had defected from the project in the interests of all-out Remain in 2019 – convinced themselves that Starmer was a genuine radical, which only shows that there is no deception like self-deception.[3] Some of the same folk also hoped that Starmer would lead some manner of pro-EU movement, which only compounded their subsequent disappointment as Starmer dropped as a lingering embarrassment the issue which had propelled him to the top. Neither Corbynism nor competence have been delivered, or even attempted. One consequence is that Starmer himself has widely and not unfairly acquired a reputation for slipperiness, a perception reinforced by further acts of dissimulation in office.

Labour polls indifferently, getting a share of the vote somewhere between Corbyn 2017 and Corbyn 2019.[4] In real votes, it has performed significantly worse than even Corbyn's Labour 2019 in by-elections and in local elections, losing parliamentary seats which Labour under Corbyn held. Starmer's personal ratings are also discouraging. The Labour coalition has continued its precipitate disintegration, with the new leadership alienating elements which had been hitherto reliable. Starmer has scored no discernible successes in winning back 'red wall' support in the North and the Midlands. Inane flag-waving has not effaced Starmer's long struggle to reverse the Brexit referendum result in voters' memories. On the other hand, the radical young in the cities and elsewhere drawn to Corbyn's Labour have been largely repulsed, the liberal end of the party's support is taking a new look at the Greens, and the party has alienated its ever-loyal Muslim voters through a combination of indulgence of Islamophobia and passivity over Palestine. The tepid admixture of New Labour and Blue Labour on offer has excited nobody. The mass membership Starmer inherited from Corbyn is in free fall. By summer 2021 the party was laying off a quarter of its staff, its healthy financial position having been transformed into near bankruptcy, while hiring dozens of special investigators to clear a backlog of complaints which did not exist at the time of his ascension. This too has generated mayhem, with midnight suspensions and investigations being issued, only to be withdrawn under pressure after daybreak.

By any ordinary political calculation, therefore, the Starmer leadership has performed poorly, as most of the left (who supported Becky Long-Bailey in the leadership election) anticipated it would. Conventional wisdom would have it that the clock was running down on his tenancy in the Leader's Office. A Tory Leader – Ian Duncan-Smith, say – would be on his last legs by now.

But not so fast.

A State's Man

By background, Starmer is less a parliamentary politician than a reliable servant of the state. He became an MP in only 2015, previously serving as director of public prosecutions (DPP).[5] In that role he did nothing to discomfort the powers-that-be. He protected undercover police officers in the spycops scandal by avoiding a wide investigation, declined to charge the police who shot Jean Charles de Menezes dead on the London Underground in 2005 or the officer who killed Ian Tomlinson with an unprovoked baton blow in 2009, and made it easier to prosecute those allegedly claiming benefits illegally 'allowing the government to waste endless resources arresting and incarcerating people who had claimed minimal amounts of money', in the words of Oliver Eagleton, who has studied his record closely.[6]

He joined the Corbyn front-bench team as shadow immigration minister, only to resign as part of the abortive MPs coup against the Leader in 2016. In what proved to be a signal miscalculation by LOTO, but understandable perhaps at the time, he was encouraged to rejoin as shadow Brexit secretary, a perch from which he would play a starring part in the campaign to drive Labour into supporting a second referendum. He was disciplined and cautious in pursuit of this, his measured outburst at the 2018 conference aside. There was none of the performative Remainia of Emily Thornberry, for example. Starmer was professional and calm in Brexit strategy meetings – on top of his brief – and careful to give no basis for charges of disloyalty. His role was to nudge policy in a pro-Remain direction and he was, alas, given the scope to do so. Even if Corbyn was a sacking type of Leader, which he emphatically wasn't, Starmer was undismissable after the 2018 conference, where his redefinition of Labour's second referendum policy had gone down a storm. He had the quality of being sufficiently vague for everyone from Tony Blair through to Momentum national organiser Laura Parker to project onto him whatever they wanted to find.[7]

As leader, Starmer's mission is to restore to the British ruling class one of the essentials for its version of democracy – a 'safe' loyal Labour opposition, which can be entrusted to exercise power, if called upon, with discretion and due regard to the famous national interest. The prerequisite for that is the destruction of Corbynism as a political trend with any purchase within the Labour Party. If that leads to short-term electoral reverses, then that seems to be acceptable collateral damage since the point of his leadership is not to secure the keys of Downing Street for himself. He is Moses restoring the party to the promised land of New Labour, even though he himself may not survive to enjoy the fruits (Moses admittedly did not discard his own ten points quite so readily). Bringing the efficiency he displayed as the state's chief prosecutor to bear on the problem, he has proved focussed, unrelenting and thus far successful in attacking the left. Let us consider first his party management measures, and then such policy positioning as he has permitted himself.

His first step as Leader was to dismiss Jennie Formby as general secretary of the party, notwithstanding that she was still recovering from having spent most of the previous year undergoing treatment for cancer.[8] David Evans, an obscure functionary from the Blair years, was chosen as Formby's successor apparently on the recommendation of Morgan McSweeney, himself Starmer's chief of staff and previously the mastermind of Liz Kendall's 2015 leadership challenge, when the Blairite MP secured all of 4.5 per cent of the members' vote. Starmer pushed through, with dubious constitutionality, a change to the system for electing constituency representatives on the NEC to benefit the right, and he broke with the system of rotation to pass over the vice-chair of the NEC, left-wing trade unionist Ian Murray, for promotion to chair in favour former foreign secretary Margaret Beckett, a veteran and reliable *routier* of Labour imperialism. Confronted with the leak of the Governance and Legal Unit report exposing a corrupted and racist party apparatus, Starmer punted for the long grass, setting up an inquiry which two years later has yet to report. The underlying problems exposed therefore have gone unaddressed.

Picking his shadow cabinet, Starmer removed nearly everyone who could fit the description 'Corbynite', replacing them with a team mainly without a past or, as it transpired, a future. Obliged to include his leadership rival Rebecca Long-Bailey as a gesture towards 'unity' (it would be the last), he sacked her as soon as possible after a confected row led by the Board of Deputies. Her crime was to have retweeted an article in the *Independent* by the actor Maxine Peake, one of her constituents. Peake had, as an aside, claimed that the US police who killed George Floyd had learned their techniques from the Israeli security forces. It was a silly thing to assert, since a moment's reflection would establish that police across the United States were killing and brutalising black people long before there was an Israel, and surely had no need for advice on that front, although if I were a supporter of Israel the conduct of its own police and military – who generally treat Palestinian civilians far worse than their US counterparts treat black people – would not be the hill I would choose to die on. But to retweet an article containing an erroneous reference to Israel was enough to make an end of Becky Long-Bailey as a member of Starmer's shadow cabinet. Every subsequent reshuffle of the front bench has further entrenched New Labour throwbacks as the party's new public face.

All this was only the hors d'oeuvre. The spearhead of Starmer's drive against the left was around anti-Semitism, unsurprisingly as that was where Corbynism had shown itself to be vulnerable. To begin with, large sums were paid to the ex-staffers who had appeared in the *Panorama* attack on the party, and who were suing the party for libel over its response to their claims. Journalists are usually averse to making use of Britain's draconian libel laws – protector of the rich and enemy of inquiring journalism as they are – but programme maker John Ware is not, so he joined in. Despite legal advice suggesting that the party could reasonably expect to win, Starmer settled. The integrity of the former employees and the impartiality of Ware's exemplary journalism are therefore now beyond question. So too is the expensive signal sent – sue us and we'll settle.

Corbyn's Suspension

This strategy reached its climax with the publication of the EHRC report into Labour's handling of anti-Semitism in October 2020. The EHRC investigation actually turned out not to be the damning indictment that had been anticipated. Labour was found to have unlawfully discriminated against Jewish members through the acts of its agents in two instances, one of them the 2016 remarks on Hitler's alleged Zionism by Ken Livingstone (an NEC member at the time), the other online remarks by a councillor in the North-West. The spin around the report, including that from the EHRC itself, put a worse construction on things, alleging that the party leadership had not dealt with anti-Semitism because it did not wish to (at the same time damning it for intervening in disciplinary cases involving anti-Semitism in order to expedite them!). This denunciation was not by-and-large sustained by the content of the report, but it served the political purpose. Corbyn was suspended on the same day, ostensibly for having observed in a statement that allegations of anti-Semitism in the Labour Party had been 'dramatically overstated for political reasons by our opponents inside and outside the Party'. This had the merit of being both true and an argument specifically identified in the EHRC report as a legitimate one to make.[9] Starmer's decision to remove his predecessor was the clearest declaration of intent to break the left and make an end of all traces of Corbynism, whatever previous promises had been made, and whatever the members' view of the matter.

Corbyn issued a clarification a few weeks later, the wording of which had been carefully negotiated with McSweeney. An NEC panel duly reinstated him in the party. Starmer, however, apparently under pressure from Margaret Hodge and others, then reversed the position and maintained Corbyn's suspension from the PLP whip, which would stop him being a Labour candidate at the next election. According to Unite's Len McCluskey among others, this was deceitful, given that the Leader had been party to the agreement reached, and had at no point indicated that restoration of the whip would not automatically follow reinstatement in the party. For McCluskey, who had helped negotiate the violated arrangement, this was the end of the road for his dealings with Starmer.[10]

General Secretary David Evans leveraged this confected drama into a crisis by suspending constituency officials who permitted their members the opportunity to express any solidarity with the man who had, just six months earlier, been the party's Leader. Likewise, debate on the just-released EHRC report was prohibited, as it was around the IHRA definition of anti-Semitism. The party membership was thus placed under a self-administered super-injunction, discussion of which was also placed off-limits. Ostensibly, this was to avoid arguments which might cause upset to Jewish members of the party. The hypocrisy is dramatised by the fact that at least three dozen Jewish members have been among those sanctioned by the party. Evidently they are the 'wrong sort' of Jews, who fail to meet the contemporary political definition of Jewishness, ethnicity notwithstanding. The uproar can be imagined had the Corbyn-period party suspended Jewish members for their views.[11]

In some parts of the country, depending on the zeal of the regional enforcers from the apparatus, the ban on debate has been extended to discussion of motions relating to the Israel–Palestine dispute, again lest some Jewish members be disturbed. Of course, no meeting on any subject should be conducted in an atmosphere of abuse and intolerance against anyone in the party, no matter what views they may hold, and there is evidence that some pro-Israel Jews have faced unpleasant behaviour at meetings. It is the job of a decent chair to ensure that conduct and rhetoric stay within acceptable limits, however deeply feelings may be held. But it is surely unprecedented for a prohibition to be placed on discussing one of the more consequential matters in world politics simply on the grounds that some members may feel uncomfortable. Such is Starmer's bleakly authoritarian party, the inverse of the vibrant and campaigning organisation that Corbyn sought to develop. While the Board of Deputies and other leading Jewish organisations urged Starmer to go still further in culling the left, leaders of the national liberation struggle in South Africa and others signed an open letter calling for Corbyn's reinstatement: 'We stand in solidarity with a man who for more than 40 years has stood by the side of liberation movements and anti-racists across the world.'[12]

By-election Blues

By-elections in summer 2020 exposed the fragility of Starmer's political project. First up was Hartlepool, an archetypical 'red wall' seat retained by Labour in 2019. It was handsomely lost to the Tories. This Starmer tried to the blame on Angela Rayner, his deputy. The patent absurdity of addressing northern working-class disaffection by demoting the senior northern working-class woman in the party forced a retreat. Lord Mandelson responded to the loss of his old constituency by urging Starmer to cut Labour's link with the trade unions – a cause he has championed for forty years or more – and be less squeamish about taking on the left. 'Hard left factions seeking to control our largest trade unions should not have a guaranteed place in the governing counsels of the party', he wrote, rebuking Starmer for wanting 'to change the party without disturbing the coalition he originally created to win the leadership.' Upholding Corbyn-era policies is 'ludicrous', Mandelson added, although that is of course what Starmer had pledged to do when seeking election.[13] Starmer did not hurry to dissociate himself from the perception that the creator of New Labour was firmly installed in the back seat of the leadership motor.

Next up was a humiliating 1.6 per cent of the vote in Tory-held Chesham and Amersham, with the Liberal democrats the benefi-ciaries of anti-government sentiment – another huge fall from the

Corbyn-era vote share. Finally, at Batley and Spen, Labour retained a seat, albeit by just 323 votes and with a vote share well down on Corbyn 2019, never mind 2017. Had it gone, then so too might Starmer. The problem here was evidence of deep disillusionment with Starmer's Labour on the part of the Muslim community, which formed a significant share of the electorate. The long-standing loyalty of this key part of the Labour electoral coalition had been tested by Starmer's reluctance to address Islamophobic racism within the party as well as his apparent indifference to the situation of the Palestinian people. Media spin claimed that Muslims were disenchanted with Labour because it was now addressing anti-Semitism, while others said it was because of homophobia in the Muslim community. If Muslims would not vote for a party opposed to anti-Semitism and homophobia then they would never have supported Labour over the last fifty years or more. These tropes served to distract from the actual reasons for Muslim dissatisfaction – Starmer's muted response to Israeli aggression against the Palestinian people and Labour's new reluctance to address critical issues of poverty and class. On top of that, the party re-admitted veteran New Labourite Trevor Phillips, who had been suspended for various remarks he had made 'othering' Britain's Muslims.[14] The media has no interest in this form of racism at all, although they noticed when, in a belated and desperate effort to appease Muslims in Batley, the party circulated a leaflet slighting the Indian Prime Minister and Hindu chauvinist Narendra Modi. This of course provoked dismay among Labour-supporting Hindu Indians. The stupidity of substituting identity-pandering for class politics has seldom been better displayed.

Having hung on to the leadership by the skin of his teeth, the empowered Starmer reached back to the 1950s right-wing playbook. He reintroduced the notorious 'proscribed list' of organisations to which Labour Party members could not belong on pain of auto-exclusion. Hitherto, only support for candidates standing against Labour was considered good enough grounds for such exclusion, as Alastair Campbell had discovered after publicly announcing that he voted Liberal Democrat in the 2019 European elections. Initially, the targets were Socialist Appeal, an entirely harmless fragment of the old Militant Tendency which Blair, Brown and Miliband had all been content to tolerate, and three groups mainly composed of the already excluded. Retrospective association with these groups was sufficient for expulsion. An open invitation was also issued for suggestions as to other organisations to be added to the list, with a Star Chamber established to consider them. Jewish Voice for Labour (which has had ten of its eleven officers sanctioned or investigated) and ultimately Momentum are surely in the frame.[15]

A Police Face

Starmer's policy passivity swiftly became the stuff of legend. His unwillingness to challenge the government over its handling of the pandemic, his incapacity in offering a vivid alternative as to how Britain could be, and his preference for a 'national' rather than a class approach to all questions have reduced Labour and himself to the point of nullity in political debate. Small wonder that footballer Marcus Rashford was often referred to as 'leader of the opposition' for his campaign against the government in support of free school meals in 2020. This at least serves as a reminder that the right wing of the Labour Party has absolutely no ideas. Nevertheless, something that might be termed essential Starmerism has peeked out from time to time, enough to sketch an outline of what he actually stands for.

The following decisions seem indicative. He initially whipped MPs to abstain on a bill to indemnify British military personnel against war crimes and torture that they may commit overseas, and sacked from the front bench those MPs who disobeyed. Likewise, he whipped abstention on the Covert Human Intelligence Sources Bill, which permitted abuses by undercover police, again losing several front-benchers as a consequence. He dismissed the Black Lives Matter movement as merely a 'moment'. He pledged in 2021 to campaign against Irish unity in any border poll that may be held, something no previous Labour Leader has done. He condemned demonstrations against Israel's racist, far-right ambassador to the UK, Tzipi Hotovely, formerly Netanyahu's settlements minister, and he repeated a range of anti-Palestinian tropes in a craven speech to Labour Friends of Israel.[16] Each of these are tokens of his loyalty to the imperialist state. As Oliver Eagleton points out, 'He has excised the final traces of Jeremy Corbyn's progressive internationalism' and aligned the party with conservative forces around the world.[17]

Further examples are not hard to find. His first pick as shadow minister for the Middle East and North Africa was Wayne David, who opined that Labour should drop its 'obsession with anti-imperialism', a striking formulation from someone holding that particular portfolio.[18] No one around the world outside the British elite could imagine that an 'obsession with anti-imperialism' was a bad thing, nor that Labour has historically suffered from an excess of it. More people would share the view expressed in 2021 by *Financial Times* columnist Jemima Kelly. She warned that then shadow foreign secretary Lisa Nandy's advocacy of Britain being a 'force for good in the world' invoked the 'image of a benevolent Britain which should steer the rest of the world in the right direction, an idea that is just as steeped in "imperial nostalgia" – perhaps even amnesia – as any Brexiteer fantasy of gunboats and military glory'.[19]

So it is wrong to say that it is unclear what Starmer stands for. He stands for the state, its servants, its perquisites and their protection from the toils of democracy. I asked my son Jack, whose career as a creative street artist has involved a number of engagements with law enforcement, what he made of Starmer. 'Dad, he's a cop,' he replied. 'He's got a police face.' And the cops recognise it. Former MI6 supremo Richard Dearlove, whom we have already encountered berating Corbyn, has been explicit: 'On Keir Starmer, he seems to me to be a Labour Leader of the type that we would expect and personally I feel quite content and happy with the fact that he's now leading the Labour Party. I may not support him politically but I don't see a repetition of the sort of problems that we had with Jeremy Corbyn, in fact not at all.'[20] Presumably MI6 and its confreres constitute the magisterial 'we' in Dearlove's endorsement. For them, Labour is once more in safe hands.

Labour's Future

Morgan McSweeney's mission as Starmer's first chief of staff as Leader has been characterised as trying 'to convince a pro-Corbyn membership to marginalise Corbynism without their realising it'.[21] In that, at least, McSweeney and Starmer failed. No one doubts any longer what is going on. This has not been a stealth war. As one earnest of that realisation, Simon Fletcher, who had been Corbyn's first chief of staff and was the most prominent left-winger to back

Starmer's leadership bid, resigned from his post in Starmer's LOTO in May 2021 and publicly repudiated him a few months later.[22]

Knowing what is happening is not the same thing as affecting the course of events, however. The response to all this has been muted. The speed and (thus far) success of the Starmer offensive has shown the weakness of the left in the Labour Party. Young Labour has proved a bastion of resistance to Starmer's dispensation and of fidelity to the spirit of 2017, but there have been few others. At the moment of Corbyn's suspension there was much talk of it constituting a 'declaration of war' – if so, only one side was really fighting. Many constituency parties wished to express support for Jeremy and opposition to Starmer, but a central lead was scarcely given. The Socialist Campaign Group of MPs was particularly feeble – only eighteen of its thirty-four members called for Corbyn to be immediately reinstated. Jeremy, true to himself as ever, did not capitulate to Starmer's demands for ever-more humiliating self-abasement as the price of restoration of the whip, but nor was there organised and purposeful resistance to the attack on him and the movement he stood for.

Clearly the transformation of the party into a campaigning, democratic organisation with some of the aspects of a social movement rooted in the communities was radically incomplete. No one was under any great illusion about the PLP or the apparatus – the latter swiftly reverted to its favoured role as the leadership's vengeful watchdog, controlling and coercing the membership as supervisor rather than servant. The primary organisation of the Labour left, Momentum, the creation of those who drove Corbyn's initial ascent to the leadership, has appeared to lose ground, with its foundational mission of defending the Corbyn leadership now otiose. Co-Chair Andrew Scattergood acknowledges:

Keir Starmer was always likely to distance himself from the left, but not many would have anticipated the speed and extent of his offensive. But in spite of the hostility, the left remains strong. We've built bigger and more organised institutions and the movement leaders whose platforms grew under Corbyn still hold influence on the left. *What is missing is a coherent strategy.*[23]

Indeed. Nor have the left-led affiliated trade unions stepped up in any meaningful way. Defeat has turned to rout, for the time being at least.

However, Starmer is not a Blair, who for one thing had a certain brio, and who ascended to the leadership at a time of economic growth and social comfort very unlike the 2020s, when harder choices are required. If he is instead playing Kinnock to Corbyn's Benn, it is far from certain that he will be given the luxury of failing twice at the polls, as Kinnock was. His franchise will not last much longer than the moment when the right wing have settled on a plausible and more authentically Blairite successor with realistic hopes of winning a party election. These will be under the new rules aimed at restoring the PLP to its erstwhile supremacy, which were adopted at the 2021 party conference (if not exactly in Starmer's preferred form, a restoration of the electoral college, and with a majority of constituency votes opposed). It is not impossible that sheer exasperation with corrupt Toryism could propel Starmer into Downing Street, but the idea of a majority Labour government under his leadership seems fanciful. More likely his place in Labour's history will be as frontman for Labour's right while they took an axe to their opponents in the party. That mission accomplished, his utility will have been exhausted.

We can anticipate what a consummated anti-Corbyn regime would look like, whether under Starmer or another. The party membership would be driven down to comfortably below 200,000 again, where it was for most of this century prior to Corbyn, and less than a third of its Corbyn-era peak. The energy and spirit that drew so many into politics for the first time would be vigorously supressed, with the young particularly excluded. The PLP's ascendancy would be re-entrenched, with the apparatus policing what remains of the membership. Even if Mandelson is still denied his maximum programme, the removal of trade unions from the party entirely, their influence would be further marginalised – indeed, Starmer appeared content to see the militant Bakers, Food and Allied Workers' Union end its 100-year affiliation to Labour in 2021. Some of Starmer's top advisors speak privately of provoking Unite into following suit. This Labour would be a party of managerial hierarchies reliant on technocratic expertise and bland spin-doctoring. Its destiny, as indicated by Tony Blair over a considerable period and with renewed zeal more recently, would be reconciliation not merely with liberalism as an ideology but with the Liberal Democrats as a party in a new 'progressive' governing coalition based on free market supremacy, an approach to the culture conflict based on 'reason and moderation' and support for the armed forces and the police.[24]

So far, the party membership has stood athwart such a scenario – it was and still is unreliable, notwithstanding an almost complete lack of leadership from the major institutions of the left in resisting the Starmer offensive and mass resignations.[25] The ghost of Corbyn takes some exorcising. Corbyn-era policies, including the reviled 2019 manifesto, remain overwhelmingly popular among party members. Starmer's notional embrace of them during his own leadership election was the tribute vice pays to virtue. Blair said his mission would not be complete until the party learned to love Peter Mandelson. That day is not imminently anticipated – indeed, getting the party to love Blair himself seems a challenge too far. In January 2020 YouGov polled Labour Party members on their attitudes to its past leaders. Remarkably, Tony Blair was the only one of thirteen Labour leaders stretching back to the 1920s to get a net negative rating among the party membership, with 62 per cent unfavourable.[26]

The prevailing faction in Labour's leadership loathes this Corbyn-ish party. London Mayor Sadiq Khan, a tepid technocrat, has said that the public were right to elect Johnson in preference to Labour in 2019, and Starmer himself has stated that Labour 'deserved to lose'.[27] Such self-loathing is no basis for renewal. Whether it is even a basis for the Labour Party's survival is a matter to be considered in the next chapter, but Starmer's purged, locked-down Labour, with its radically diminished vision, its lurch back to stale centrist bromides, its renewed fealty to state imperatives, its anti-Muslim racism, its neo-imperialism and knee-jerk authoritarianism is already a world away from Corbyn's movement. At any event, the question of whether socialism is possible in Britain and whether the Labour Party can be the vehicle for its attainment are not coterminous.

10

Legacy and Lessons

Corbynism is receding in the rear-view mirror of politics. Could it, however, like a well-bred subatomic particle, be in front of us, too? That is a counter-intuitive argument, given both the scale of the 2019 election defeat and the scorched-earth approach of Starmer towards his predecessor and those who supported him, but then almost everything about Corbyn's leadership of Labour was counter-intuitive.

The ground that seeded Corbyn's ascent remains fertile. Though austerity has been at least temporarily and partially abated as of 2021, the more profound crisis of capitalist society, scoping climate change, the pandemic, rampant inequality and the decay of both democracy and the international political order, is if anything deeper than it was six years ago. Johnson-or-Starmer is not a choice that offers any possibility of a durable solution to dislocations on this imposing scale. Corbynism did embody such a possibility, and it struck a popular chord, earning the hatred of those who know the price of everything but the value of nothing.

That is not to say that the 2015–19 river can be crossed again. The shortcomings of the Corbyn endeavour, both in conception and execution, proved too profound to form any basis for a do-over – one more time with feeling, except with a different front-of-house team, would be a parody of a programme for the left. What can be retrieved from Corbynism is important. Key is the potential popularity of a break with the reigning conventions of neoliberalism, as ratified by Labour's 40 per cent vote in 2017, and some of the specific policies as already outlined – as well as at least a fleeting sense of renewed agency in a democratic politics normally restricted to a stultifying conformism and an elite bereft of an imagination remotely corresponding to the scale of the challenge. However, it is not sufficient. For our movement to build back better, we need to go deeper. One of the attainments of the Corbyn period is the emergence of a newer, younger, left cadre open to the experiences of the past but unencumbered by the imperative to repeat it.

As argued in chapter 2, Corbynism's ascent and its demise were likewise conditioned by the reconfiguring of classes over the last forty years, and the resultant instability of class relations. The middle class has felt its own position shaken by globalisation. Its familiar institutions – commercial, religious, cultural – have seen their influence diminished almost as much as trade unionism. Its rising generation is generally lost to conservative politics and attracted by a radicalism that, paradoxically, holds out the promise of the economic stability and security which their parents regarded as their birthright. While the ruling class still likes socialism as much as Dracula craves garlic, the middle class en masse does not fear the working-class movement as it once did.

Corbynism began by advancing through those fissures, which had among other things unmoored radical politics from its historic institutions to a significant extent. It attained an unforeseen ascendancy, and ended by stretching itself in vain to bridge the new chasms that had opened within the working class, and between the working class (or most of it) and the progressive middle class. A working-class project, it was to a large extent powered by a middle-class left, a divide which dogged its steps.

There is nothing here that has not been emulated, with variations, in all the countries of first-wave capitalism. There is no coherent modern framework for class politics, although there is every good reason for one to develop. Nativist populism often fills the gap. In 2019 Labour attempted to narrate a list of grievances common to working people in both the metropolis and the disenfranchised industrial communities, grievances that a social democratic government would address. This attempt failed, but arguably only because it forsook the terrain of democracy and hence disrespected too many whose votes it needed.

Class and Mass

How is a class vested in a socialist future reconstituted for itself? And what would be its political field of operation? These are the critical issues for addressing the question on this book's cover. As we saw in chapter 1, Marx and Engels mandated the first task of socialists as being to organise the proletariat as a class. That, as it turns out, was not to be a once-and-for-all accomplishment which, once ticked off, opened the way for the constituted class to return the favour by struggling for socialism. Rather, class-constitution has proved to be the work of the repeated, open-ended renewal and recomposition of the historical agency charged with digging capital's grave. No working class organised for itself, no graves dug.

On the one hand, Panitch and Leys note, uncontroversially enough, that 'it is hard to imagine that any socialist project can make headway unless organised labour plays a major role in it'.[1] On the other, Neal Lawson observes that 'a Labour government expected to re-enact '45 will have to do so without the agency that was Labour's historic engine, a unified and purposeful working class ... There is no solid working-class base, in quantity and quality, to power a traditional left project.'[2] That, too, is not wide of the mark, particularly if the word 'solid' is emphasised.

The reconstitution of the working class as a social agent in its own right is the *sine qua non* for a socialist project. Perhaps it is not entirely necessary for the formation of a radical social democratic government. For that, the 40 per cent or so of the vote secured by Corbynism would be quite sufficient, if that was the way the parliamentary cookies crumbled. Socialism requires more – including a majority of the population behind it. Corbynism in power would have helped in that reconstitution, by re-empowering existing working-class organisations, by strengthening the stability of working-class communities, and by laying the basis of a new class politics, through its from-Tottenham-to-Tyneside orientation towards popular needs. It would not have been enough, however – class composition cannot be the work of government alone.

Socialism is not just the icing on the working-class cake. A class which does not carry within it a project for the remaking of society is a class diminished, more of a sociological category. Class political independence is not a sectarian shibboleth but a precondition for transforming the conditions of our existence. The 'progressive alliance', which would lash the Labour Party, the Liberal Democrats, the Greens, Scottish and Welsh nationalism and who knows what else together in a governing coalition, is a means neither to electoral success nor socialism. Rather it is the death-knell of socialism as a class project, which already faces challenges enough with the 'progressive alliance' *within* the Labour Party, precariously uniting supporters and opponents of systemic change. It would involve the labour movement politically vacating much of the country, probably never to return. Its electoral potency assumes a willingness to transfer votes tactically which is yet to be seriously tested as an articulated strategy, some spontaneous local dabbling notwithstanding. And the only governing party the Liberal Democrats have actually allied with since their formation is, of course, the Tories.

The 'progressive alliance' is sometimes advocated in *Guardian*-ista circles as a necessary defensive measure to secure democracy from the populist/authoritarian right endangering it. The threat is not fanciful. However, it is plain that democracy cannot be success-fully defended if it stands on the ground of the liberal centrism of the 1991–2008 period. A democracy that cannot deal with inequal-ity, climate change or economic stagnation, and which writes its record in blood from Libya to Afghanistan, will not now secure the support needed for its survival. Protecting democracy demands superseding such centrism, not entrenching it in a 'progressive' bundling together with the LibDems. The 'progressive alliance' actually constitutes the political expression of the prioritisation of culture/identity referents over class. Nothing could do more to further fuel the nativist jihadis of the populist right, serving the Establishment they claim to despise.

Today, the diminution of the working class as a social actor is writ in the ruins of the 'red walls' laid low by recalibrated identi-ties. The same phenomenon sees bastions of French communism vote for Le Pen, left strongholds in Italy back Salvini, and areas of the industrial Midwest come out for Trump. Some of the blame for this in Britain can doubtless be laid at the door of the complacent indifference of New Labour's panjandrums, but the core of the problem, politically, *is that the labour movement has ceased to exist in many of these communities.* Not Brexit, not Jeremy Corbyn, nor even simply New Labour. The 2019 debacle was a record in votes of changes which had occurred much earlier as factories and mines closed and the connective tissue of proletarian Britain correspondingly withered and weakened. As Alex Niven wrote in the *New York Times* shortly after the election, 'At the root of Labour's waning support in England's postindustrial regions is a basic historical fact: the industrial communities that gave rise to the birth of the labour movement no longer exist.' Labour's 'rediscovery of its radical roots following Jeremy Corbyn's election as its Leader in 2015 arrived too little and too late to check these long-term processes of fraction and disillusion'.[3]

Tackling this rupture is not, however, as imposing a task as it may sound. Some of what is required can sound almost routine. The labour movement still exists, to state the obvious. Stronger trade unions are essential, and the unions do not lack the capacity to advance. Unite's community membership initiative, and Labour's now-redundant community organisers, point in the right direction, but they will not cover enough territory on their own. The movement needs to be part of the life of post-industrial towns and villages, as well as never-heartland areas today savaged by capitalist crisis and a decade of austerity. Why, for example, does the left merely condemn the existence of food banks but not also seek to organise those dependent on them to make demands on local and national government, making them the centre of a transition from charity to class solidarity? It also needs to follow the exploitation into its new centres in the cities, where casualised labour, usually in the service and distribution sectors and often of the young and the migrant, is increasingly the norm. It is incongruous that the only unions to have taken the gig economy sufficiently seriously so far are small, under-resourced and outside the TUC. Automation too is giving exploitation new forms, challenging traditional notions of work in a way which leaves some form of democratic social planning or mass destitution the most likely options facing humanity.

A Momentum organiser, Harriet Soltani, who argues that the organisation should refocus on direct political interventions outside Labour's internal agonies, 'creating a movement that stretches across workplaces and communities', is on the right track.[4] The synthesis of the unions' social weight with the vibrancy and initiative of the mass movements against austerity, war, climate change and more remains the holy grail of left politics. Corbynism was a taste of it.

Corbynism was also correct in appealing to common experiences of exploitation, social dispossession and alienation. However, it lacked the entrenchment in society identified by Lawson. It was underpinned by the lived reality of many people, including young workers in city and country alike, but not by the structures of an organised class which could transcend otherwise divergent cultural attitudes. As *Tribune* editor Ronan Burtenshaw puts it, Corbynism 'hoped to convince working people that Labour would fight for them in government again. It aimed for a coalition of those whose *interests* lay in social change, not one of those whose *views* aligned broadly with progressivism; a coalition of the exploited rather than a coalition of the enlightened.' This more or less reverses the position championed by Paul Mason and others. It entails not just reviving the labour movement but 'rebuilding the social institutions that give us a day-to-day presence in working-class communities, which were allowed to wither over decades and were then largely ignored in favour of Westminster in more recent times'.[5] A Corbyn government could and would have done something to fill in the gaps in its own foundations by re-establishing a degree of cohesion and stability in the life of working-class communities through its housing, industrial and welfare policies. It would also have re-empowered workers and unions in the workplaces through its legislative commitments. By devolving power to regions and communities it would have created new catalysts for political regeneration. Such measures can make radicalism part of people's daily lives.

Culture and Imperialism

Learning nothing from the Brexit schism, parts of the left now seek to impale themselves on the spike of identity politics, despite enough flashing warning signs to illuminate Piccadilly Circus. This is a trap set by the Establishment aiming to perpetuate the Brexit divisions within the working class through the promotion of largely spurious 'issues' that can separate progressives from the rest.[6] It is not necessary. Citing an IPSOS/MORI poll, even the *Telegraph* acknowledged that half the country has heard little or nothing about the term 'woke'. Journalist Stephen Armstrong continued: 'You know what the IPSOS/MORI poll found British people really think divides the country? Wealth and class. The same thing we think has divided the country for years.'[7] A vindication of the Corbyn approach in fact.

That is not to suggest that neutrality in all 'culture war' controversies is a proper or viable approach for socialists. We should be opposed to the celebration of British imperialism and its heroes, likewise to the marginalisation of the lived experience of black people. These are scarcely new arguments within the labour movement. They are important because they reinforce the foundations of a living class unity, and embody the perspectives of a socialist future. In fact, such arguments are not unpopular either. Three in four 'red wall' voters agree that it is important to educate children about Britain's role in the slave trade and colonialism. Most do not believe that immigration has been a bad thing for the country.[8] But it is to class, the 'fundamental basis on which our lives are structured', in Burtenshaw's words, that we should connect these issues, rather than posing them as an alternative foundation for the left's politics on a cross-class 'progressive' basis, joined with a number of less compelling imperatives. As for those on the left who obsessively echo the anti-'woke' agenda of the Tories, they are simply playing the elite's game with the elite's ideas. Rather than constructing a narrative for the left's hegemony in 'culture wars', they entrench that of the right, something inimical to class regroupment.

Class unity will not emerge through a process of invocation. Corbynism drew its original strength from the sort of mass movements and social campaigns which constitute the beginnings of the transformation of people's consciousness of their potential to change society, and it grew weaker the more it retreated into parliamentarism. Such movements may be against the consequences of austerity or other economic questions, but they may just as likely be against imperialist war, or against populist-authoritarian racism and threats to democracy, or climate change. The Labour Party has no central role here, for sure. The development of the mass struggles which will actually power progress towards socialism is the work of mass campaigns, from CND and Stop the War to Black Lives Matter and Extinction Rebellion – organic social movements embedded in the people. Corbynism drew on their traditions and showed a glimpse of the potential of aligning their transformational energy with electoral politics. It was no more than a glimpse, but it is a world in advance of the constipated centrism of Starmerism. Such movements, their connexions and cross-currents, can seed a new class politics, a new movement of all the exploited and oppressed against the capitalist system. There are parts which parliamentary procedure does not reach, yet the streets can refresh.

The Necessity of Opposing Empire

As the imperialist occupation of Afghanistan collapses in ignominy, its wreckage a monument to its own pointless failure, on the one hand; and as Britain joins the US and Australia in a huge escalation of the arms race and cold war confrontation with China in the Pacific region, it is evident that Corbyn's anti-imperialism is no eccentric posture, but instead of vital contemporary relevance. In the face of the strident internal opposition from the social-imperialist right of the Labour Party, there was an element among Corbyn's support who that felt the foreign policy game wasn't worth the candle, and that radicalism should be exclusively concentrated on domestic economic and social policies. 'Give the generals what they want', was the inscription on that particular white flag. It is an argument that has been revived in some of Corbynism's autopsies.

There was never the slightest chance that Corbyn would fly that standard – its advocacy by some allies was merely one of the debilitating distractions that beset his leadership. The larger point is that political life does not fall into such easily separable compartments, least of all in a world shaped by more than thirty years of uninhibited capitalist globalisation. This anti-imperialism was so bitterly opposed because imperialism has to a large extent made Britain and British capitalism what it is, and is key to the identity of the elite and its place in the world, as well as to its profits. Opposing it is also key to the reconstituted working-class politics which might offer a hope of transcending contemporary capitalism.

We have a state heavily over-invested in globalisation and the imperialist force structures underpinning it. As Cain and Hopkins explained in their definitive review of the subject, British imperialism's roots lie in the City halls of high finance, and those roots run deep.[9] Relative to the size of the domestic economy, British finance is greater than any other centre of international capital. It is, in Grace Blakeley's words 'engorged on capital sucked in from every corner of the globe'.[10] Tackling the City is tackling imperialism – conversely, hostility to anti-imperialism generally corresponds with acquiescence in City power within Labour's ranks.

Consider, too, the huge and corrupting influence of the arms sector on government, and the fact that making weaponry to be sold to foreign regimes, including the least savoury, occupies a considerable slice of manufacturing industry, distorting diplomacy and industrial strategy alike – and Labour's own policies too, since trade unions will unavoidably prioritise the protection of their members' skilled jobs in an economy offering few alternatives. Here is another way in which imperialism disorganises the working-class movement here at home. The same point could be made in relation to the giant oil monopolies, the quintessential imperial industry. If two industrial (as opposed to finance-sector) companies enjoyed privileged access to Blair's Downing Street, they were British Aerospace and BP. Defence diversification and ending fossil fuel consumption – the latter a favourite investment choice for the City – will never advance under a regime of international exploitation and despoliation.

Above all there is racism, and the resurgent struggle against it. No one can really separate Black Lives Matter or Islamophobia (now an issue within the Labour Party itself) from the recurring global divisions engendered by imperialism. 'We are here because you were there' begins to explain the dynamic of mass Commonwealth immigration, promoted by the state as a source of cheap labour drawing on the same racist assumptions as were used to justify colonialism. Black Lives Matter reminds us that while it is right to tear down the statues of Colston and other slave-traders, it is also necessary to acknowledge that British society has at least one foot on that same plinth. Our capitalism is a racialised capitalism, and has been so from its earliest days, reinforced by the project of a British imperialism which emerged amid slavery and genocide and then matured into mere authoritarian repressive violence and exploitation. The history of the Empire is more contested than ever before, to the discomfort of the right, with a deepening awareness of its record of slavery, massacre, hyper-exploitation and denial of basic rights to millions over generations.[11] That is a record that lives on in racist discrimination today, and in the neo-imperial structuring of the world economy. These are not barnacles on the hull of British capitalist society, they are among its timbers.

Is it seriously possible to challenge unabashed Islamophobia while supporting wars targeted at Muslim-majority countries and buying into anti-Islam demonology? Can the economy be rebuilt and reoriented without breaking from the warped priorities of militarism? Can the refugee crisis be addressed without ending catastrophic military interventions like those in Afghanistan, Libya and Syria, as well as global impoverishment and climate despoliation? The answers are pretty obvious. So in sum: you may not be interested in imperialism, but imperialism is certainly interested in you, as Trotsky almost said. Some find this painful, so deeply are assumptions based on Britain's imperial role woven into the culture, above all in terms of an imagined British exceptionalism, but it is a barrier that needs to be crossed by any genuinely socialist project.

Even if all this was not true, and the ills of British society could be addressed in isolation from its world position – to repeat, an absurd position – it would still be wrong to assert that joining a US-led war in the Middle East is an acceptable price to pay for enhancing welfare benefits in Britain. That would not be socialism, but chauvinistic reformism.

'Corbynism' was about confronting these integral challenges. Its anti-imperialism was not a specialist side-show relating to foreign policy, but core to remaking British society around a vision for social and economic transformation. It understood that this would be a cramped and limited project if it did not embrace addressing Britain's place in the world and the consequences that flow from it. It is not by chance that Corbyn's strongest critics among the liberal centre, like the *Observer*'s Nick Cohen, have also been the most vocal champions of the twenty-first-century wars of intervention. The political defeat of such views is one of the British left's major achievements of this century, and one the left needs to defend staunchly if it is to offer a plausible socialist perspective.

Even Labour's conference 2021 showed the strength of attachment to anti-imperialism on the left today in its votes, against the leadership, on Palestine and the AUKUS pact.

Labour in Vain?

Shortly after 9/11 I found myself agitating one Saturday morning in Walthamstow Market in east London. The Communist Party group I was with turned up with leaflets and other materials protesting against the impending war on Afghanistan, ingloriously terminated twenty years later. A couple of far-left groups also showed up, likewise campaigning against the looming conflict. Finally, a few local Labour Party activists arrived in the market – distributing leaflets concerning the illegal resale of tickets at the local tube station. Here was the humdrum pragmatism, the thinking small in the face of big events, which characterises the history of British social democracy.

However, that is only one side of the picture. It is not that the Labour Party was ignoring Afghanistan. The Blair government was even then preparing to bomb and invade the country alongside George Bush's USA. This little vignette displays the Labour Party in all its glory – serving the British imperial state with fire and thunder while immersed in the daily concerns, even the minor ones, of the people.

Jeremy Corbyn offered a different Labour Party. It proposed big solutions to the quotidian problems of society, while breaking, at least to the greatest extent possible, with the traditional notions of what constitutes the 'national interest' (slipperiest of concepts). The near-pathological resistance he encountered within his own party and the vehemence of the Starmer-led counter-offensive against the left speak to the threat this represented. This at least has a certain pedagogical value in understanding the essence of Labour's usually hegemonic right wing. They are not latent social-ists who have yet to see the light, nor are they potential allies in the great work of socialist transformation. They remain what they have always been – the expression of imperialism within the labour movement – with today the added handicap of having no original ideas whatsoever. That is not to say they lack vigour, but it is a vigour powered solely by venom against the left. In Starmer they have lighted upon a most serviceable vehicle for their campaign to crush socialism within the Labour Party.

So is Labour either use or ornament as it rows back to the barren centre of politics? Its collapse as a serious governing force is far from inconceivable. Of course, the last rites have been read over the party many times before, from 1931 onwards, invariably prematurely. However, the global trend dubbed 'PASOK-ification' after the elimination as an electoral force of the traditional party of Greek social democracy could reach British shores yet. It has occurred in France, Italy and the Netherlands. Other parties, including the once-mighty German SPD, have merely endured persistent erosion of their electoral base. Quirks of electoral systems and the possibility of coalitions may yet give a blush of rouge to the ailing patient, as it has in Germany, where the SPD can lead a government despite polling little more than 25 per cent of the vote (down from over 40 per cent earlier this century).

Labour faces challenges which it displays very little capacity to meet at present. First, as we have seen, its electoral coalition is unravelling. A large section of the working class has abandoned it, for either apathy or Tory populism, and there is small sign of it 'returning home'. Its base among ethnic minorities seems increasingly precarious, as a result both of growing class differentiation among them and the party's own neglect. The Starmer dispensation is alienating the younger voters who Corbyn attracted in such numbers, in the cities in particular, disinclined as they are to vote for the coalition of 'there is no alternative' neoliberals. They may prefer to vote Green or simply not to bother. The overarching themes of social change which bound together that coalition in 2017 have been discarded, to be replaced by next-to-nothing. Scotland, even if it remains in the Union, looks unlikely to be a reservoir of Labour seats once again – indeed, Scottish Labour keeps finding new lows to slump to. Only in Wales can the party hope to remain quasi-hegemonic for now, and it is led by a Corbyn sympathiser. Remember – Labour secured well over 40 per cent of the vote in all of the eight general elections from 1945 to 1970, but achieved this in just three out of the thirteen since, most recently under Corbyn's leadership.

Second, the presently hegemonic right-wing faction has created a vacuum of ideas and inspiration which it is incapable of filling. Consider the deterioration of Peter Mandelson. For New Labour Mark One he was fizzing with ideas at least, penning a book with Roger Liddle setting out what became Blair's agenda.[12] Today he makes scant pretence of having a programme to offer beyond the extermination of Corbynism. His allies on the right, sheltering under the tattered Starmer umbrella, unite the characteristics of support for imperialism and intellectual incapacity as they incant the totality of their programme in the words 'NATO, Trident, Israel; Israel, Trident, NATO'. The passage of thirteen years from the collapse of their socio-economic model under the impulse of the banker's crash is apparently insufficient time to allow the brains trusts of reformism to develop a new positive agenda. Instead it clings with ever-greater fervour to the main signifiers of the global order which has privileged them. The capitulation of social democracy in the face of capitalist globalisation over the last generation, abandoning the use of the powers of the nation-state for social improvement in significant part and placing traditional reforms out-of-bounds because of likely market opposition – all the hallmarks of centrism, in fact – has both cut parties like Labour off from much of their long-time electoral base and left it bereft of any cards to play other than 'managerial competence'. Perhaps that could work against Boris Johnson, but it is far from a surefire winner. Even were the political tides to propel Starmer into Downing Street, we can be sure that it would add nothing to the chronicles of socialism.

Third, while divisions within the Labour Party are scarcely a novelty, there can seldom if ever have been a time when its principal factions have been so estranged from each other, really bound together by nothing except a mutual loathing and a determination to obliterate their internal opponents. The left does this in the name of changing the world, the right in the cause of not doing so. The democracy of the party, which could in theory provide the means of meditating even such deep divisions, is increasingly strangulated in the hands of an authoritarian and socially reactionary bureaucracy.

Not every sow's ear has silk purse potential. The challenge is more than a mere unfortunate conjuncture of circumstances. It is hard to believe that anyone seeking political agency for social change would found the Labour Party in its existing form today did it not already exist. The world that brought Labour into being has passed. Its main constituents, perhaps other than socialist intellectuals, do not carry the social heft they did a century (or even forty years) ago. If history would oblige by presenting a blank sheet of paper for the construction of a broad electoral organisation aiming at socialist transformation it would seek to inscribe new ways of connecting Unison to Black Lives Matter, Stop the War to the Socialist Health Association, Young Labour to Extinction Rebellion, Walthamstow to Wakefield, Glasgow to Grimsby. That would be an act of class recomposition in itself. Labour has a future only to the extent that it makes itself serviceable to that project. Otherwise, it is a declining psephological phenomenon and there are only so many times socialists need use the Labour Party to verify Einstein's definition of insanity.

However, none of the parties launched to the left of Labour during the New Labour period have even begun to fill the vacancy.[13] Tariq Ali, surveying the wreckage of Corbynism, has argued that 'an independent Labour party with even half a dozen MPs and a membership base of perhaps 50,000 ... could mark a real advance'.[14] That would be the case, the more so if trade union support could be added. However, it would require Corbyn or McDonnell to place themselves at the head of such an initiative for it to secure even such a minimal level of support, and of that there is no sign. The electoral system would make it a gamble, a supervening consideration for those whose livelihood depends on parliamentary electoral success.

If the question is finding an electoral champion for the working-class interest and progressive politics – there isn't one presently, merely an establishment Opposition party with a large if diminishing number of socialists in it, and a historic if scarcely vital connection with significant parts of the trade union movement. If the question is reframed as needing a governing alternative to the Tories, then the Labour Party remains the most plausible offer, distant as a majority Starmer administration seems. While the great majority of socialists – ethical, scientific, public bar, drawing room, activist and academic – focus their endeavours to some extent through its structures these matters cannot be discounted.

But there is also a need for conscious socialist activity which, even if it mostly coalesces around Labour candidates at election time for want of anything better, cannot be collapsed into imperialist Labourism. Other organisations have their part to play in political education, the spread of socialist ideas, mass campaigning on the great issues and the practical unification of the manifold struggles engendered by capitalist society. If all these latter organisations and initiatives are at full flood, then Labour might be swept along with it, rather than constituting itself as a sort of dam. Corbynism hinted at this.

As for the perennial question of the parliamentary road to socialism, does the twenty-first century and the experience of Corbynism provide fresh scope for reflection? To offer a very short stab at an answer: in the present state of political activity in Britain, any thought of bypassing Parliament, or introducing socialism through entirely different means, is purely fanciful. The change from one regime of class power to another – the essential first step towards socialism – depends on a variety of factors far beyond majorities in the House of Commons, of course, and above all on the mass activity of working people in a kaleidoscope of struggles. But at the very least, Parliament is required to register in some form the changes introduced in society by such struggle, and it must be a Parliament chosen by democratic election for it to be recognised as such by the British people. The working-class project depends on deepening democracy, not negating it. The relationship of the Commons to the people it purportedly represents will surely change dramatically, but the idea of it being reduced to a purely formal role cannot be taken any more seriously than the idea that a parliamentary majority is alone sufficient to secure profound social change. Challenging state power, the indispensable prerequisite for socialism, was not an issue that Corbynism really grappled with. 'Preparing for government' meant trying to order priorities for Labour in office and finding some means for imposing direction on the existing machinery of the state, with little anticipation of the likely recalcitrance of the latter. New forms of popular power were not considered. The decay of parliamentarism and of the esteem in which it is held, the continuing development of mass movements of resistance added to the potential of new technology in driving organisation and communication, all mandate that they should be. So too does the broadening critique of the state itself, an organisation frequently in a simmering civil war with wider society. This was a truth imposed for previous generations by the role of police and judiciary in great industrial struggles, or the racist coercion of black communities. Its entrenched misogyny and immersion in permitting (when not actually conducting) violence against women teaches the same lesson today.

Yet Corbynism's message was that the state in Britain could be repurposed, after forty years of neoliberalism, to ameliorate life for working people. That, too, was supported by the great majority of Labour Party members, and also by most working-class voters across all other inflated divisions. Yet in volunteering the nation-state's continued subordination to the external restrictions imposed by the EU, the party parted company with most of the class. If anyone asks why the Tories outpolled Labour among the working class for the first time in generations, at least part of the answer may be that Boris Johnson was able to pass himself off, however fraudulently, as wielding nation-state power to protect the economic interests of the people, the traditional tune of social democracy. This attachment of working people to the nation-state and its potentials may appear an aberration of nostalgia to the high priesthood of liberals and ultra-lefts alike, but not only is it a presently intractable electoral fact – it is also one which Corbynism sought to embrace before drowning itself in Euro-equivocation. It would be tiresome perhaps to rerun the twentieth-century debates around the possibility of 'socialism in one country', but a radical social democracy has no viable locus other than the nation-state, at least pending the establishment of a democratic international political apparatus.

Socialism

There is no Corbynism, only socialism. A balance sheet of 2015–19 that discusses the personalities, office gossip, parliamentary arithmetic and swings-and-roundabouts of polling would be a tedious triviality. These are pebbles dropped in history's swell. Moreover, they are available in profusion elsewhere.

But what then of socialism? Perhaps the failure of the 2019 election campaign may at least have helped clarify what it is and isn't. It isn't tax-and-spend, even on an imposing scale, nor is it eat-drink-and-be-merry-for-free. The transformative message of socialism, of a different form of society, got lost in 2019 beneath a clutter of gratis goodies, bestowed on the public at bewildering speed. Important policy advances like the Green New Deal, which offers sustainable renewal and future-proofed work and is such a good idea that even Keir Starmer still advocates it perforce, were occluded by the special offer of the day. There is something to be said for the language of priorities, and also for the distinction between left-wing social democracy and socialism, even if only to better highlight the transitional connections.

Socialism is the elimination of social inequality and ultimately the attainment of a classless society, with gender, racial and national differences no longer consequential. The road there leads through the progressive decommodification of the essentials of life, from housing to culture, extending the founding principles of the NHS to the other necessities of a real *human* existence. The Right to Food campaign, which also found support at the Labour Party conference, is a move in that direction. It is both possible and popular. But every advance for decommodification will depend on the political defeat of those who profit from the domination of commodity production and seek the extension of market principles into all aspects of life. As those battles are won, something which can only be delivered by new forms of popular power ultimately spreading across national boundaries, humanity passes beyond the realm of necessity into the flowering of real human history.

Everything essential in Corbynism strained in that direction, despite its own weaknesses, vacillations and blunders. It held its own for four years in a class struggle that was still a class struggle even if not generally being named as such, exactly because those essentials cut with the needs of the hour. They still do. Indeed, a right-wing think-tank, the Institute for Economic Affairs, glumly reports that younger people in Britain blamed capitalism for the housing crisis (80 per cent), climate change (75 per cent) and wanted 'sweeping nationalisation' (72 per cent) and to 'live under a socialist economic system' (67 per cent).[15] Imposing figures, which explain Labour's overwhelming hegemony among the under-forties under Corbyn's leadership.

So we can be sure that, establishment efforts to avert a repetition notwithstanding, there will be another '–ism' replacing Corbynism before long, and it will still only be socialism. Corbynism went down to defeat in the bicentenary year of the British ruling class massacring those demonstrating peacefully for democracy at Peterloo. The survivors of that outrage saw the first steps at least towards elected government in Britain. And it was the centenary year of the same class shooting dead hundreds of Indians demanding national freedom at Amritsar. If you were not among those slaughtered by that imperial atrocity, you likely lived to see the end of the Raj and its torments. This defeat – a bloodless one – will be overcome as well. The alternative is accommodating capitalism, if anyone prefers. It's never been easy, and never will be, and let's not forget, Corbynism worked – almost.

Appendix:
Report to Labour Leadership on the
2017 General Election Campaign

*These, lightly edited, are the core conclusions of the report I submitted
to the party leadership in Parliament and at Southside HQ in June
2017, on the general election campaign which I had co-managed.*

Two factors above all seem to have contributed to the turnaround
[from the start of the campaign]. The first was the publication of
Labour's manifesto. This proved to be an extremely popular document, which resonated more with the electorate than any Party
manifesto for decades. Andrew Fisher and his team cannot be
praised too highly for the work they did on an exceptionally-tight
schedule (so too the Treasury team who provided costings and
revenue plans for all the pledges). The main pledges in the document helped secure Labour support immediately, and maintained
their impact throughout the campaign.

The second was the personal role of Jeremy Corbyn, whose
campaign and conduct helped overturn the impact of two years of
sustained abuse from much of the mass media, and of internal criticisms from the PLP. The judgement that the neutrality requirement

imposed on broadcasters during the campaign, with its guarantee of a degree of unmediated access to the electorate, would help people see the 'real' Jeremy Corbyn – straightforward, decent and taking the electorate seriously – was vindicated. No such obligations are imposed on the newspapers, of course, and the failure of their pages of hostile coverage of Jeremy to make a difference is a landmark. It would seem that progressive politicians no longer need to go in fear of Rupert Murdoch or Paul Dacre . . .

Within the overall context of those two over-riding factors, a number of things clearly went right during the campaign. I would like to list those I believe came into that category:

1   The emphasis on voter registration was very successful. 1.7 million people registered to vote in the course of the campaign up to the deadline, a number equivalent to about 24 parliamentary constituencies. It would be likely that those voters were disproportionately young and/or poor, and would mostly have voted Labour . . .

2   The Party's seat targeting strategy appeared to work – eventually. This has been a matter of controversy. Until May 11, the Party appeared to be exclusively targeting already Labour-held seats for direct mail and social media support. This was essentially a defensive strategy. That was not entirely irrational given the polling numbers at the time. However, the political leadership had clearly and correctly determined that Labour must fight the election to win, which obviously meant focussing resources on Tory-held seats as well. Even within the context of a defensive strategy the direction of resources to some of the seats targeted appeared eccentric. In the end, a strategy of at least targeting sufficient constituencies to deprive

the Tories of a parliamentary majority was adopted and this, of course, was successful. Whether an earlier shift could have achieved more is not certain, but it would not be impossible. The easy aspect of this issue is agreeing a target list for the next election – clearly a more ambitious approach will be appropriate. The trickier part is ensuring that the decisions of the political leadership on strategy are carried through by all parts of the Party, despite whatever reservations may be held . . .

3 A strategic decision was taken at around the same time to focus political messaging on northern working-class voters who appeared to be in danger of defecting directly to the Tories (or via previous brief support for UKIP) from Labour. These were identified as above all firm supporters of Brexit. Albeit this strategy was only implemented in a fairly unsystematic way . . . it appears to have worked. While the first wave of voters abandoning UKIP appear to have overwhelmingly gone to the Tories, the evidence of the final vote would indicate that there was a second wave, pushing UKIP to the point of collapse, which returned to Labour. Given the overall result in a number of northern and Midlands constituencies, which showed swings against Labour, had this not happened there could have been more Labour losses. This strategic choice was made the easier by the fatuity and feebleness of the Liberal Democrat campaign which meant that the spectre of having to campaign on two fronts – against UKIP/ Tory 'Leavers' in the north, and against Lib Dem 'Remainers' in London and elsewhere did not materialise. We therefore escaped the 'strategic vice' which had been an evident risk since the 2015 election and an acute one since the referendum on EU membership.

4 Following on from this strategic focus, the message on Brexit was sharpened to make it beyond doubt that Labour was not seeking to hold a second referendum or otherwise call Britain's departure from the EU into question, but was instead framing the question as a choice between a Labour Brexit which put jobs first, or a Tory Brexit which would have turned Britain into a low-wage offshore tax haven . . . this messaging, added to the popular manifesto commitments addressing the concerns of voters in 'left-behind' communities, staunched and reversed the loss of Labour votes in many parts of the country without compromising our support in 'Remain' areas.

5 We moved fast to exploit the disastrous Tory manifesto launch, which was successfully framed as a sustained attack on older people, via the 'dementia tax', the scrapping of the pensions triple-lock and the cuts in the Winter Fuel Allowance. The expectation was that this would dissuade older voters, a category in which the Conservatives enjoy a very big advantage, from continuing to support the Tory Party, whether or not they would switch over to Labour . . . the fact that the Prime Minister was forced into a rapid U-turn (or more likely confusion) on some of this only added to the Tories' chaos, and provided a contrast with Labour's own manifesto. A welcome side-effect of this was that May's 'red Tory' proposals on fuel prices, workers on boards, caps on executive pay etc., pledges which could have had some resonance with Labour voters, got almost no attention at all.

6 Jeremy Corbyn's response to the two terrorist atrocities during the campaign was pitch-perfect. In particular, his speech resuming campaigning after the Manchester bombing worked well, even though some perceived it as 'risky' at the time. It

framed the debate around terrorism in a mature and thoughtful way, without conceding any ground to the perpetrators of the attack. Polling showed that a big majority agreed with Jeremy's contention that there is a connection between some foreign policy decisions made by the West and the apparent persistence of the terrorist menace here at home. This enhanced Jeremy's standing and denied the Tories the accretion of support they might have anticipated as the traditional law-and-order party. It is noteworthy that, overall, the terror attacks do not seem to have made any very obvious difference to voting intentions.

7 The decision that Jeremy should attend the Leaders' Debate in Cambridge, despite the absence of the Prime Minister, also paid off on balance. It became evident in the course of the last two weeks that Jeremy's television appearances were going down very well, and that keeping him in front of the cameras was an asset. His attendance at the debate showed Labour taking the electorate seriously, and of course highlighted Theresa May's absence, consistent with her wooden, scripted campaign throughout.

8 While I would not claim any authority on the matter, it seems that the twin-track social media focus, by the Party's team and the JC team, worked brilliantly. It succeeded on both the organic front and the paid digital front (with precise voter targeting systems), although in the latter respect we were of course heavily outspent by the Tories ... The role of Momentum was important here (as it was in ground mobilisation in many seats) and this should be recognised and built on.

9 The final focus on mobilising the youth vote by spending on key social media channels clearly paid off handsomely. The use

of Snapchat and the provision of information on where voters could find their local polling station were vital to this.

10 Labour fought a positive, mature campaign focussed on policy and on a dialogue with the voters, who appear to prefer being treated as adults rather than as Pavlovian dogs. We attacked the Tories of course, but without scare-mongering or personal smears.

11 By contrast, the Tory campaign failed on every level. As is common with right-wing parties the democratic world over at present, it relied almost exclusively on smear and fear to persuade voters to ignore substantive issues and their own economic and social interests. Lynton Crosby is, it would seem, a one-trick pony. When smear-and-fear fail, as they did last year in the London Mayor election, and again in 2017, he has nothing left in the locker. It remains to be seen whether the Conservative Party can rise to the challenge of a positive-message campaign, but it is a long time since they last tried.

Notes

Introduction

1 'Keir Starmer's Labour Is Not Yet a Credible Alternative', editorial, *Financial Times*, 22 September 2020.

2 Editorial, *Telegraph*, 1 August 2021. Corbyn himself has said that 'the way in which the government *eventually* responded to the corona crisis indicates that everything I was saying in the general election . . . about investment in housing, health, education and support for manufacturing industry jobs has now come full circle.' *Middle East Eye*, 2 June 2020.

3 Martin Wolf, 'Covid Exposes Society's Dysfunctions', *Financial Times*, 15 July 2020.

4 Gabriel Pogrund and Patrick Maguire, *Left Out: The Inside Story of Labour Under Corbyn* (London 2020); Owen Jones, *This Land: The Struggle for the Left* (London 2020). Jones covers the entirety of the Corbyn leadership, Pogrund and Maguire focus on the post-2017 period.

5 Sebastian Payne, *Broken Heartlands: A Journey Through Labour's Lost England* (London 2021); Deborah Mattinson, *Beyond the Red Wall: Why Labour Lost, How the Conservatives Won and What Will Happen Next?* (London 2020). Mattinson's account is more coloured by her personal anti-Corbyn views than Payne's is. She is now an advisor to Keir Starmer.

6   Alex Nunns, *The Candidate: Jeremy Corbyn's Improbable Path to Power* (New York/London 2018); Len McCluskey, *Always Red* (New York/London 2021).

7   Matt Bolton and Frederick Harry Pitts, *Corbynism: A Critical Approach* (Bingley, UK 2018). Pitts is, in particular, a zealous opponent of anti-imperialism.

8   Mark Perryman, ed., *Corbynism from Below* (London 2019).

9   Cited in Christopher Hill, *The Experience of Defeat: Milton and Some Contemporaries* (London 1984), p. 37.

1. New Adventures on the Parliamentary Road

1   '"There Is No Such Thing as Corbynism" – Jeremy Corbyn', *BBC News*, 13 December 2019. See also James Schneider, 'Bridging the Gap: Corbynism After Corbyn', in Grace Blakeley, ed., *Futures of Socialism: The Pandemic and the Post-Corbyn Era* (London 2020), pp. 226–35, for a further exploration.

2   Friedrich Engels, *The Condition of the Working Class in England*, preface to the English edition (London 2009 [1892]), p. 48. A *causeuse* is a love-seat.

3   Andrew Murray, *The Fall and Rise of the British Left* (London 2019), p. 183. Kinnock's own career combines parliamentary non-socialism and electoral failure in a paradox he has not really confronted.

4   Ralph Miliband, *Parliamentary Socialism: A Study in the Politics of Labour*, 2nd edn (Pontypool, UK 1972). The story was carried forward into the New Labour years by Leo Panitch and Colin Leys in *The End of Parliamentary Socialism* (London 2001) and beyond in their *Searching for Socialism: The Project of the Labour New Left from Benn to Corbyn* (London 2020).

5   *The Communist Manifesto*, in *Marx/Engels Collected Works*, vol. 6 (London 1976), p. 498.

6   Engels had formed a more practical intimacy with the new-born class in 1840s Manchester.

7   David Howell, *British Workers and the Independent Labour Party, 1888–1906* (Manchester 1983), pp. 352–7.

8   Max Beer, *A History of British Socialism*, vol. 2 (London 1919), p. 304.

9   Boris Ponomarev, et al., eds, *The International Working-Class Movement*, vol. 3, *Revolutionary Battles of the Early Twentieth Century* (Moscow 1983), p. 336.

10   Nicholas Owen, 'Critics of Empire in Britain', in Judith Brown and Wm Roger Louis, eds, *The Oxford History of the British Empire*, vol. 4, *The Twentieth Century* (Oxford 1999), p. 191; James Joll, *The Second International 1889–1914* (London and Boston 1974 [1955]), p. 125.

11   *Official Report of the Socialist Unity Conference* (London 1911), p. 11.

12   The 1918 constitution provided for individual membership, allowing the ILP to give itself a sharper political profile now that it was no longer the main avenue for non–trade union members to join the party. It sought to straddle the division between the Leninism of the Bolsheviks and the reformism of the Second International, distancing itself from the authoritarianism of the former and the class collaboration of the latter (above all in the prosecution of the war). The ILP joined the Two-and-a-Half International briefly established by various like-minded socialist parties and became more vehemently anticapitalist. Predictably, it was pulled in different directions and suffered several splits of members leaving in the direction of the Communist Party. Nevertheless, it remained an organised force on the Labour left, with a particular base on Clydeside, throughout the interwar years, despite rashly disaffiliating from Labour in the aftermath of MacDonald's final surrender to the capitalist class in 1931.

13   Ken Coates and Tony Topham, *The Making of the Transport and General Workers Union*, part 2, *1912–1922: From Federation to Amalgamation* (Oxford 1991), p. 720.

14   This programme is well summarised by Luke Akehurst, leading organiser of the party's right wing today and a member of Labour's National Executive Committee, who inscribes as the first item in a social democratic credo: 'We are not seeking to abolish capitalism but to promote social justice and greater inequality within a liberal democratic political system and a capitalist economic system': Akehurst, 'Is Social Democracy in Crisis?', labourlist.org, 28 February 2018.

15   Kenneth Harris, *Attlee* (London 1982), p. 56.

16   Jon Cruddas, 'ILP@120: George Lansbury, the ILP and a Re-Imagined Labour Party', independentlabour.org.uk, 15 November 2013. Under

Lansbury's leadership, perhaps the last real effort was made by the Labour hierarchy to address the realities of class power. In a 1933 compendium *Problems of a Socialist Government*, Labour frontbencher Stafford Cripps warned that 'the ruling class will go to almost any length to defeat parliamentary action if the issue is . . . the continuance of their financial and political control. If the change to Socialism is to be brought about peacefully a Socialist party must be fully prepared to deal with every kind of opposition direct and indirect and with financial and political sabotage of the most thorough and ingenious kind': Cripps, 'Can Socialism Come by Constitutional Methods?', in Christopher Addison, ed., *Problems of a Socialist Government* (London 1933). Cripps's solution was to take emergency powers. By the time he next held office under Attlee he was to be found among the saboteurs instead.

17   See Andrew Adonis, *Ernest Bevin: Labour's Churchill* (London 2020), pp. 294ff. Bevin himself was a racist and an anti-Semite, something that has not prevented his subsequent lionisation by Labour's right wing, for whom his anticommunism is far more consequential.

18   See John Saville, *The Politics of Continuity: British Foreign Policy and the Labour Government, 1945–6* (London 1993) for a comprehensive picture.

19   Stalin advised CPGB leader Harry Pollitt that 'England shall come to socialism through its own path and not through Soviet Power', as its previous programme had assumed. Later versions of the CPGB's 'British Road to Socialism' programme embedded the idea of a peaceful, even placid, advance to socialism still further. See 'On the British Road to Socialism', in *Revolutionary Democracy* 12, no. 2 (September 2007), p. 188. The Soviet leader implored a delegation of Labour MPs in Moscow: 'We all advance to the same goal, which is socialism. Therefore it would be surprising if our two countries were not friends'. See the London School of Economics archive *Record of Comrade J.V. Stalin's Conversation with the Delegation of the British Labour Party*. He also observed that 'the British bourgeoisie are cleverer, richer and more experienced than the Russian, and will be a very strong opponent.' This proved true.

20   Simon Hannah, *A Party with Socialists in It: A History of the Labour Left* (London 2018), p. 145.

21   Benn described the Labour government's embrace of an IMF loan and huge cuts in public spending in preference to his economic strategy as the 'moment of defeat', *Against the Tide: Diaries 1973–1976* (London 1989), p. 679. By 1983 this had become a 'sense of overpowering tragedy in respect of Britain and the Labour Party', *The End of an Era: Diaries 1980–90* (London 1992), p. 271.

22   Neoliberalism, the doctrine associated with Hayek and Friedman, has two grand objectives. First, to extend market processes to as many human interactions as possible. Second, to insulate as much as possible the rights of property and the workings of the market economy from any form of democratic control or intervention. Governments which pursue policy along these two lines justify being described as neoliberal.

23   See the Labour Party, *Labour's Programme 1982* (London 1982). It was adopted by a conference vote of 6,420,000 to 224,000.

24   The themes in the remainder of this chapter are treated much more comprehensively in *Fall and Rise*.

2. Context of Crisis, Crisis of Context

1   Jon Meacham, 'We Are All Socialists Now', *Newsweek*, 16 February 2009.

2   Said to executives in Silicon Valley in 1999.

3   For a more detailed review of the anti-war movement, see Murray, *The Fall and Rise of the British Left*, chapter 5; and Andrew Murray and Lindsey German, *Stop the War: The Story of Britain's Biggest Mass Movement* (London 2005).

4   Paul Lewis and Tim Newburn, 'Introducing Phase Two of Reading the Riots: Police, Victims and the Courts', *Guardian*, 1 July 2012.

5   'Corbynism' might now be known as 'Abbottism' had the left's candidate succeeded in 2010, but Diane Abbott came last, although she outpolled former ministers Andy Burnham and Ed Balls in the trade union members' section of the college.

6   See Andrew Murray, 'Left Unity or Class Unity? Working-Class Politics in Britain', in Leo Panitch, Greg Albo and Vivek Chibber, eds, *Registering Class: Socialist Register 2014* (London 2013), pp. 266–86.

3. Radicalism without a Route Map

1   Simon Fletcher, chief of staff to Jeremy Corbyn, 2015–16; previously held the same position for Ken Livingstone as mayor of London, 2000–08; later, strategic advisor to Keir Starmer, a commission he resigned from in 2021.

2   Andrew Fisher: executive director of policy, 2016–20; previously Jeremy Corbyn's speechwriter.

3   Mark Perryman, ed., *Corbynism from Below* (London 2019). See Grace Blakeley, *Stolen: How to Save the World from Financialisation* (London 2019) and Aaron Bastani, *Fully Automated Luxury Communism* (London 2019). Bastani heads up Novara; Blakeley is a staff writer at *Tribune*.

4   Eagle put herself forward to run against Corbyn in the 2016 leadership election rerun, but lost out to Owen Smith.

5   'John McDonnell Seeks to Reassure City over Capital Control Fears', *Financial Times*, 23 January 2019.

6   Victor Kiernan, *America: The New Imperialism* (London 2005 [1978]), p. xv.

7   Brockway was a Leader of the ILP in the 1920s and 1930s and a Labour MP best known for anticolonial campaigning thereafter. He was president of Liberation, previously the Movement for Colonial Freedom.

8   It is also true that both organisations include anti-Semitic formulations in their charters, which they have declined to modify, a symptom of how a desperate situation can lead to a recrudescence of reactionary and self-defeating political ideas.

9   Austin was then a Labour MP, but he has now been placed in the House of Lords by Boris Johnson, having established a front organisation – Mainstream – to support the Tories in the 2019 election. Nothing disgraceful there, of course.

10 This and subsequent quotations are from my notes taken at the time. The strategic team included John McDonnell, Diane Abbott, John Trickett and Ian Lavery from among Labour politicians (as well as Corbyn himself) and myself, Seumas Milne, Andrew Fisher, Amy Jackson, Niall Sookoo and Karie Murphy from among the staff. Jennie Formby also became a member. Later the committee expanded further,

to the point of being unwieldy, and then stopped meeting altogether, for reasons never made clear.

11 'International Strategy', LOTO Strategy Meeting, 8 April 2019.

12 Thornberry made some particularly dreadful remarks on the anniversary of the Balfour Declaration, omitting to mention its consequences for the Palestinians, which earned her a rare rebuke from Corbyn.

13 Errors may have been made – as the response to the attempted murder of Sergei Skripal in Salisbury by Russian military intelligence showed – but they would have been errors in the direction of avoiding international confrontation wherever possible.

4. 2017: Oh, Jeremy Corbyn

1   Blair won more across the UK as a whole in 1997, thanks to Labour's strength in Scotland at the time, which had been radically diminished before Corbyn became Leader.

2   Extraordinarily, the Tory vote share has increased in all six general elections this century, with the biggest single improvement being between 2015 and 2017.

3   With this and its 'enemies of the people' headline attacking the judiciary, the *Mail* was channelling the 1937 *Pravda*.

4   John Stuart Mill, 'Chapters on Socialism' in *Principles of Political Economy* (Oxford 1994), p. 375; Daniel Finkelstein 'The Corbynistas Always Spoke of Success. They Were Right', *The Times*, 10 June 2017.

5   'Stalin's Sycophant', *The Times*, 16 May 2017. Another editorial devoted to the Murray question, which was clearly vexing the newspaper, appeared on 9 March 2019, this time headed 'Corbyn's Communist', which I suppose was an upgrade. 'The dictatorship of the proletariat' is a much debated and surely much-misunderstood term. I take its meaning to be that the working class is constituted as the state power, in place of the existing capitalist state.

6   Steve Howell, deputy to Seumas Milne in 2017, and advisor during the 2019 general election campaign. He was earlier a journalist and founder/chief executive of Freshwater communications consultancy. His book *Game Changer: Eight Weeks That Transformed British Politics* (London 2018) is a detailed review of Labour's 2017 campaign.

7   'General Election 2017: Strategy', Office of the Leader of the Labour Party, p. 1.

8   John Rentoul, 'Peter Mandelson: "It's Simply a Myth That Labour Can Win from the Left" ', *Independent*, 3 April 2021.

9   Ed Fieldhouse and Chris Prosser, 'The Brexit Election? The 2017 General Election in Ten Charts', British Election Study, 1 August 2017.

10   'How Many Labour Supporters Voted Leave?', BBC News, 29 April 2019.

11   Payne, *Broken Heartlands*, p. 330.

12   The party's report – 'The Work of the Labour Party's Governance and Legal Unit in Relation to Antisemitism, 2014–2019', March 2020 – has been to some extent submerged under a blizzard of actual and threatened lawsuits by those whose conduct was exposed in it, which has led to a convenient media blackout. It is, however, still accessible on the internet. Seek and ye shall find.

13   'The Work of the Labour Party's Governance and Legal Unit in Relation to Antisemitism', p. 102.

14   'The Work of the Labour Party's Governance and Legal Unit in Relation to Antisemitism', pp. 92–3.

15   'Corbyn's Office Ordered 2017 Election Campaign Funding Cuts For "Moderate" Labour MPs, Ex-Campaigns Chief Reveals', *Huffington Post*, 27 August 2020.

16   Steve Howell, 'Don't Let Labour's Right Do Any More Wrecking', Labouroutlook.org, 19 August 2020.

17   An independent inquiry was set up, headed by Martin Forde QC, to investigate the contents of the GLU report. The findings of the inquiry have not been released as at the time of writing.

18   See Andrew Murray, 'Unite: How Do We Build on Labour's Election Results? Not by Misunderstanding Our Position with Working Class Voters,' Labourlist.org, 14 July 2017, for a lengthier analysis of this problem and how the right wing of the party tried to misrepresent it in order to challenge Corbyn's foreign policy. My conclusion: 'If working-class people stopped voting Labour in 2005 or 2010 because of defence-related reasons, it would have been because "New Labour" fought too many wars, not too few.'

19   Strategy meeting, Leader of the Opposition, December 2017.

20 'More Scots saw the independence debate as primary and the Brexit debate as secondary', Maria Sobolewska and Robert Ford, *Brexitland: Identity, Diversity and the Reshaping of British Politics* (Cambridge 2020), p. 278.

21 The phrase is Tariq Ali's, denoting the dominant centre-right/centre-left political bloc of the neoliberal age. See Ali, *The Extreme Centre: A Second Warning* (London 2018).

5. Corbynism versus Labourism

1 After the unforeseen outcome of the 2015 leadership ballot, a stunned Labour right and a popped media bubble turned their eyes longingly to Watson to engineer a return to their preferred version of normal. He did not disappoint, in effort if not in reward. Could he have been handled differently? My view (although I had very little to do with him) is that he is both a more nuanced and sensitive man and a less successful plotter than his image allows. Certainly, he was not hugged close by Corbyn's LOTO, nor was any effort made to intimidate him – neither love nor fear was deployed, a serious omission. While Corbyn had no power to dismiss him as deputy leader, he could have been removed from his shadow cabinet portfolio at any time, or otherwise censured for his escalating disruptions. Every time Corbyn came to the point of acting he was talked out of it (or talked himself out of it). Of course, any move to clip Watson's wings would have been resented by much of the PLP, but then there are always abundant rationalisations for passivity, and disloyalty to Corbyn became an activity that carried no cost. There was, it is true, a cockamamie scheme to abolish the post of deputy leader altogether, briefly floated and swiftly abandoned on the eve of the 2019 conference. It was an attempt to introduce a bureaucratic fix, abolishing overnight a post which had existed for generations, to cure a political ailment.

2 The PLP had already resented Ed Miliband winning the 2010 leadership election largely by dint of the votes of trade union members. The modifications to the system which then produced Corbyn as Leader had been engineered to prevent a repetition: an irony.

3   Jon Stone, 'Tony Blair Says He Wouldn't Want a Left-Wing Labour Party to Win an Election', *Independent*, 22 July 2015.

4   See *Hansard*, 26 June 1975.

5   'Legal Documents Reveal Depth of Split between Jeremy Corbyn and Party's General Secretary', *Telegraph*, 25 July 2016; 'Labour Rebels Fail to Break Rule of Corbyn', *Financial Times*, 12 July 2016.

6   A significant number of right-wing Labour MPs did quit during the Corbyn years because of political opposition, thwarted ambition, or early retirement, but none because of deselection.

7   Corbyn himself sometimes spoke of moving LOTO out of its claustrophobic accommodation in the House of Commons to offices nearby to signal detachment from parliamentary priorities.

8   As summarised by Leo Panitch and Colin Leys, 'The Labour Party Machine versus Corbyn', Socialist Project, 9 May 2020, socialistproject.ca.

9   Pogrund and Maguire, *Left Out*, p. 241.

10 'Watson Mocks Lib Dem "Brexit Deniers" and Vows Labour Will Not "Disrespect" Public by Trying to Overturn EU Vote', labourlist.org, 25 November 2016.

11 'Labour's Civil War over Brexit Deepens: Tom Watson Claims Vote to Leave the EU Is No Longer "Valid" and Calls for a Second Referendum to Be Held BEFORE a General Election', *Daily Mail*, 11 September 2019.

12 As of summer 2021, all the community organisers were facing redundancy under the new Labour restorationist regime of Starmer and party General Secretary David Evans. Starmer has also rolled back the democratic reforms introduced in 2018.

13 Leo Panitch and Colin Leys, *Searching for Socialism: The Project of the Labour New Left from Benn to Corbyn* (London and New York 2020), p. 253.

6. The Campaign against Corbynism

1   Richard Dearlove, 'Don't Even Think of Handing Jeremy Corbyn the Keys to Number 10', *Mail on Sunday*, 24 November 2019.

2   'Former Head of MI6 Sir Richard Dearlove "Troubled" by Corbyn', *The Times*, 7 October 2018.

3   'Communists Spied on by MI5 Are Now Senior Corbyn Advisors',
    Mail Online, 14 October 2017.

4   Gavin Gordon, 'Ex-Defence Chief: Corbyn Can't Be Trusted to
    Protect Nation', *Huffington Post*, 24 April 2017.

5   Tim Shipman et al., 'Corbyn Hit by Mutiny on Airstrikes', *Sunday
    Times*, 20 September 2015. The report even identified the general as
    having served in Northern Ireland in the 1980s and 1990s, but he
    remains unnamed.

6   Matt Kennard, 'How the UK Military and Intelligence Establishment Is
    Working to Stop Jeremy Corbyn from Becoming Prime Minister',
    dailymaverick.co.za, 4 December 2019.

7   Jake Ryan and Ian Gallagher, 'Revealed: Top Corbyn Aide Held Four
    Meetings with Czech Spy in the 1980s and Was Viewed as a "Friend of
    the Soviet Embassy" and an "Enemy" of US', *Mail on Sunday*, 10
    November 2019.

8   'Corbyn's ex-Communist Top Adviser is Banned from Entering the
    Ukraine for Three Years After Intelligence Officials Brand Him a
    National Security Risk "Over Links to Putin" ', *Mail on Sunday*, 15
    September 2018.

9   Andrew Murray, 'Is the "Deep State" Trying to Undermine Corbyn?',
    New Statesman, 19 September 2018.

10 Jack Brewster, '6 Bombshells from New Trump Book: From Coup
    Threat to Calling Angela Merkel a "Kraut" ', forbes.com, 15 July 2021.

11 Dan Hodges 'Forcing Jeremy Corbyn to Kneel Before the Queen
    Would Be Cruel and Distasteful', *Telegraph*, 17 September 2015.

12 'BBC's Kuenssberg removes tweet about activist punching Tory aide',
    The National, 10 December 2019. Robert Peston also retailed the smear.

13 Bert Cammaerts et al., 'Journalistic Representations of Jeremy Corbyn
    in the British Press: From Watchdog to Attackdog', Media@LSE, July
    2016.

14 David Deacon, 'Press Hostility to Labour Reaches New Levels in 2019
    Election Campaign', Loughborough University, 19 December 2019.

15 Peter Oborne, 'Jeremy Corbyn: British Media Waged Campaign to
    Destroy Me', middleeasteye.net, 2 June 2020.

16 Tom Bower, *Dangerous Hero: Corbyn's Ruthless Plot for Power* (London
    2019), p. 300.

17 Peter Oborne, 'Jeremy Corbyn and the Truth About Tom Bower's Book', middleeasteye.net, 9 March 2019.

18 See Murray, *Fall and Rise*, pp. 187–9, for gory details.

19 'Britain Deserves Better', *New Statesman*, 4 December 2019.

20 Greg Philo et al., *Bad News for Labour: Antisemitism, the Party and Public Belief* (London 2019).

21 The *Mail*'s campaign against Ed Miliband's father, Ralph, a Jewish refugee to Britain who the paper said 'hated Britain', was almost universally regarded as anti-Semitic. The *Telegraph* has been criticised for its treatment of leading Jewish figures from Anthony Julius to George Soros. See Rafael Behr, 'A Secret Plot to Stop Brexit, or an Anti-Semitic Dog Whistle?', *Guardian*, 8 February 2018, and Anthony Julius, *Trials of the Diaspora: A History of Anti-Semitism in England* (Oxford 2010), pp. xxxv–xl.

22 See Julius, *Trials of the Diaspora*, esp. pp. 271–81.

23 House of Commons Home Affairs Committee, 'Antisemitism in the UK', 16 October 2016, p. 46.

24 'Ken Livingstone Stands by Hitler Comments', *BBC News*, 30 April 2016; Evgeny Finkel, 'Netanyahu Blames a Palestinian for the Holocaust. What Does the Evidence Say?', *Washington Post*, 22 October 2015.

25 Deborah Lipstadt, *Antisemitism: Here and Now* (London 2019), pp. 55–67 in particular; Julia Neuberger, *Antisemitism: What It Is. What It Isn't. Why It Matters* (London 2019), pp. 104–25.

26 See the thread on @daverich1, 1 April 2020. See also his *The Left's Jewish Problem: Jeremy Corbyn, Israel and Anti-Semitism* (London 2016) for an influential narrative on left anti-Semitism, purported and actual.

27 Peter Walker, 'Corbyn's Comments Most Offensive Since Enoch Powell, Says Ex-Chief Rabbi', *Guardian*, 28 August 2018.

28 Greg Philo and Mike Berry, 'What Could Have Been Done and Why It Wasn't and Will It End?' in Philo et al., *Bad News for Labour*, p. 60.

29 Emphasis in original. 'Summary Note of Telephone Conversation re Antisemitism with Tony Klug and Jeremy Corbyn', 3 April 2018. I am grateful to Prof. Klug for his consent to quote this note.

30 'Maureen Lipman Drops Long-Standing Support for Labour Party', *Guardian*, 29 October 2014. Lipman left her trade union, Equity, for similar reasons in 2021.

31   Marcus Dysch, 'Huge Majority of British Jews Will Vote Tory, *JC* Poll Reveals'; 'Blame Toxic Ed for Labour's Loss of Support', *Jewish Chronicle*, 7 April 2015.

32   The idea that Labour is the 'natural home' for Jewish voters is questionable, and rooted in long-departed days of a substantial Jewish proletariat in east London and elsewhere. Possibly only a minority of Jewish voters have supported Labour since the 1960s, with an upward blip during the leaderships of Blair and Brown, both of whom were very pro-Israel, although perhaps for different reasons – neoconservatism in Blair's case and a family background in Christian Zionism in Brown's. Almost as questionable is the view that Labour has always been 'antiracist'. That is not so, and could never be so for a party as embedded in imperialism from its formation. It is, however, definitely the less racist of the two main parties of government.

33   Ewen MacAskill and Ian Cobain, 'Israeli Diplomat Who Plotted Against MPs Also Set Up Political Groups', *Guardian*, 8 January 2017; Alex MacDonald and Simon Hooper, 'Israeli Diplomat Worked Inside Labour to Discredit "Crazy" Corbyn', middleeasteye.net, 13 January 2017.

34   Strangely, the Labour NEC did as well.

35   Letter from Simon Johnson, Jewish Leadership Council, and Mark Gardner, Community Security Trust, to Jennie Formby, 29 August 2018.

36   What might constitute 'appropriate action' is elucidated by a resource page on the Board of Deputies website headed 'Standing up for British Jews'. This includes their work to 'Challenge councils that fly Palestinian flags', a position that is not so much pro-Israeli as anti-Palestinian and consistent with the most reactionary expressions of Zionism, which deny legitimacy to any expression of Palestinian identity.

37   All of the Jewish people I have known across my life, a large and diverse group, would be united in having no regard whatsoever for the Board of Deputies.

38   David Hirsh, *Contemporary Left Antisemitism* (Oxford 2018), p. 261. Hirsh's book repays careful study, despite his hostility to Corbyn and much of the left. It addresses the left's often poor grasp of the

significance of the Holocaust 'as something which profoundly altered the history of the Jews' (p. 79); its weaknesses include anti-Communism and the frequent elision of Jews with Israel and Zionism.

39   Cited in Hirsh, *Contemporary Left Antisemitism*, p. 89.

40   The text can be found at 'Working Definition of Antisemitism', holocaustremembrance.com.

41   'IHRA Definition of Anti-Semitism Has Been Weaponised, Warns Lead Drafter', middleeastmonitor.com, 11 December 2020. Others involved in the drafting dispute Stern's position.

42   In an almost comedic aside, two members of the Board of Deputies proposed, at the height of this controversy, to censure its vice president, who had made mild criticisms of Israel's racist nation-state law, for having violated the IHRA code. Someone must have realised that this would make the case for those who saw the IHRA as gagging criticism of Israel, and the matter was dropped. 'Deputies Push No Confidence Motion Against Board Vice President for Criticising Israel's Nation State Law', Jewish Chronicle, thejc.com, 28 September 2018.

43   See 'A Threshold Crossed: Israeli Authorities and the Crimes of Apartheid and Persecution', Human Rights Watch, hrw.org, 27 April 2021.

44   Ban Ki-moon, 'The US Should Back a New Approach to the Israel–Palestine Conflict', *Financial Times*, 30 June 2021.

45   House of Commons Home Affairs Committee, 'Antisemitism in the UK'.

46   Rayson, *The Fall of the Red Wall*, p. 169.

47   'Jeremy Corbyn: What I'm Doing to Banish Anti-Semitism from the Labour Party', *Evening Standard*, 24 April 2018.

48   As of August 2021, the *Jewish Chronicle* had sustained four libel settlements and twenty-eight recorded breaches of the Independent Press Standard Organisation's editors' code in the preceding three years, many of them related to Labour Party members. Brian Cathcart, 'Will the Independent Press Standards Organisation Ever Uphold Any Standards?', *Byline Times*, 4 August 2021.

49   'Siobhain McDonagh Links Anti-Capitalism to Antisemitism in Labour', labourlist.org, 4 March 2019; John McTernan, 'Labour's Mistake Is to Believe There Are No Enemies to the Left', *Financial*

Times, 1 March 2019. In the midst of the Tories' internal Brexit wars right-wing agitator Toby Young claimed that former Chancellor Philip Hammond's use of the word 'speculator' employed an anti-Semitic trope. He beat a speedy legally inspired retreat. Haroon Siddique. 'Toby Young Apologises for Accusing Hammond of Antisemitism', *Guardian*, 30 September 2019.

50 Tweet @DavidHirsh 22 February 2021. Emphasis added.

51 Raphael Ahern, 'With Netanyahu in Town, Hungary's Jews Lament Israel "Deserting" Them', timesofisrael.com, 17 July 2017.

52 'Push Against Anti-Semitism "Purging Jews from Labour" ', jewish-voiceforlabour.org.uk, 7 August 2021.

53 David Hirsh, 'JVL Has Been an Effective Voice for Anti-Semitic Policies in Britain', *Jewish Chronicle*, 10 December 2020.

7. Class and Culture

1 Wolfgang Streeck, *Critical Encounters: Capitalism, Democracy, Ideas* (London and New York 2020), p. 123.

2 Richard Tuck, *The Left Case for Brexit: Reflections on the Current Crisis* (Cambridge 2020), p. 118.

3 Costas Lapavitsas, *The Left Case Against the EU* (Cambridge 2019), p. 126.

4 Danny Dorling and Sally Tomlinson, *Rule Britannia: Brexit and the End of Empire* (London 2019); Maria Sobolewska and Robert Ford, *Brexitland: Identity, Diversity and the Reshaping of British Politics* (Cambridge 2020).

5 Paul Mason, 'Corbynism Is Now in Crisis: The Only Way Forward Is to Oppose Brexit', *Guardian*, 27 May 2019.

6 'Labour Should Ignore Voters Who "Hate Blacks, Women and Gays", Says Paul Mason', *Huffington Post*, 29 May 2019.

7 Labour narrowly retained the constituency I was in at the 2019 election. Two adjacent ex-mining seats were lost.

8 *Guardian*, Letters, 14 January 2020.

9 Sobolewska and Ford, *Brexitland*, pp. 153, 125.

10 'Brexit Votes in the United Kingdom by Social Class 2016', Statista, 24 June 2016. Definitions of class vary. On conventional sociological

categories 64 per cent of skilled and unskilled workers voted to leave the EU.

11 'Brexit Witness Archive: John McDonnell', UK in a Changing Europe, ukandeu.ac.uk, 19 February 2021.

12 Payne, *Broken Heartlands*, pp. 96, 89, 179.

13 In the event, Emily Thornberry happily retained her seat in December 2019, squeaking in with a majority of 17,328.

14 'Brexit Witness Archive: James Schneider', UK in a Changing Europe, ukandeu.ac.uk, 11 January 2021.

15 Tuck, *The Left Case for Brexit*, p. 85.

16 See Murray, *Fall and Rise*, pp. 192, 193–4.

17 Payne, *Broken Heartlands*, p. 168.

18 Heather Stewart and Lisa O'Carroll, 'Labour Delegates Back Keir Starmer Push for Public Vote on Brexit', *Guardian*, 25 September 2018.

19 I contributed to Jeremy's conference speeches in 2016, 2017 and 2018, but I did not draft the words quoted.

8. 2019: The Road to Defeat

1 'A Year on, Did Change UK Change Anything?', *Guardian*, 19 April 2020.

2 Daniel Finn, 'Crosscurrents: Corbyn Labour and the Brexit Crisis', *New Left Review* 118, (July/August 2019), p. 5.

3 Ibid., p. 30.

4 Pogrund and Maguire, *Left Out*, pp. 239–41.

5 Paul Mason, 'Corbynism Is Now in Crisis: The Only Way Forward Is to Oppose Brexit', *Guardian*, 27 May 2019. Mason did outline a programme for addressing the Leave-voting Labour areas: '[Labour] needs to fight personal insecurity, crime, drugs, antisocial behaviour and organised crime as enthusiastically as it fights racism. It needs to sideline all voices who believe having a strong national security policy is somehow "imperialist". It needs to forget scrapping Trident.' Mason's crime/racism juxtaposition is particularly noteworthy. The chance of Corbyn embracing this approach was zero.

6 In September 2019 Mason and others met Starmer to anoint him head of a pro-Remain government if Johnson could be displaced, brushing

Corbyn aside in the process, according to Pogrund and Maguire, *Left Out*, pp. 334–5. If true (and the book has not been challenged on any point of fact), this testifies to the detachment from political reality of all involved. As of 2021, Starmer continues to let down his Europhile supporters by walking away from his previous Remain-y commitments.

7 Carl Shoben, 'Summary of Current Electoral Data', June 2019.

8 McDonnell had taken charge of election preparations during the summer. Normally this would have been the role of the party's general secretary, but Jennie Formby alas had to spend most of 2019 undergoing extensive and debilitating treatment for cancer. McDonnell injected a sense of focus and purpose into the work and broadly made the best of a bad job. I myself played no part in proceedings from August until the election campaign itself as a result of a heart attack and subsequent bypass surgery.

9 'General Election Strategy', August 2019.

10 As Tom Hazeldine notes, the 'promise of "real change" rang oddly for a Party that had spent the past twelve months attempting to preserve the pre-2016 European status quo.' Tom Hazeldine, *The Northern Question: A History of Divided Country* (London 2020), p. 206.

11 For the most part – Putney did fall to Labour on the night.

12 Streeck, *Critical Encounters*, pp. 187–8.

13 Aditya Chakrabortty, 'Corbyn Still Plays the Crowds – but Spirit of 2017 Remains Elusive', *Guardian*, 6 December 2019.

14 Rayson, *The Fall of the Red Wall*, p. 190.

15 Deborah Mattinson, *Beyond the Red Wall: Why Labour Lost, How the Conservatives Won and What Will Happen Next?* (London 2020), pp. 122, 107, 109.

16 Labour retained 79 per cent of its Remain voters but only 52 per cent of its Leave voters. Hazeldine, *The Northern Question*, p. 207.

9. The Starmer Counter-revolution

1 Keir Starmer, *The Road Ahead* (London 2021). Responses from usually supportive mainstream media included 'a necklace of platitudes strung together with banalities, fastened with clichés' (Rafael Behr, *Guardian*);

'29 mentions of "business", zero mentions of "socialism", "socialist", "nationalise", "public ownership" . . .' (Jim Pickard, *Financial Times*); 'It is not impossible to imagine Boris Johnson saying almost all of it' (Robert Peston, ITV).

2   David Rosenberg, 'What Happened to the Anger and the Hope?', *Morning Star*, 10 June 2021.

3   In the media Paul Mason was the main proponent of this point of view. Among campaigners, Simon Fletcher, once Corbyn's chief of staff, was the most prominent example.

4   As of January 2022, Labour does seem to be inching into a modest lead, which may, however, not last any longer than the Tories continue to tolerate Johnson, now widely seen as feckless and untrustworthy, as their Leader.

5   He had overcome a 1980s flirtation with one of the more insipid varieties of Trotskyism by then.

6   Oliver Eagleton, 'The Case Against Keir Starmer', Verso Blog, 27 January 2020; see also Eagleton, 'Keir Starmer Is a Long-Time Servant of the British Security State', Novara Media, 2 March 2021, and *The Starmer Project: A Journey to the Right*, forthcoming from Verso.

7   Laura Parker, Corbyn's private secretary in 2016–17, and subsequently Momentum National Organiser. As of September 2021 she repented her support for Starmer.

8   Starmer was assisted by infantile divisions on the left that had allowed him to secure a working majority on the National Executive Committee through by-election victories for the right announced on the same day as he took the leadership.

9   EHRC, 'Investigation into Antisemitism in the Labour Party', October 2020, p. 27.

10   See Len McCluskey, *Always Red* (New York and London 2021), pp. 276–80.

11   'How Labour's Claim of Countering Antisemitism Has Resulted in a Purge of Jews', jewishvoiceforlabour.org.uk, 5 August 2021.

12   'Starmer Warned over Far-Left Push to Hinder Party Clean Up', *Jewish Chronicle*, 4 November 2020. John McDonnell and Len McCluskey were specified by the BoD; 'Anti-Racists Stand Together with Former Labour Leader', *Morning Star*, 10 July 2021.

13　Peter Mandelson, 'After Hartlepool, Starmer Must Listen to Voters Not Labour's actions', *Financial Times*, 10 May 2021.

14　Haroon Siddique, 'Labour Lifts Trevor Phillips' Suspension for Alleged Islamophobia', *Guardian*, 6 July 2021.

15　'Equality Commission Steps in After Labour Accuses Nearly Entire Jewish Voice for Labour Board of Antisemitism', *Canary*, 2 December 2021.

16　'Keir Starmer's Speech to LFI'S Annual Lunch 2021', Labour Friends of Israel, lfi.org.uk, 16 November 2021.

17　Eagleton, 'Keir Starmer Is a Long-Time Servant of the British Security State'.

18　'Labour's Foreign Policy Must Avoid Corbyn's "Obsession with Anti-imperialism", Frontbencher Says', *Redaction Report*, 17 December 2020.

19　Jemima Kelly, 'Jibes About Brexiter "Imperial Nostalgia" Are Disingenuous', *Financial Times*, 7 January 2021.

20　'Ex-M16 Boss Relieved Jeremy Corbyn Is No Longer Labour Leader', *Shropshire Star*, 12 July 2020.

21　Pogrund and Maguire, *Left Out*, p. 346.

22　Simon Fletcher, 'I Went to Work for Keir Starmer Because He Said He Would Unite the Party. I Regret It Now', *Guardian*, 28 September 2021.

23　Andrew Scattergood, 'Momentum Is Still Leading the Labour Left', *Morning Star*, 9 January 2021. Emphasis added.

24　Tony Blair, 'The Progressive Challenge,' *New Statesman*, 14 May 2021.

25　Estimated at around 180,000 as of January 2022.

26　Even Ramsay MacDonald got a net plus-six, which he really does not deserve, although the further back you reach into history the more the uninformed influence the outcome, and around 58 per cent of members surveyed had no view on Labour's first prime minister. 'Five More Things We Discovered About Labour Members', YouGov, 21 January 2020.

27　Matt Zarb-Cousins, 'Why Does Keir Starmer Keep Telling Voters That Labour Deserves to Lose?', *Guardian*, 23 June 2021.

10. Legacy and Lessons

1   Leo Panitch and Colin Leys, *The End of Parliamentary Socialism: From New Left to New Labour* (London 1997), p. 265.

2   Neal Lawson, 'Labouring Under Illusions', in Mark Perryman, ed. *Corbynism from Below* (London 2019), p. 173.

3   Alex Niven, 'The Labour Party's Spectacular Defeat Had Been Coming for Decades', *New York Times*, 20 December 2019; see also Payne, *Broken Heartlands*, for a journalistic exploration of this phenomenon.

4   Heather Stewart, 'Where Now for Labour's Corbyn Supporters?', *Guardian*, 12 December 2020.

5   Ronan Burtenshaw, 'Class Politics, or Class Dealignment', *Tribune* (Summer 2021), p. 9.

6   This is true internationally as well. Sevim Dagdelen, an MP for Die Linke in Germany, attributed her party's disastrous showing in the September 2021 elections to 'thinking that we could address issues increasingly in terms of identity politics instead of class'. Jamshid Ahmadi, 'Die Linke Needs to Focus on Its Core Topics, Namely Social Justice and Peace', *Morning Star*, 16 November 2021.

7   Stephen Armstrong, 'GB News Should Speak for Right-of-Centre Britain, Not Culture Warrior Weirdos on Twitter,' *Telegraph*, 17 July 2021.

8   Henry Mance, 'Britain's Culture War Is Not Really Taking Place', *Financial Times*, 22 May 2021.

9   See P.J. Cain and A.G. Hopkins, *British Imperialism: 1688–2015* (Abingdon, UK 2016 [1993]) for an exposition of this.

10 Grace Blakeley, introduction, in Blakeley, ed., *Futures of Socialism: The Pandemic and the Post-Corbyn Era* (London 2020), p. xiv.

11 Andrew Murray, *The Imperial Controversy: Challenging the Empire Apologists* (Croydon, UK 2009), expands on the present author's view of this history and those who defend it.

12 Peter Mandelson and Roger Liddle, *The Blair Revolution: Can New Labour Deliver?*, (London1996).

13 See Murray, *Fall and Rise*, pp. 146–9, for a fuller consideration of this problem.

14   Tariq Ali, 'Starmer's War', NLR/Sidecar, newleftreview.org/sidecar, 15 December 2020.

15   Owen Jones, 'Eat the Rich! Why Millennials and Generation Z Have Turned Their Backs on Capitalism', *Guardian*, 20 September 2021.

Index